A Survey of the Bible

A Survey of the Bible

An Overview of the Sixty-Six Canonical Books of Sacred Scripture

Ronald F. Satta

WIPF & STOCK · Eugene, Oregon

A SURVEY OF THE BIBLE
An Overview of the Sixty-Six Canonical Books of Sacred Scripture

Copyright © 2009 Ronald F. Satta. All rights reserved. Except for brief quotations in critical publications or reviews, no part of this book may be reproduced in any manner without prior written permission from the publisher. Write: Permissions, Wipf and Stock Publishers, 199 W. 8th Ave., Suite 3, Eugene, OR 97401.

Wipf & Stock
A Division of Wipf and Stock Publishers
199 W. 8th Ave., Suite 3
Eugene, OR 97401

www.wipfandstock.com

ISBN 13: 978-1-60608-068-9

Manufactured in the U.S.A.

Scripture taken from the HOLY BIBLE, NEW INTERNATIONAL VERSION © 1973, 1978, 1984 by International Bible Society. Used by Permission of Zondervan. All rights reserved.

*This book is dedicated to my wife, Carol,
a faithful student of the Word of God,
and the one who first "inspired" me with the idea in the first place.*

Contents

Acknowledgments ix

Introduction xi

Chapter 1   The Pentateuch (Genesis through Deuteronomy)   1

Chapter 2   The Historical Books (Joshua through Esther)   21

Chapter 3   The Poetical Books (Job through Song of Solomon)   79

Chapter 4   The Prophetical Books (Isaiah through Malachi)   98

Chapter 5   The Gospels and Acts   126

Chapter 6   The Pauline Literature (Romans through Philemon)   149

Chapter 7   Hebrews through Revelation   204

Acknowledgments

I WISH TO THANK some of the pivotal individuals and resources to which I have turned for help in studying the Bible over the years and in producing this Bible Survey. As I look back over nearly 20 years of ministry as the senior pastor of Webster Bible Church, I realize that I am indebted to many positive influences.

Faculty members at both Capital Bible Seminary and Trinity Evangelical Divinity School helped me formulate a consistent hermeneutic, an exegetical method, and a systematic and historical theological grid which has served me well over the years and for which I am thankful.

A host of trusted commentators have served quietly at my side as I have endeavored to understand and expound the Word of God. In particular, I would like to thank the faculty of Dallas Theological Seminary who contributed to *The Bible Knowledge Commentary* edited by John Walvoord and Roy Zuck, and the scholars who produced *The Bible Knowledge Commentary* edited by Frank Gaebelein. These are both fine examples of technically sound and clearly expressed commentary sets. I have also benefited from many other scholars, linguists, theologians, and commentators who have invested their lives producing written works which elucidate the meaning of the text.

The Elder Board and congregation of Webster Bible Church receive my heart felt thanks as well. They have provided consistent encouragement to me in my written endeavors and have allowed me ample time to pursue them fully. This work is only possible because our church values my gifts and calling—thank you for that.

Finally, I would like to thank my wife, Carol, with whom I have spent many hours discussing the Bible, and who has consistently offered valuable insight into the Scripture. She is a trusted counselor and friend, who is truly a student of the Word. I would also like to thank her for "inspiring" me with the idea of writing "A Survey of the Bible" in the first place and encouraging me to pursue its publication.

Many thanks to all,
RFS

Introduction

The Bible is the greatest of all books because it is the only one authored by God. The apostle Paul stated this very thing to his young colleague Timothy, writing, "All Scripture is God-breathed" (2 Tim 3:16). Yet, this Sacred Text remains largely mysterious for many Christians, a daunting volume filled with ancient literature whose meaning is often elusive and enigmatic. This work is intended to help interested students of the Bible acquire a clearer and more comprehensive understanding of the sixty-six canonical books of Scripture, making their personal Bible study more productive and meaningful.

These summaries were produced over a two-year period of time, during which I studied the biblical books, wrote the surveys, and taught them to our people at Webster Bible Church. Each Sunday night from September to May we explored one book of the Bible in survey fashion-- in about 50 minutes. By nature, a survey includes and excludes. Other than some cosmetic editing and revising, I have tried to keep the work authentic to its occasion. Thus, these studies are not detailed commentaries but are concise synopses of the biblical books, laying a foundation upon which to expand one's understanding of and facility with the Scripture.

Occasionally, we would consider more than one book in an evening, such as when we studied the Minor Prophets. On rare occasions, we took two nights to study a book, as in the case of the Gospel of John and the books of Acts, Romans, and Revelation. However, I intentionally refused to spend longer than two sessions on any one book, remaining committed to providing a broad overview. I hope that these studies will serve as helpful tools for serious Bible students of all ages and church leaders committed to educating and equipping God's people with a greater knowledge of the greatest book in the world—the Bible.

Sola Scriptura,
RFS

1

The Pentateuch
(Genesis through Deuteronomy)

GENESIS

The book of Genesis is the book of beginnings. It reveals the beginning of the universe, the beginning of our world, and the beginning of life in all its varied forms, including the beginning of human life (Gen 1–2). God created it all out of nothing by the power and authority of his word. While we marvel at the created order and the vastness of the universe, God summarized its formation in only two chapters.

- It also reveals that human beings are special, being made in the image of God (Gen 1:26–27). This means that we have an intellect, emotions, and a will.
- It describes the fall, the beginning of corruption, and God's redemptive plan to restore fallen humanity to fellowship (Gen 3:15).
- It reveals God's patience with sinners and judgment of sin, most particularly in the cataclysmic, worldwide flood of Noah (Gen. 6—8).
- It recounts the beginning of the nation of Israel.
- God called Abraham, promising him a special land, a vast number of descendants, fame throughout the earth, and the eventual appearance of a Savior.
- This promise is called the Abrahamic Covenant (Gen 12:1–3).
- It was an unconditional covenant with conditional blessings attached. In this way it mirrors our salvation experience, which is a gift with additional benefits for obedience and faithful service.

- The book of Genesis then recounts the slow and steady development of the nation of Israel right up to their entrance into Egypt under Joseph.
- Much of Genesis is constructed around biographies—Abraham, Isaac, Jacob, and Joseph, detailing the tests, struggles, experiences, and victories associated with each character. We discover that the great patriarchs were not perfect, nor did they have easy lives, but they were men of great faith and perseverance.
- The Abraham narrative stretches from Genesis chapters 12 through 25. Here we learn the value God places upon faith, as Abraham and Sarah waited twenty-five years for the birth of their promised son.
- We also encounter one of the great tests of Abraham's life in Genesis 22, in which God told Abraham to offer up his son Isaac as a burnt offering. Incredibly, the patriarch followed God's instructions precisely, preparing to sacrifice his precious son of promise for whom he had waited so long. The New Testament offers insight into Abraham's thoughts at this crucial time of testing: "Abraham reasoned that God could raise the dead. . ." (Heb 11:19). God stopped Abraham from harming his son by providing a different sacrifice.
- When Abraham died, the great nation he was promised amounted to one son and a pair of twin grandsons. However, God's promises are always reliable, and Israel did develop into a great nation, principally during their time of enslavement in Egypt. Furthermore, Abraham's name is revered among the three great world religions today—Christianity, Judaism, and Islam. Also, Messiah, the Prince, came through Abraham's descendants, just as God promised. Indeed, God is always trustworthy.
- The story then continues with Isaac in chapters 24 through 27. Sadly, Isaac and Rebekah played favorites with their children; Isaac loved Esau, and Rebekah loved Jacob. This led to division in their home and eventually to a cruel piece of deception on the part of Rebekah and Jacob, deceiving Isaac to transfer the birthright to Jacob (Gen 27). Esau was outraged, and this fact led Jacob to flee home for a long time. He stayed with his uncle Laban, learning that we reap what we sow—as Jacob deceived, he was likewise deceived by his uncle.
- The Jacob narrative is found in chapters 28 through 35. While serving his uncle, Jacob fell in love with Rachel. He served Laban for seven years to acquire her in marriage; however, Laban deceived his nephew. Jacob ended up marrying Leah rather than Rachel. Distraught,

Jacob confronted Laban, who told him custom demanded that the eldest first be wed.

- Jacob would work another seven years for Rachel (Gen 28). Polygamy always produced intense feelings of animosity. As his parents, Jacob played favorites too. Upon his eventual return home, Jacob, fearing his brother's wrath, deployed his family members according to his affection for them. The text records, "And he put the handmaids and their children foremost, and Leah and her children next, and Rachel and Joseph last of all" (Gen 33:2). To his credit, he at least went out first to humbly meet Esau, discovering that his brother had forgiven him, warmly welcoming him back home.

- Much of the rest of the book deals with Joseph (Gen 37—50), recounting how he was called by God, hated by his brothers, sold into slavery, falsely accused, imprisoned, and eventually released, elevated to a position of authority, and finally reunited with his family in the land of Egypt.

- Wonderfully, Joseph held no bitterness against his brothers, living contentedly together with his reunited family for many years. This was because he realized that all he had experienced was part of God's plan for him and his family, writing, "You intended to harm me, but God intended it for good to accomplish what is now being done, the saving of many lives" (Gen 50:20). And Joseph lived to the ripe old age of 110 years, enjoying his children, grandchildren, and great-grandchildren! He never allowed the root of bitterness to entrench, and God blessed him for it.

Key verse: "And he believed in the LORD, and he credited it to him as righteousness" (Gen 15:6). This is the first occurrence of the condition of justification with God.

EXODUS

Exodus details the exit of the Jews from their bondage in Egypt until the completion of the Tabernacle and the appearance of the Shekinah glory of God.

- The three main sections of Exodus are: (1) The deliverance from bondage (Exod 1—19), emphasizing redemption; (2) the giving of the law (Exod 20—24), emphasizing obedience; and (3) instructions for building the Tabernacle (Exod 25—40), emphasizing worship.
- During their four hundred years of bondage, God fulfilled his seed promise to Abraham. The nation had multiplied from around seventy to about two million in number (Exod 1:7). This approximate calculation is derived from Numbers 1:46, in which there were 603,550 men tallied among the tribes who were twenty years and older and ready to go to war.
- Four hundred years of Israelite history passed in silence. Just because God is quiet does not mean he is disinterested.
- The book opens by reminding the reader of the names of the initial immigrants to Egypt, thereby connecting it with the closing narrative of Genesis (Exod 1).
- A new pharaoh, who never knew Joseph, both impressed and fearful of the rapid proliferation of the Jews, enslaved them (Exod 1).
- Just as Genesis is a story told via biography, so Exodus focuses upon a person—Moses. His birth, protection by Pharaoh's daughter, and defense of a fellow Israelite are explained in chapter 2.
- Moses fled to the land of Midian after killing an Egyptian and there met his future father-in-law, Jethro, and wife, Zipporah (Exod 2).
- God appeared to Moses in the burning bush and commissioned him to deliver the nation of Israel from the Egyptians (Exod 3).
- Moses was in no hurry to comply with God's request, naming both the stubbornness of the people and his own speech deficiencies as notable reasons to decline God's offer (Exod 4).
- However, God was not dissuaded and appointed him a helper—Aaron—and offered Moses the assurance of God's fellowship and protection (Exod 4).

- Chapters 5 through 12 recount the contest between Moses and Pharaoh, in which God is shown to be far more powerful than any adversary, natural or supernatural.
- As a sign of God's commissioning, Moses's staff became a serpent (Exod 7). While this miracle was duplicated by the magicians in Egypt, the magicians' serpents were devoured by the serpent of Moses.
- The plagues brought upon the land of Egypt were in increasing severity and force. In order, they were:
    - Water turned to blood (Exod 7)
    - Frogs plague the land (Exod 8)
    - Lice (Exod 8)
    - Swarms of flies (Exod 8)
    - Egyptian livestock stricken (Exod 9)
    - Boils afflict the Egyptians (Exod 9)
    - Hail and fire fall upon the Egyptians (Exod 9)
    - Plague of locusts (Exod 10)
    - Judgment of darkness and light (Exod 10)
    - The death of the firstborn in Egypt (Exod 11—12)
- Some of the plagues did not fall upon the children of Israel, but others did. For instance, the land of Goshen where the Israelites lived was spared the swarm of flies (Exod 8:22–25), the judgment of the hail and fire (Exod 9:26), and the judgment of darkness (Exod 10:23). Israel's cattle were also delivered from the consequences of the fifth plague (Exod 9:4). Of course, they were also rescued from the agony of the tenth plague, the death of the firstborn, because they followed the command of the Lord and placed blood on their doorposts (Exod 12).
- Chapter 12 explains the very first Passover, in which the people were instructed to sacrifice a spotless lamb and sprinkle the blood on their doorposts. When the Destroyer passed through the land, the blood protected them from judgment. Jesus was crucified on the Passover, fulfilling the symbolism to which this event looked forward.
- The children of Israel were then released from Egypt (Exod 12:31–13).

- Pharaoh pursued them in anger and was destroyed, along with his army, in the Red Sea (Exod 14).
- The people responded with thanksgiving for protection and deliverance (Exod 15).
- God provided for his wandering people with manna and water from the rock (Exod 16—17).
- Moses received leadership advice from Jethro, his father-in-law, focusing on the wisdom of appropriate delegation of responsibility and authority (Exod 18).
- The people arrived at Sinai under the direction of divine guidance (Exod 19).
- God revealed himself to the people but did not permit any of them to touch the Mount (Exod 19).
- The Ten Commandments were given (Exod 20).
- Civil laws were enacted to govern the affairs of society (Exod 21—23).
- Ceremonial laws framed the religious life of the nation, most particularly exacting details regarding the construction of the Tabernacle, the priestly garments, and the priesthood (Exod 24—28).
- The consecration of the priests and their provisions and the continual sacrifice were explained (Exod 29).
- Various practices and sacrifices were prescribed for the priests (Exod 30).
- God prepared spirit-filled craftsmen to build the Tabernacle and all that was associated with it (Exod 31).
- The Sabbath was established (Exod 31).
- The golden calf fiasco occurred in Exodus 32. We cannot properly appreciate the abrupt disappointment of both God and Moses unless we see this incident in the context. God was carefully revealing to Moses the manner in which his people should worship him, while down below the nation fell into worshipping idols and committing immorality.
- Moses interceded for the rebellious people (Exod 32).
- Moses received the second tablet of the law (Exod 33—34), and God gave Moses a fresh vision of his glory to sustain him in the work (Exod 33:18-23).

- Further instructions were issued regarding the feasts, Sabbath, dimension and construction of the Tabernacle and the courts, and the priests' garments (Exod 35—39). Interestingly, God received the offering from those who had willing hearts to give—and they had more than they needed (Exod 35:4—36:7).
- God was pleased by the attitude of the people and demonstrated this by appearing in a glorious cloud—the Shekinah—and visibly dwelling in the Tabernacle (Exod 40).

Key Verse: "The blood shall be a sign for you on the houses where you are; and when I see the blood, I will pass over you. No destructive plague will touch you when I strike Egypt" (Exod 12:13).

LEVITICUS

Leviticus is named after Levi, one of the sons of Jacob, who was assigned to the priestly role.

- The book opens with a lengthy description explaining a number of sacrificial offerings (Lev 1—7). This list includes the burnt offering (Lev 1), the grain offering (Lev 2), the fellowship offering (Lev 3), the sin offering (Lev 4), and the guilt offering (Lev 5).
- Moses instructed the priests how to offer these various sacrifices in chapters 5 through 7.
- The pattern for offering is the same throughout; a repentant sinner willingly took a sacrifice to the priests, who offered it as atonement for the sin of the violator.
- The sacrifices offered had to be without defect, as stated expressly in Lev 1:3, 10; 3:1, 6; 4:3, 23, 32; 5:15, 18; and 6:6.
- The priests had charge of offering the sacrifices. Their consecration for service was outlined in chapters 8 through 10.
- Aaron and his sons were sanctified for their priestly function. After he washed with water, Aaron donned the priestly garments. Then Moses anointed the Tabernacle with oil, and then he presented Aaron's sons with their priestly robes. Moses offered a number of sacrifices on behalf of the priests.
- After a seven-day period of isolation/consecration, the priests began their ministry of offering sacrifices on behalf of the people (Lev 9). The Lord sanctioned their ministry by visibly devouring the burnt offering laid on the altar (Lev 9:24).
- Chapter 10 chronicles the death of Aaron's sons at the hand of the Lord for trespassing into the Holy of Holies without making proper preparation (Lev 10). In chapter 16, God revealed the steps necessary in order for the high priest to pass beyond the veil. One must meet with God on God's terms, for God is holy.
- In chapter 11, clean and unclean foods were described and explained. The Israelites were commanded to be different from the nations round about them, and that seems to be the principal reason for these dietary distinctions. (These restrictions would be revoked in the Church Age, as evidenced by the vision of the sheet revealed to Peter in Acts 10).

- The purification of women following childbirth was set forth in chapter 12.
- Leprosy was one of the great scourges of the day, and chapters 13 through 15 explained how to diagnose it and isolate it from the people as a whole. Of course, this required isolating the infected person. It also explained how to disinfect a home wherein leprosy or some other contagious disease had festered.
- As a corrective to the irreverent intrusion into the Holy of Holies by Aaron's sons, God explained to Moses how the high priest must prepare himself to enter God's presence in chapter 16. Here the Day of Atonement, or Yom Kippur, was described. The high priest had to do the following in order to be acceptable.
    - First, he had to bring a bull for a sin offering and a ram for a burnt offering.
    - Second, he had to wash with water and wear the appropriate holy clothing.
    - Third, the bull and ram were offered for himself and his house.
    - Fourth, he presented two goats at the door of the Tabernacle—one to sacrifice and one to act as the scapegoat.
    - Next, he took incense and put it on the fire on the altar, creating a cloud of smoke that covered the mercy seat until he could apply the blood of the offerings to the mercy seat.
    - Then he sprinkled the blood of both the bull and the goat upon the mercy seat seven times with his finger, making atonement for the sins of the children of Israel.
    - Finally, Aaron laid his hands upon the scapegoat, confessing the sins of the people, after which he sent it away.
- He then changed clothes and washed himself, finishing the offerings for himself and the people.
- God told Moses that the people of God had to worship at the House of God. Some apparently took to sacrificing animals to pagan gods themselves out in the fields and not by means of the priests. God condemned this as an idolatrous practice (Lev 17).

- Chapters 18 through 20 discuss a variety of regulations governing interpersonal relationships. Various forms of immorality, idolatry, and occultism were rampant among the nations surrounding the Israelites. God wanted his people to be different and separate from these sorts of practices. The reason, repeatedly stated, was, "Be holy because I, the LORD your God, am holy" (Lev 19:2; 20:7; 20:26).
- Chapters 21 through 22 discuss the laws pertaining to the priests. Interestingly, priests were free to marry, but their wives needed to be honorable and virtuous. Furthermore, the priests could only offer unblemished sacrifices to the Lord (Lev 22:17–33).
- The special feasts (or holy celebrations) for the nation were established in chapter 23. They are as follows:
    - The Passover, celebrated on the fourteenth day of the first month, Nisan
    - The Feast of Unleavened Bread, beginning on the day after the Passover and lasting for a week
    - The Feast of First-fruits on the sixteenth of Nisan
    - Pentecost, which occurred fifty days after the Feast of First-fruits. (These first four feasts all anticipated the events surrounding the sacrifice and resurrection of Jesus Christ. He was slain on Passover, died as the sinless lamb, rose again as the first fruits from the dead on the Feast of First-fruits, and sent the Holy Spirit in fullness at Pentecost to begin the Church Age.)
    - The Feast of Trumpets, celebrated on the first day of the seventh month, Tishri
    - The Day of Atonement, celebrated on the tenth day of the seventh month
    - The Feast of Tabernacles or Booths, celebrated on the fifteenth day of the seventh month
- The Feast of Trumpets looks ahead to a final restoration of the nation of Israel, the Day of Atonement was when the blood of the sacrifice was applied to the mercy seat, and the Feast of Booths was instituted to serve as a reminder of the great work of God in bringing his people out of bondage from Egypt. It is good to remember what God has done.

The Pentateuch (Genesis through Deuteronomy)

- Additional laws and warnings for the nation appear in chapters 24 through 27. God clearly explained that if the people would listen and obey, they would be blessed, but if they would not listen and obey, they would be cursed (Lev 26).
- The book concludes, noting the importance of the tithe, which was generally paid in terms of agricultural goods.

Key Verse: "I am the LORD your God; consecrate yourselves and be holy, because I am holy..." (Lev 11:44).

NUMBERS

The book of Numbers derives its name from the two numberings of the people, as recorded in chapters 1 and 26.

- In chapter 1, God directed Moses to take a census and number all the men of the twelve tribes who were twenty years old or older. Moses delegated this responsibility to twelve key leaders, one over each of the tribes of Israel.
- The twelve tribes were: Reuben, Simeon, Gad, Judah, Issachar, Zebulon, Ephraim, Manasseh, Benjamin, Dan, Asher, and Naphtali.
- The men of war totaled 603,550 (Num 1:46).
- However, the Levites were not numbered in this census.
- In chapter 2, God arranged the twelve tribes around the Tabernacle—three tribes on the east, three tribes on the south, three tribes on the west, and three tribes on the north. These tribes formed an outer circle, and the Levites formed the inner circle, the core of which was the Tabernacle. Spatially, God was at the center of the nation; He desired to occupy that position spiritually as well.
- In chapters 3 through 5, the Levites from one month old upwards were numbered, and their work defined and explained. Men between thirty and fifty did the primary work in the Tabernacle, assisted by others (Num 4:1–3). The Levites were given to the Lord in lieu of the firstborn (Num 3:45–46). The difference between the number of Levites and the total number of the firstborn in Israel was compensated for by a tax of five shekels of silver each.
- The jealousy offering was explained in chapter 5, and the Nazarite vow in chapter 6. Typically taken only for a short time, the Nazarite vow included abstaining from wine or other alcoholic beverages and from shaving one's head. It represented a time of consecration to the Lord.
- The twelve leaders over the twelve tribes brought their dedication offering to the Tabernacle in chapter 7. They each brought an abundance, and their offerings were made publicly—they led by example (Num 7:13–17, etc.). Each offering was made on a single day for twelve consecutive days.
- The ceremonial cleansing and preparation of the Levites occurred in chapter 8.

- A reminder of the Passover and of God's divine guidance by means of the cloud was discussed in chapter 9. Moses was instructed to make two trumpets of silver. They would serve as both an alarm and a signal to the people.
- From Numbers 10:11 to 13:1, the people moved from Sinai to Kadesh-barnea (about two hundred miles). They began this journey on the twentieth day of the second month of the second year after the exodus from Egypt (10:11). When the cloud moved, the people followed and when it stopped, so did they.
- It is sobering to chronicle stubborn people—and highly instructive. The Jews regularly complained, murmured, challenged Moses's leadership, and blamed both Moses and God for their various trials and struggles.
- Chapter 11 is one such instance. The people were disgruntled about their food supplies, complaining about the manna. The text tells us that God heard their murmuring and was angry (Num 11: 1). His judgment fell on some, killing them. Moses intervened, as he did several times in the book, and God's anger was quelled.
- The people lusted for better food, and God gave them their desire and more. He sent quail for the people, but he also sent a plague with it.
- Moses became so weary of the complaining people that he asked God to kill him—if he had found favor with the Lord (Num 11:14–15)! This is a poignant reminder of the inevitable struggles and disappointments associated with leadership.
- Moses was regularly challenged concerning his right to lead. In chapter 12, his own brother and sister rose up against him. Aaron and Miriam wanted more power. They were angry at Moses for marrying an Ethiopian woman (Num 12:1). God legitimized the leadership of Moses by striking Miriam with leprosy (Num 12:10).
- Twelve spies were sent out on a reconnaissance mission to assess the land in chapter 13. Only Caleb and Joshua encouraged the conquest. All the others were awed by the inhabitants of the land (Num 13:33). The journey of faith is only successful when we focus on God and his promises rather than our circumstances.
- Once again the children of Israel murmured against Moses in chapter 14, trying to appoint new leaders to take them back to Egypt (Num 14:2–4).

- The Lord was deeply disappointed with their lack of faith (Num 14:11) but respected their decision to refuse to possess the land. However, as with all decisions, consequences followed. Their lack of obedience resulted in a forty-year forced march in the wilderness—until all the rebels had died (Num 14:28–33).

- Hearing this, the people declared their readiness to obey, but it was too late. We must take the opportunity while it is offered.

- In chapters 15 through 20, the years of wandering are recorded. How sad to witness these people marching on the longest funeral procession in history.

- Another rebellion against Moses is recorded in chapter 16, this time spearheaded by Korah. Carnality is often cloaked in spiritual language, and such was the case here. Korah argued that all the people were holy and so Moses had no exclusive rights to leadership. God endorsed the leadership of Moses by means of an earthquake and a consuming fire (Num 16:31–35).

- Amazingly, the very next day the people were once more murmuring against Moses and Aaron, asserting that they had killed the people of God (Num 16:41). God sent a plague against the people, which was intercepted by Moses and Aaron, but not before 14,700 people had died.

- God confirmed Aaron as the high priest by means of the rod that budded in chapter 17.

- In chapter 18, the inheritance of the Levites was reiterated. They had no land inheritance. Instead, they received the tithe of the people. They were responsible to tithe of the tithe. Everyone should participate in giving.

- The sacrifice of the red heifer is presented in chapter 19. This was a type of the sacrifice of Christ for cleansing as we walk as pilgrims through the world.

- In chapter 20, both the death of Miriam and the death of Aaron are recorded. The people were complaining again about a lack of water.

- The Edomites refused to allow the Israelites to pass through their land, thus bringing upon themselves a curse.

- Following the death of Aaron, the people stopped wandering and started marching toward the promised land. They defeated the Canaanites (Num 21:1–4).
- The people once again spoke out against God and Moses regarding their food supplies, inciting God to send fiery serpents into the camp. Moses made a bronze snake upon which the bitten people could look to receive healing (Num 21:8–9).
- Victory against the Amorites followed.
- The prophecies of Balaam given to Balak, king of Moab, are recorded in chapters 22 through 24.
- While Balaam was forbidden by the Lord from cursing Israel, he suggested an alternative plan. He advised Balak to form alliances with the Jews, inviting them to intermarry and attend their pagan festivals. Worldliness always weakens God's people, and such was the case here.
- Instead of destroying the Moabites, Israel intermarried with them, resulting in Israel's adoption of many of their idolatrous practices (Num 25: 1). The leaders of this movement were killed, and all those joined to Baal died in a plague (Num 25:1-9).
- The second numbering was recorded in chapter 26. The number of all the males twenty years and older who were fit for war now totaled 601,730 (Num 26:51).
- Moses prepared for death, as recorded in chapter 27. His concern was for continued godly leadership over Israel. God appointed Joshua as eventual successor to Moses.
- From chapter 28 to chapter 36, a variety of topics are addressed: the order of the feasts and offerings (Num 28—29), the law concerning taking a vow (Num 30), war with the children of Midian and the division of the booty, the settling of Reuben and Gad in Gilead, a summary of the journeying from Egypt to Jordan (Num 33), the forty-eight Levitical cities and the six cities of refuge (Num 35), and laws of land inheritance (Num 36).

Key Verse: "Then Caleb silenced the people before Moses and said, 'We should go up and take possession of the land, for we can certainly do it'" (Num 13:30).

DEUTERONOMY

Deuteronomy literally means "the Second Law," referring to the fact that Moses recounted the law to the new generation preparing to enter the promised land.

- Chapters 1 through 4 are reflective, reminding the new generation of their recent past. Moses discussed the years of wandering. What would have taken only eleven days for a faithful nation became a forty-year sojourn because of the refusal of the first generation to obey the voice of the Lord (Deut 1:2).

- The failure of the people to exercise faith and possess the land as well as the loyalty of both Caleb and Joshua are recounted in chapter 1.

- God told the children of Israel to deal kindly with both the children of Esau (the Edomites) and the children of Lot (the Moabites and the Ammonites), leaving their land alone. However, they were to wage war against the Amorites, specifically against Sihon, the King of Heshbon. This marks the beginning siege of the promised land, as described in chapter 2. The battle for conquest began immediately following the death of the last rebellious warrior (Deut 2:16).

- In chapter three, the conquest of Og, King of Bashan, is described. Though Israel had feared confronting giants in the past, their disobedience had only prolonged the inevitable. Indeed, the giants were still waiting to be removed. Og, King of Bashan, was apparently significantly larger than Goliath of Gath, measuring about nine cubits in height (approximately 162 inches tall or nearly 14 feet!), nor was he lean, having an iron bed about seventy-two inches wide (Deut 3:11). They also had to contend with fortified cities.

- Nonetheless, Israel conquered the land of the giants (including sixty fortified cities and many unfortified towns) because the Lord fought on their side. Reuben, Gad, and the half tribe of Manasseh received their land on the east side of the Jordan (Deut 3:12–22).

- In chapter four, Moses reminded the new generation of their responsibility to worship the Lord alone when they possessed the land, condemning idolatry of any kind or the making of any image to worship. He mentioned that God is a jealous God who deserves the loyalty of his people. This phrase is repeated many times in the book.

- Moses reiterated the Ten Commandments in chapter five, reminding the people of his role as mediator between them and God at Sinai.
- The heart of the law is stated in chapter 6: "Hear, O Israel: The LORD our God, the LORD is one. Love the LORD your God with all your heart and with all your soul and with all your strength" (Deut 6:4–5).
- Moses commanded parents to faithfully transmit the word of the Lord to their children, teaching them in all appropriate times and seasons (Deut 6:7).
- Moses was deeply concerned that prosperity would produce apathy toward God. He constantly challenged the new generation to resist the temptations associated with affluence, forgetting its source and taking it for granted (Deut 6:10–12).
- Seven specific nations were targeted in Israel's crusade: the Hittites, the Girgashites, the Amorites, the Canaanites, the Perizzites, the Hivites, and the Jebusites. These nations occupied the territory that God intended for Israel. They had been an exceedingly wicked group, and God used the Jews as an instrument of his judgment against them (Deut 7:1–3).
- Moses commanded that they not intermarry with these people, knowing that such a practice would only turn the hearts of the people toward false gods.
- The Lord will repay those who hate him—face to face (Deut 7:10).
- Blessing for obedience is a continual theme throughout the book, as in Deut 7:12ff.
- Moses reminded the people of God's faithfulness during their years of wandering. Neither their clothes nor their shoes wore out during their forty-year sojourn. He brought this up as a tribute to God's trustworthy character.
- Again Moses enjoined them to honor the one who prospered them: "But remember the LORD your God, for it is he who gives you the ability to produce wealth..." (Deut 8:18).
- Moses sadly reflected upon some of the more prominent failings of the people, directly addressing their refusal to confront the Anakim and their readiness to construct the molten calf. He did so to remind them that it was not their righteousness that had earned them their inheritance but God's faithfulness. Moreover, Israel was functioning

as a divine tool of judgment against the incredible wickedness of the nations they would drive out (Deut 9:4–5).

- God's gracious replacement of the initial set of tablets upon which the Commandments were inscribed was set forth in chapter 10.

- Chapter 11 outlines the importance of listening to the word of God. Listening, obeying, and transmitting to future generations is the key to success and blessing.

- Moses instructed the people to destroy all the sacred shrines and places of worship used by the people of the land. They were told not to inquire after these false gods or practice any of the abominable activities of the corrupt nations, most especially child sacrifice (Deut 12:30–31).

- God prescribed the death penalty for false prophets who would deceive the people. All prophecies needed to be tested by how they harmonized with the revealed word of God (Deut 13:1–3). Signs and wonders were not considered reliable tests of truth.

- Dietary restrictions were repeated in chapter 14, as well as the command not to mark one's self in the manner of the pagan people.

- The sabbatical year was established again in chapter 15, calling for the release of any Hebrew servants in the seventh year. Once the servant was freed, the former master was to give the servant a liberal offering from the flock and winepress (Deut 15:12–15). One could remain a perpetual servant by choice, if one wished to do so (Deut 15:16ff).

- The observance of the Passover, Feast of Weeks, and Feast of Tabernacles was discussed in chapter 16. Delegating judges and other officers to assist in ruling the people was established as well. It was considered vital that those who were chosen would judge without showing partiality.

- Chapter 17 discussed the importance of unblemished offerings, the penalty for idolaters, and the prescription for future monarchs in Israel. Interestingly, Solomon violated many of the prescriptive warnings set forth here (Deut 17:15–20).

- Chapter 18 proscribed occult activity and set forth the tests of a true prophet.

- The cities of refuge were endorsed in chapter 19, as was the principle of reciprocity or "an eye for an eye."
- Regulations for warfare were established in chapter 20. Only those who wanted to engage in warfare were enjoined to participate. Those who expressed fear were relieved of responsibility, because they might discourage others (Deut 20:8).
- Utter destruction was the prescription for dealing with the seven nations previously named.
- Various domestic relationships were prescribed in chapters 21 through 23, including those regarding disobedient and stubborn children (Deut 21:18). The Old Covenant stressed justice, not mercy.
- The Mosaic law of divorce appears in chapter 24. Divorce was permitted for "uncleanness," and remarriage was assumed—just as Jesus assumed it in Matt 19:8–11.
- Newlyweds were excused from most responsibilities during their first year of marriage (Deut 24:5). Also, those who owned farms were told to leave some of the harvest behind for the homeless and poor.
- Appropriate justice was the topic of Chapter 25.
- Only forty stripes could be administered against a criminal.
- God desires us to offer him the first fruits of our prosperity, not what is left over, as is outlined in chapter 26.
- The people were told to erect a stone monument when they crossed over the Jordan as a perpetual reminder of God's faithfulness (Deut 27:1–8).
- The Palestinian Covenant is set forth in chapters 28 through 30, citing the conditions under which the nation would secure the inheritance and maintain it.
- Obedience would bring blessing, and disobedience would result in cursing. Israel would be distressed and dispersed if they refused to comply with God's directives. History has testified to the truth of these warnings. If Israel repented and turned to the Lord, he would forgive and restore them.

- Moses called the people to a point of decision after clearly delineating their options. He viewed them as free to choose and responsible for choosing the right path—the path of life and blessing (Deut 30:14–20).
- Joshua was installed as the replacement for Moses. Moses prepared to die and to be gathered together with those who had gone on before him. Sadly, Moses learned of the eventual disobedience and dispersion awaiting his people (Deut 30:14ff). He was instructed to compose a prophetic song against them as a witness of their coming rebellion.
- Moses offered his blessing upon the tribes in chapter 33.
- Finally, Moses viewed the promised land from a distance. His death was recorded, and Joshua rose as his successor. His epitaph honors him as a truly great prophet and leader: "Since then, no prophet has risen in Israel like Moses, whom the LORD knew face to face" (Deut 34:10).

Key Verse: "Love the LORD your God with all your heart and with all your soul and with all your strength . . . ." (Deut 6:5).

2

The Historical Books
(Joshua through Esther)

The twelve historical books are Joshua through Esther (Joshua, Judges, Ruth, 1 and 2 Samuel, 1 and 2 Kings, 1 and 2 Chronicles, Ezra, Nehemiah, and Esther). The Old Testament consists of the law, history, poetry, and prophecy.

JOSHUA

- The book of Joshua is named after the key leader through whom Israel took possession of the promised land.
- Chapter 1 records the charge given to Joshua by God to lead the people valiantly into the new land. On three occasions God commanded Joshua to be strong and to have great courage. The key to success is meditating on the word of God and obeying it (Josh 1:8).
- Joshua sent only two spies to assess the land. They arrived at Jericho and found protection from Rahab the harlot. Rahab is illustrative, teaching us that all who turn to God in faith receive mercy from God. Both James and the writer of Hebrews praised Rahab for her gracious protection of the spies without explicitly sanctioning her lie, though it seems clear that deception in war or to protect human life is simply a case of promoting the greater good. The scarlet cord served as the sign for the invading army to show mercy.
- The reputation of the Israelites had preceded them. All the inhabitants of Jericho quaked in fear at their arrival because they had heard of their Red Sea experience and of their conquest of the Amorite kings on the other side of Jordan (Josh 2:10). What kind of reputation do we have?
- Chapter 3 reveals the strategy for crossing the first major obstacle in their path—the Jordan River. The plan required the priests, carrying

the Ark of the Covenant, to walk feet-first into the surging Jordan, causing it to immediately dry up. Of course, this required a robust faith. This scenario demonstrates the truth of Hebrews 11:6: "And without faith it is impossible to please God, because anyone who comes to him must believe that he exists and that he rewards those who earnestly seek him." And indeed, God proved true to his word. As soon as the soles of their feet touched the water, the Jordan dried up.

- Following their successful passage across Jordan, Joshua commanded twelve men to take twelve stones from the Jordan River bed and set them up on the other side as a witness to God's faithfulness and power. He twice commanded the people to refer to this stone monument to instruct their children about the true God and his great wonders (Josh 4). It is wise to remember significant moments in which we witness the gracious intervention of God.

- Once on the other side, the new generation was circumcised as a witness to their consecrated status. They had not performed circumcision during the years of wandering, so all those born during this time were still uncircumcised.

- Once the people had entered the land and were able to eat of the agricultural produce therein, the manna stopped. God provides for us when we cannot provide for ourselves, but he has a strong work ethic and expects us to be responsible when we have the ability to do so.

- The captain of the Lord's hosts met with Joshua at the end of chapter 5, most likely to encourage him for the battle (Josh 5).

- The plan for taking Jericho was set forth in chapter 6. The Israelites were to compass the city about one time each day for six days. Seven priests were instructed to bear the Ark and the trumpets. On the seventh day, the people compassed the city seven times. When the priests blew the trumpets and the people shouted out, the walls collapsed and the Israelites stormed the city, successfully destroying all its inhabitants—all except Rahab and those with her.

- God instructed the Israelites to take the precious metals (gold, silver, brass, and iron) for the Lord's treasury, but they were to destroy everything else. No one was to take any of the spoils.

- However, Achan transgressed the command not to keep any of the spoils, coveting silver, gold, and garments. He took some and hid it in the ground under his tent. This led to an Israelite defeat at the hands of a minimal force at Ai. Achan was found out, and he and his family were stoned to death (Josh 7). We never sin exclusively to ourselves; our sins always influence others.

- Israel set an ambush for the people of Ai, conquering them as recorded in chapter 8. In the course of the conflict, over twelve thousand men and women were slain—all the men and women of Ai.

- The deception of the Gibeonites is recorded in chapter 9. Fearing for their lives, the Gibeonites concocted a scheme, making an agreement with the Israelites, alleging that they came from a distant land. Donning old clothing, they convinced the Jews that they had traveled from afar to unite peacefully with them and learn of their God. Without consulting the Lord, the leaders agreed to this coalition. They later learned of the deception and made the Gibeonites their perpetual servants.

- The Southern and Northern Palestinian campaigns are detailed in chapters 10 and 11. God gave repeated victory to Joshua and the Israelites. In no other book is the conquest so complete and thorough. The Israelites moved systematically, conquering one king after the next. They utterly destroyed all that breathed. God had endured the wickedness of the people of the land for a long time, but eventually, as is always the case, judgment fell. The Jews served as divine tools of God's wrath upon those people.

- In chapter 12, a recounting of the kings conquered appears. In all, Israel conquered thirty-one kings in taking possession of the promised land (Josh 12:24).

- Though great progress had been made, there was still much to do, as chapter 13 records. Joshua was getting older and beginning to flag. The chapter outlines the areas and people groups yet to be conquered and also specifically states the inheritance of Reuben, Gad, and the half tribe of Manasseh.

- God keeps his promises. In chapter 14, Caleb finally secured the land of Hebron (a stronghold for the Anakim). He was eighty-five at the time, and according to his testimony, he was as strong and vibrant at that age as he had been forty-five years earlier! Undoubtedly, both the land and his good health were gifts from the Lord for his faithfulness.

- In chapters 15 through 17, the land inheritance was specifically divided up for Judah, Ephraim, and Manasseh. Unfortunately, all three left remnants of the people of the land without eradicating their influences entirely. History reminds us that partial obedience is disobedience and dangerous as well (Josh 15:63; 16:10; 17:12–13).

- The centrality of the Tabernacle was established in chapter 18. It was located at Shiloh, which was situated in the tribal allotment of Ephraim. This was to be the central place of worship for the Jews.

- The inheritance by lot for the remaining seven tribes appears in the rest of chapter 18 through chapter 19 (Benjamin, Simeon, Zebulon, Issachar, Asher, Naphtali, and Dan).

- Joshua received a special inheritance—the city of Timnath-serah in Mount Ephraim. Apparently, Joshua had requested this location, and his request was honored (Josh 19:49–51).

- The six cities of refuge were staked out in chapter 20, as were the forty-eight Levitical cities in chapter 21. The close of chapter 21 asserts that God had fulfilled all his goodness to the obedient nation. He withheld nothing from them and kept all his promises in giving them the promised land.

- Following the essential completion of the conquest, the two and a half tribes were sent home with hearty thanks for their help in securing the land over Jordan (Josh 22).

- Once they arrived home, they constructed their own altar upon which to worship the Lord. However, word reached the tribes on the other side of Jordan, and they concluded that their friends had become apostate. Thus, they prepared for war against them. Fortunately, Phinehas the priest and the heads of the ten tribes had the good sense to talk things over with the leaders of the two and a half tribes. They discovered that no such apostasy was intended and that their commitment to worship the Lord alone was firmly consecrated. They parted as friends. Our assumptions are frequently incorrect.

- From chapter 23 through chapter 24:28, Joshua proclaimed his final message to the nation of Israel and their elders, judges, and officers. He exhorted them with very much the same message that God gave him at the outset of the campaign to be brave and obedient. He also commanded them to remain undefiled by the people of the land who remained.

- Like a good preacher, Joshua brought his message to a point of decision in which he asked the people to "... choose for yourselves this day whom you will serve ... But as for me and my household, we will serve the LORD" (Josh 24:15).
- The people stoutly affirmed their loyalty to God and their commitment to serve him.
- Chapter 24:29–33 records the deaths of both Joshua and Eleazar. Leadership is influential. The text tells us that the people of Israel followed the Lord as long as Joshua lived and as long as the elders who served with him and who witnessed all the great deeds of God lived. The book closes with their burials and that of the remains of Joseph in Shechem.

Key Verse: "Do not let this Book of the Law depart from your mouth; meditate on it day and night, so that you may be careful to do everything written in it. Then you will be prosperous and successful" (Josh 1:8).

JUDGES

The book of Judges is so named after the special leaders employed by God who delivered Israel from oppression and bondage.

- Chapter 1 clearly indicates that this book is a continuation of the book of Joshua, resuming the story immediately following his death.
- The opening chapter recounts the conquest of Judah over the Canaanites and most particularly the failure of the tribes to thoroughly purge the land of its delinquent residents. Of course, this partial catharsis resulted in continual trouble for the Jews, who constantly struggled with syncreticism, idolatry, and spiritual treason of various sorts.
- They put the pagan people to forced labor, thinking they could control and contain them. However, the Jews ended up being controlled by them; such is often the case with sin.
- The new generation who rose up after Joshua died turned against the Lord and did evil (Judg 2:10–11). A content summary occurs in 2:14–23 that offers an overview of the rest of the book: the people rebel, God punishes them through an intermediary, they repent and call on God, God raises up a judge to deliver them, and once delivered (generally after the judge dies), the people return to their disobedience. This pattern is habitual throughout the book.
- One recurring phrase is particularly sobering: "And the anger of the Lord burned against Israel."
- Through intermarrying, Israel became polluted, and God brought them into servitude to the king of Mesopotamia for eight years (Judg 3:8–9).
- The people cried out to the Lord, who sent forth a judge—Othniel. Othniel delivered the people through war, and the land rested for forty years.
- After Othniel died, the people returned to their evil ways and were once again subdued by the Moabites for eighteen years (Judg 3:12–14). Again the people cried unto the Lord, who sent another judge to rescue them.

- Ehud assassinated Eglon, the king of Moab, using a concealed dagger. This was the first step in a siege led by Ehud against the Moabites, in which Israel conquered them.
- Shamgar was the third judge, of which little is said except that he killed six hundred Philistines with an ox goad and delivered Israel (Judg 3:31).
- Chapter 4 focuses on the rescue afforded by Deborah and Barak.
- Sisera, the captain of the hosts of the Canaanites, had nine hundred chariots of iron with which he oppressed the people of God. Of course, this oppression, like all the others, resulted from Israel's wickedness in turning from the Lord.
- The judges waged war against Sisera. A great torrent rendered their chariots immobile, giving the Jews victory. Sisera fled to the home of Jael, in which he met his doom. She assassinated him by driving a large nail through his temple (Judg 4:21).
- Chapter 5 records the song of Deborah and Barak, in which they praised God for the victory and Jael for her bravery in killing Sisera.
- Chapters 6 through 8 deal principally with Gideon, the sixth judge. Once again the people of Israel had abandoned the Lord, who delivered them into the hands of the Midianites for seven years.
- Their oppression was so severe that many Jews were living in caves. When the Israelites had sown their crops, the Amalekites and Midianites came and destroyed them, causing a severe famine. Thus they turned to the Lord for help again. An angel appeared to Gideon, charging him with the task of delivering the people.
- Gideon was hesitant to say the least, employing some of the same tactics as Moses when God recruited him.
- Gideon had reason to fear, because his own father and many of his close associates had turned to Baal (Judg 6:25–27).
- He was instructed to destroy his father's altar to Baal and replace it with one to the Lord.
- In obedience, he did so in the secrecy of night. Upon awakening, the men of the city wanted to kill Gideon for this blasphemous act. However, his father shielded him, asserting that Baal should do his own avenging.

- Gideon began preparing the rebellion against the oppressors. However, before initiating it, he respectfully asked God for a sign. Gideon put out the fleece, asking that in the morning the dew might only be upon the fleece and not the ground. This happened. Gideon asked for another sign regarding the fleece. He requested that on the next day the fleece might be dry and the ground wet; God graciously consented again.
- God whittled down the fighting force from about thirty-two thousand to three hundred men (Josh 7). God did not want Israel to take credit for the victory he was about to give them.
- The strategy for the battle was laid out to Gideon, sounding somewhat like the plan at Jericho. Trumpets, pitchers, and lamps served as the weapons. When the trumpets sounded and the lamps were broken, God wrought confusion in the enemy camp. They ended up fighting each other.
- You just can't please everyone. The tribe of Ephraim was insulted that they had not been invited to fight (Judg 8:1). Interestingly, they would make the same complaint later in the book regarding another war. Perhaps they were just difficult to work with.
- As a reward for his service, Gideon requested the earrings of the vanquished. They placed them upon a garment, and Gideon gathered them up and made an ephod from them. (An ephod was a close-fitting, armless vest.)
- Sadly, this object became a stumbling block for Israel and Gideon (Judg 8:27). As soon as Gideon died, Israel turned again to Baal. They did not remember the Lord, nor did they show kindness to the household of Gideon.
- Chapter 9 records the reign of Israel's first king (though it was a very limited monarchy), Abimelech. As a son of one of Gideon's concubines, he sought the right to rule. Hiring worthless mercenaries, he killed all the sons of Gideon (seventy in number). Only Jotham, the youngest son, survived the attack.
- However, treachery was rewarded with treachery, and the co-conspirators fell into arguing. Abimelech was killed trying to hold on to his power. A woman dropped a millstone upon his head. In order to avoid the humiliation of being killed by a female, he ordered his armor bearer to finish him off.

- Chapter 10 very briefly records the judgeship periods of Tola and Jair, the seventh and eighth judges. After Jair died, the children of Israel again did evil in the sight of the Lord, serving other gods. In his anger, God brought the people into servitude to the Philistines and the Ammonites. This set the stage for the emergence of the ninth judge, Jephthah.

- Jephthah, the son of Gilead, was the son of a prostitute, but the legitimate sons of Gilead expelled their half-brother Jephthah, not wishing to share their inheritance with him. However, he was an effective fighter and leader, and the people turned to him for help in their bondage. Jephthah tried reasoning with the king of Ammon, which failed. So Jephthah and his troops invaded the Ammonites, defeating them.

- His tragic vow led to the sacrifice of his daughter. It is unclear if he actually offered her as a sacrifice or whether he made her a perpetual virgin. Either way, his haste led to grave consequences.

- Once again the children of Ephraim were angry about being omitted from the fray. However, Jephthah asserted that he had called them, but they did not respond. Thus he fought with his own men. Angered by their insolence, Jephthah and company fought with Ephraim, using their native speech impediment against them. The Ephraimites apparently could not pronounce the "sh" sound. Once discovered, they were slain.

- Chapter 12 concludes with a brief summary of the next three judges: Ibzan, Elon, and Abdon (Judg 12:8–15).

- The story of Samson is set forth in Judges 13 through 16.

- His birth was announced by the angel of the Lord.

- He was born of a woman who had previously been barren, so his was a special birth.

- Samson was born into a godly family, as evidenced by Manoah's concern to raise him properly (Judg 13:8f).

- He was assigned a special mission by God.

- The Spirit of God came upon him, giving him super-human strength.

- He was a Nazarite—one who could not consume wine or strong drink or eat any unclean thing. These restrictions applied to his mother while Samson was in her womb.

- Yet Samson, the strongest man who ever lived, allowed his carnal nature to rule over him. His first recorded words, "I have seen a woman," summarize his life.
- He was conformed to the spirit of his day and chose to form relationships with pagan women who did in fact turn his heart away from God.
- His parents encouraged him to marry a woman from Israel, but he would not listen.
- Though Delilah was obviously intent on betraying him, he finally revealed the source of his strength—his hair. Once cut off, he became as an ordinary man.
- He was imprisoned by the Philistines, who plucked out his eyes and turned him to forced labor.
- They mocked God and celebrated Samson's defeat.
- At the last, Samson prayed and was restored, receiving super-human strength, killing many Philistines as he pulled down the pillars of a building in which they reveled.
- Though God did restore and use him at the last, Samson wasted much of his life. The paths we choose determine our destiny.
- Chapters 17 through 21 vividly illustrate the religious and moral decline that occurred throughout Israel in the latter days of the judges. Idolatry, superstition, and syncretism characterized the land. A man named Micah created images of gods and worshipped them in a family temple. He hired a traveling Levite, believing that his presence would bring him blessings.
- The tribe of Dan was dissatisfied with their land inheritance and sought to expand their land holdings, ravaging Micah's household in the process and absconding with the Levite and his false gods. When Micah objected, the Danites warned him to leave or be killed.
- The tribe then invaded a peaceful area and killed all the inhabitants of the city, burning the place to the ground (Judg 18).
- Chapter 19 outlines the shameful abuse of a concubine by the people of Gibeah, who were members of the tribe of Benjamin. She was unfaithful to her husband and left him for four months. However, he pursued her and persuaded her to return home with him. He was a Levite. They stopped for rest in Gibeah.

- The men of the city converged on the place in which they stayed, demanding immoral relations with them, representing something of a return to Sodom. The woman was sent out, raped, and abused. She died, and the husband dismembered her, sending her in pieces to the twelve tribes of Israel.
- This horrific scene shocked the other tribes, who converged against the tribe of Benjamin. Rather than expressing remorse, Benjamin gathered together to defend themselves and their actions, assembling twenty-six thousand warriors.
- Civil war ensued. After three days of fighting, Benjamin was defeated.
- Only six hundred warriors escaped to the wilderness. The other tribes swore that they would not permit their daughters to marry anyone of the tribe of Benjamin.
- Making oaths in haste is unwise, and they later regretted it. However, they could not renege on their promise, so they slaughtered the people of Jabesh-Gilead, taking four hundred women back to the tribe of Benjamin. They also devised a scheme for the sons of Benjamin to kidnap other women to become their wives—this they did!

The concluding verse is the key verse: "In those days Israel had no king; everyone did as he saw fit" (Judg 21:25). When objective authority is lost, anarchy reigns

RUTH

The book of Ruth is named after the principal heroine of the story, Naomi's daughter-in-law, Ruth.

- Chapter 1 recounts the migration of Naomi's family from Judah to Moab during the days of the Judges. A famine drove them to relocate. It is possible that this was the very famine encountered by Gideon in the book of Judges.
- Naomi's husband, Elimelech, and both her grown sons, Mahlon and Kilion, died during their stay in Moab, leaving behind three widows.
- News arrived in Moab that the famine had abated in Judah, so Naomi made plans to return home. She urged her daughters-in-law to remain in their homeland, even encouraging them to return to their ancestral pagan worship. The reason for this is that Naomi was bereft of all hope. Certainly she would never again bear sons, and the girls, in her opinion, would be much better attended in their native environment.
- They had established very close bonds. Neither woman wanted to depart at first; however, finally Orpah consented and kissed Naomi goodbye. But Ruth refused to desert her, clinging to her and declaring, "Where you go I will go, and where you stay I will stay. Your people will be my people and your God my God" (Ruth 1:16b).
- When Naomi saw the sincerity and determination of Ruth, she relented and allowed her to come to Judah with her.
- Naomi returned to Bethlehem feeling very depressed. She lamented, "... Call me Mara, because the Almighty has made my life very bitter. I went away full, but the LORD has brought me back empty ..." (Ruth 1:20–21).
- An important detail is mentioned at the close of chapter 1—the women's return coincided with the beginning of barley harvest.
- Chapter 2 begins by introducing another character to the story—Boaz. He was a kinsman of the house of Elimelech, Naomi's deceased husband.
- Ruth was a hard worker who was willing to humble herself and gather scraps in order to survive and care for Naomi. Had she been

- too proud to do so, she never would have met her future husband. Life unfolds in steps, and sometimes those steps are rather halting.
- After settling in to their new home, Ruth asked permission to go to a local field and gather food after the reapers. The landowners hired reapers or employed family members to harvest their agricultural goods. Some scraps were missed along the way, and these were to be left for the community poor, a group to which Ruth belonged.
- The field to which Ruth went belonged to Boaz. He came to the field to survey the harvesting process and saw Ruth. Her reputation had preceded her, and Boaz determined to treat her with kindness and generosity. He gave her instructions to continue gleaning in his fields and to take water any time she was thirsty. Ruth responded with gratitude and humility, thanking him for his gracious reception (Ruth 2:10). Ruth's commitment to Naomi and to the God of Israel was well known (2:11–12).
- Sometimes God provides for his people through other people. Ruth had placed her trust in God, and Boaz determined to honor that commitment and show her kindness. Boaz placed her under the protection of his other maidens and warned his male workers not to bother her. He also invited her to eat with the reapers at mealtime and instructed his harvesters to intentionally drop handfuls of grain at various intervals so that Ruth would have a sufficient supply.
- At the end of this day of hard work, Ruth had beaten out the grain from the stalks and had accumulated an ephah of barley—about half a bushel, or the equivalent of roughly thirty pounds (Ruth 2:17). This was a very successful effort, representing enough food to feed both Ruth and Naomi for several days.
- Not surprisingly, Naomi was thrilled with the success of the day. Upon hearing that Ruth worked in the field of Boaz, she was doubly delighted, telling Ruth that he was a near kinsman. This seems to indicate that Ruth was quite unaware of this fact, and that God did providentially steer her to him. Ruth continued to work in the fields daily throughout the barley and wheat harvest, a period representing several weeks.
- But what would happen to the women once the harvest had ended?
- Boaz was a close relative to the family and could serve as a kinsman redeemer if he so desired—that means he could redeem property or

persons in the name of the family and raise up a son to the family name (Deut. 25:5–10).

- Boaz was threshing his harvest on a particular day. The people generally took turns using the threshing floor, which was a flat, hard area on an elevated surface. Threshing was the process of beating the grain out from the stalks. Winnowing involved throwing the grain in the air and allowing the wind to remove the chaff. The grain was then removed from the threshing floor and stored, to be consumed or sold later.

- Naomi instructed Ruth to present herself to Boaz on this particular day. She prepared herself and then went to the threshing floor and waited.

- After Boaz had finished eating, he found a place to lie down and fell asleep. Typically, the thresher stayed with his produce to protect it from thieves. About midnight, Ruth went, uncovered his feet, and lay down at his feet. Boaz awoke with a start, and Ruth explained that it was she and requested that Boaz fulfill the role of kinsman redeemer for her.

- Some speculate that something immoral happened here; however, the text does not support that idea. Boaz acted responsibly, and so did Ruth. Her integrity was affirmed by Boaz (Ruth 3:11). He accepted her invitation to marriage but only if a closer relative in the town refused this option.

- Very early, before sunup, Boaz instructed Ruth to return home. However, he would not send her away empty-handed, placing six measures of barley in her shawl (about sixty pounds worth!). Ruth likely carried this load upon her head. The first thing Boaz would do the next day, as Naomi knew, was determine if he could marry Ruth by discussing the issue with the nearer relative who remained unnamed.

- Boaz greeted this near kin and invited him to the village gate to sit down and discuss the issue. The business of a community was often conducted by the men at the gate of the city. He also gathered ten respected leaders of the town to meet with them, making the proceedings legal and formal.

- Boaz approached the issue shrewdly, demonstrating that he had thought carefully about his plan. He began by explaining that Naomi had a parcel of land that needed to be redeemed. If the other relative wanted it, he could buy it, and if not, Boaz said he would do so. The unnamed relative stated that he would buy it.

- However, there was more to the deal. If he bought the field, he also had to buy Ruth and raise up children to the family name. This he was unwilling to do. Why? Most probably because in bearing male sons, Ruth's children would take possession of the land and perhaps contest for other possessions in the unnamed person's family. He was not interested in taking such risks. Thus, he backed out of the deal.

- One of them drew off his shoe and gave it to the other, sealing the deal. (Cultural customs are indeed interesting!)

- The elders acknowledged that the agreement was official. By now a crowd had gathered and the women cheered, asking God's blessing upon Boaz and Ruth's union, most especially that Ruth would be as fruitful as Rachel and Leah.

- And indeed she was fruitful, bearing a son. Wonderfully, Naomi was charged with taking care of this little baby. Hope was restored—Naomi had found security, love, and family. Even in the darkness of despair and loss, God had been faithfully watching, leading, and providing.

- God had worked through the faithful devotion of a young woman named Ruth and the generosity and kindness of a wealthy landowner named Boaz.

- Indeed, the theme of the book is discovered at the end of the book where the reader learns that even in the uncertain and perilous days of the judges, God was at work. The lineage through which the blessing of the world would arrive was growing.

Key verse: "The women living there said, 'Naomi has a son.' And they named him Obed. He was the father of Jesse, the father of David" (Ruth 4:17). Ruth, the Moabitess, was King David's great grandmother and an important ancestor of Messiah the Prince, the blessing of the whole world.

1 SAMUEL

The book of 1 Samuel chronicles the revival of the priesthood under Samuel, the introduction of monarchy in Israel under Saul, and the jealousy of Saul toward David, his eventual successor.

- Chapters 1 through 8 focus upon Samuel. Elkanah and his wife Hannah went up to worship and sacrifice at Shiloh yearly. Hannah, one of two wives, was childless. She was mocked by Elkanah's second wife, Peninnah, who did bear children.

- In depression, Hannah made a vow unto the Lord at the temple that if God gave her a son, she would devote him back to the Lord. Eli the priest thought she was drunk because of her great sorrow. After Hannah explained herself, Eli realized his mistake and asked for God's blessing on her. Indeed, God answered Hannah's prayer and she conceived, bearing a son.

- After Samuel was weaned, Hannah brought him to Eli and asked him to mentor her son, whom she had devoted to the Lord.

- She then offered a song of praise to God for his wonderful kindness and power (1 Sam 2:1-9).

- Eli took the young boy and put him to work in the temple.

- Samuel was a good boy who worked diligently and served Eli faithfully; Eli thanked Samuel's parents for bringing Samuel to him. God graciously gave Hannah more children—three sons and two daughters. (One can never out give God.)

- Eli's sons, Hophni and Phinehas, were evil. They were gluttonous and immoral in their dealings as priests, dishonoring the sacrificial system and those who came to sacrifice.

- God sent a prophet to rebuke Eli for his lack of parental control over his grown sons, saying that he had honored them above the Lord. Therefore, God was going to slay them both in one day (1 Sam 2:27-36).

- God called out to Samuel three times on one particular night. At first, the child thought it was Eli; however, it was not. Samuel made himself available to God, and God affirmed his plan to replace the corrupt priests with Samuel. God judged Eli and his household—the sons because of their inveterate sin and the father for his failure to restrain them (1 Sam 3:13).

- Samuel continued to grow, finding favor with God and man.
- Chapters 4 through 8 recount Israel's warfare with the Philistines, particularly the lost Ark of the Covenant. In chapter 4, the Philistines waged war against Israel, defeating them and stealing the Ark of the Covenant. In this war, the two sons of Eli were slain and upon hearing the news from the battle, Eli fell backward, breaking his neck. Also, his pregnant daughter-in-law went into premature labor and died giving birth to a child she named Ichabod, which means, "The glory has departed from Israel."
- In chapters 5 through 6, God punished the Philistines for defiling the Ark, sending tumors of various sorts to torment them. Thus, they kept moving the Ark from one place to the next. At first they placed it in Ashdod before their god Dagon. However, Dagon did obeisance before the Ark, and God finally severed the hands and the head of Dagon as it lay helpless before the Ark. The Philistines knew they were in trouble at this point. Finally they returned the Ark with an offering, hoping to quell God's displeasure with them.
- Finally, after twenty years of stalemate, Israel repented of its idolatry and turned whole-heartedly to the Lord. Samuel offered sacrifice and earnest prayer for the warriors in their confrontation with the Philistines, and Israel prevailed. Samuel faithfully judged Israel all the days of his life. He made his sons judges too, but they failed to follow the Lord! They became corrupt, taking bribes and perverting justice. Therefore, Israel rejected their leadership and demanded a king.
- Samuel was disappointed at their request, because he considered Israel a theocracy. However, God told him to fulfill their request for a king, but not before warning them of all this would mean (taxation, conscription, etc.). But the people would not relent; "Give us a king as the other nations" was their united cry, and Samuel did so.
- Chapters 9 through 15 chronicle the call of Saul to be the first king of Israel.
- Saul was an imposing physical specimen who stood taller than anyone else from the shoulders upward.
- God told Samuel that Saul was his choice. Samuel encountered Saul as he was attempting to locate some missing livestock.

- In chapter 10, Samuel privately anointed Saul as king, giving him a number of specific signs as a means of assuring his heart. All the signs came to pass, including the sign that Saul too would prophesy.
- Chapter 10:17–27 records the public installation of Saul as the first king of Israel. He began as a very humble and sincere leader. They had to literally pull him into the limelight, as he apparently had a strong aversion to it (1 Sam 10:21–23).
- Saul led the Israelites against the Ammonites, utterly destroying them. The Ammonites wanted to put out the right eyes of all the men of Jabesh-gilead, making them their servants and insulting Israel.
- Following Saul's great victory, the people wanted to kill those who had questioned Saul's commissioning as king, but Saul rebuked them. Instead, all the people celebrated the victory and publicly proclaimed Saul as their rightful king, offering sacrifices to the Lord.
- Samuel enjoined the people to continue following the Lord, though they had sinned and made many mistakes. He also promised them that his prayers would continue on their behalf (1 Sam 12).
- Chapter 13 records Saul's rash disobedience of offering a burnt offering and a peace offering to the Lord, a privilege established for the priests alone. Saul had good reason to be impatient—the Philistines were set in array against him and Samuel was late. However, his rash actions were not justifiable, even in an emergency situation. Samuel informed Saul that the kingdom would be taken from him and given to another. (It would have been established forever had he been patient.)
- In chapter 14, the daring account of Jonathan and his armor bearer against the Philistines is recorded. They snuck into a stronghold and smote about twenty of the enemy, creating confusion throughout the ranks. Indeed, the Philistines ended up fighting each other, and Israel was rescued.
- Saul had issued an order that none should eat that day, lest they die. Jonathan had not heard the edict and had eaten some honey after his battle. Sadly, Saul was prepared to kill even his son, but the people intervened for Jonathan, and he was delivered from the hand of his father.
- Unremitting warfare characterized the reign of Saul. They fought against Moab, Ammon, Edom, and the Philistines throughout his reign.

- God commanded Saul to utterly destroy Amalek, including women, children, and livestock. However, Saul left King Agag alive and kept much of the booty. When confronted by Samuel, Saul pointed fingers. First, he denied any wrongdoing. Then, when that didn't work, he blamed the people for the transgression. Finally, Saul admitted his sin but was principally concerned with his image before the elders of Israel, asking Samuel to honor him by worshipping together with him. After agreeing to Saul's request, Samuel fulfilled God's command and killed Agag. Then the elder statesman left Saul and returned to his home in Ramah. Samuel would never see Saul again and left him with a heavy heart.

- Saul illustrates the fallacy of rationalizing disobedience for a "good reason." Even a "good reason" does not legitimize disobedience to God.

- Samuel was led of the Lord to privately anoint a new king in Israel. This mission took him to the home of Jesse, where we learn that God looks on the heart while humans tend to judge by appearance.

- After viewing seven sons of Jesse, Samuel asked if there were any others. After a puzzled pause, Jesse remembered there was one other—the youngest, David. He was out watching the sheep. Samuel anointed him in the presence of his brothers (1 Sam 16:1–11). One wonders what they thought of all this!

- Saul was suffering from depression and other ailments to such an extent that his counselors advised retaining a musician to soothe his troubled spirit. David was employed at the court of Saul (1 Sam 16:14–23).

- The champion of the Philistines, Goliath, challenged the army of Israel in chapter 17. This huge warrior paralyzed the entire army for forty days. Each morning and evening he issued his intimidating message, asking for a man to come and fight with him; there were no takers.

- On an errand from his father, David entered the camp and confronted the problem. He offered to go down and fight the Philistine intruder. Saul, who should have fought Goliath, offered David his war equipment. However, it didn't fit. So, David fought Goliath with a sling and stones. Interestingly, he took five stones. This was most likely in case Goliath's brothers sought to intrude.

- This brave act incited respect, admiration, and love on the part of Jonathan, Saul's son, toward David. They became the best of friends. Jonathan demonstrated great humility by giving David his royal garments. Of course, Jonathan was next in the royal succession after Saul. But his actions indicate that he felt David was the better qualified to become the next king. Unlike his father, Jonathan was not jealous of David nor threatened by him (1 Sam 18).
- Saul became very jealous of David's success and popularity (1 Sam 18:6–9).
- Saul's daughter Michal also loved David, and Saul, knowing the character of his daughter, decided to give her to David as a snare to him (1 Sam 18:20–21).
- Saul sought to kill David, as recorded in chapter 19, but David fled to Samuel and the two hid at Naioth.
- Jonathan and David developed a plan by which David would be warned of Saul's temper, as recorded in chapter 20.
- Indeed, Saul was bent on killing David, so David and Jonathan said a sad farewell (1 Sam 20:1–42).
- David went to Nob, seeking refuge among the priests. He pretended that he was on business from the king and secured a weapon—Goliath's sword. He then fled to Gath, feigning insanity in the presence of Achish, the king of Gath.
- David hid in a cave in Adullam, gathering to him all those who were in distress about the reign of Saul—about four hundred men. He became their leader.
- Doeg the Edomite informed Saul of David's respite in Nob with the priests. Angered about an alleged conspiracy, Saul went there and commanded Doeg to slay all the priests of the Lord. He killed eighty-five priests, as well as women and children along with livestock. Saul had become quite mad. Of the priests, Abiathar escaped and warned David.
- David saved the inhabitants of Keilah from the Philistines, but they were prepared to deliver him to Saul, so he fled. Saul surrounded David at En-gedi but was prevented from finding him due to an attack at another location by the Philistines (1 Sam 23).
- After Saul dealt with the Philistine incursion, he returned to En-gedi to seek David. Saul entered the very cave in which David was hiding,

making himself an easy prey. However, David refused to kill his enemy. As Saul was leaving the area, David revealed his location saying he could have killed him. Instead, he had spared his life. "Doesn't this reveal my loyalty?" David asked. Saul repented of his jealous rage, momentarily realizing his folly. However, his repentance would not last long.

- The death of Samuel is recorded in chapter 25
- David and his men were hiding out on Mt. Carmel
- Here the account of the foolishness of Nabal and the wisdom of Abigail his wife is recorded. Her quick action and humility spared many lives. She became David's wife.
- Again David spared Saul, this time in the wilderness of Ziph (1 Sam 26). Abishai and David crept into the camp and took Saul's spear and cruise of water and then exited. Then David woke the camp and told them of his exploits, seeking to prove his loyalty. Again Saul praised David and promised to pursue him no more.
- In chapter 27, David sought refuge in Gath under Achish, the king. The king received David, believing that he fought against his own people. However, David actually led campaigns against the enemies of Israel. He lived there for sixteen months.
- The Philistines prepared for war with Israel, and Saul consulted the witch at Endor in chapter 28. The witch seemed genuinely surprised that she actually conjured up Samuel. Samuel told Saul that on the morrow the Philistines would conquer Israel's army and that Saul and his sons would die.
- In chapter 29, the Philistine generals rejected David, and Achish the king sadly expelled him from Gath.
- David and his men left Achish and went to their camp to make preparations to leave the area. However, when they arrived, they discovered that their camp had been ransacked by the Amalekites and all the people had been taken.
- David's men were so anguished that they spoke of killing David, but David encouraged himself in the Lord. They pursued the invaders, receiving assistance from an Egyptian servant who the Amalekites had abandoned. David and his men defeated the invaders and recovered all that had been taken. They divided the booty among those who participated in the conflict and those who stayed behind guarding the stuff.

- In chapter 31, the words of Samuel came true—the Philistines defeated the Israelites in a major offensive and Saul and his sons, Jonathan, Abinadab, and Melchishua, all died. Saul died of a self-inflicted stab wound upon realizing the inevitable defeat.
- The enemy decapitated Saul and put his armor in the house of Ashtaroth. A group of brave warriors from Israel rescued the bodies of Saul and his sons and burned them and buried their bones at Jabesh, fasting for seven days out of respect for them.
- Thus ended the life and the reign of Israel's first king, Saul. A new chapter was about to begin.

Key verse: "... The LORD does not look at the things man looks at. Man looks on the outward appearance, but the LORD looks on the heart" (1 Sam 16:7).

2 SAMUEL

David did not have long to celebrate the recovery of his family, because three days later he received word of the Philistine victory over Israel and the death of Saul and his three sons.

- The message came via an Amalekite who claimed to be the agent of Saul's death. It is likely that he lied, hoping to ingratiate himself to David.
- Little did he know that in spite of all the ill treatment by Saul, David still loved and respected Saul and of course, his son Jonathan.
- Instead of giving the messenger honor, David executed him.
- The rest of chapter 1 records David's elegy of Saul and Jonathan.
- A breach in the nation occurred in chapter 2. Judah received David as their king but Israel (the ten tribes) received Ishbosheth, Saul's surviving son, as their new monarch, leading the nation into civil war. David reigned from Hebron, a city in Judah, for seven and a half years (2 Sam 2:11).
- But Abner, the captain of Saul's army, made Ishbosheth king over Israel (2 Sam 2:8–10).
- Joab, the general of David's army, fought a war against Abner in which they soundly defeated the opposing force. However, in the battle, Joab's brother, Asahel, was killed by Abner.
- Abner's troops were forced to retreat.
- Over time, the house of David gained superiority over the house of Saul (2 Sam 3).
- David had multiple wives, and he had six sons born in Hebron.
- Ishbosheth made a strategic error by accusing Abner of violating one of Saul's concubines. Abner deeply resented this and transferred his allegiance to David, weakening Saul's house even more.
- Abner communicated his intentions to David by means of messengers. David was thrilled at this turn of events and told Abner to come to see him, including one caveat. He was to bring Michal, Saul's daughter, to him when he came. She was already married, but this fact did not dissuade Abner, who tore her from her husband and took her to David.

- David and Abner had a cordial meeting in which Abner pledged his loyalty to David. David sent him away in peace. When Joab returned from a campaign and heard this news, he was troubled. Joab retrieved Abner via messengers and once Abner returned to Joab, Joab murdered Abner. Joab would brook no rivals.
- David was distraught, participating in the funeral and fasting out of respect for this fallen warrior. David lamented, "...These sons of Zeruiah are too strong for me. May the LORD repay the evildoer according to his evil deeds!" (2 Sam 3:39). This would certainly come true for Joab years later.
- Ishbosheth was murdered in his own house by two men (2 Sam 4). Apparently Baanah and Recab, two captains in the army, perceived that things were going badly and decided to end the war by assassinating Ishbosheth. They decapitated him and took his head to David. They thought he would be pleased—but he wasn't. David had these two murderers killed, cutting off their hands and feet and hanging them up over a pool in Hebron. He then had the head of his former enemy buried in the tomb of Abner.
- Following the death of Ishbosheth, the nation united under David as their rightful king. He moved his throne from Hebron to Jerusalem. David became king at age thirty, and he reigned for forty years (2 Sam 5:4).
- David multiplied his wives and concubines while in Jerusalem, and they bore him many children. David was a great king and had a heart after God, but he also made many mistakes, which created no small amount of turmoil in his personal life.
- David successfully led Israel on two campaigns against the Philistines in the rest of chapter 5.
- The Ark of the Lord was transported by the people by means of a cart. As Uzzah tried to steady the Ark, he touched it, and the Lord slew him. This confused and saddened David and the people.
- Finally, they brought the Ark to Jerusalem with great fanfare. David danced before the Ark and celebrated its return. This action displeased Michal, Saul's daughter, as she no doubt felt his behavior demeaned his office. David was angry with her response, cutting himself off from her. She died childless.
- David desired to build God a fitting house. God communicated through Nathan the prophet that David's son would build God a

house of great splendor. Furthermore, Nathan communicated God would build David an everlasting house, making what is known as the Davidic Covenant with David in 2 Samuel 7:15–17.

- This led David to offer a prayer of thanksgiving, praise, and adoration to God, thanking him for his kindness and mercy.
- David extended Israel's borders, glory, and fame through military conquests (2 Sam 8). He defeated the Philistines, Moabites, Syrians, and Ammonites, bringing them all into subjection to him.
- David wanted to show kindness to any surviving relatives of the house of Saul for Jonathan's sake. Mephibosheth was Saul's grandson and Jonathan's son. He had suffered a crippling injury following the death of his father and grandfather and remained lame in his feet. David brought him to his house and set him at his own table as one of his own sons—quite unlike what typically happened to relatives of a deposed competitor.
- David sought to extend comfort to Hanun, the new king of Ammon, following his father's death (2 Sam 10). However, Hanun had poor counselors who told him that David had ulterior motives for sending representatives to him. So, they humiliated David's messengers and sent them home. Upon hearing this, David led troops against both Syria and Ammon, defeating them both under the leadership of Joab and Abishai, his brother. It really matters from whom we receive counsel.
- Chapter 11 records David's great sin with Bath-sheba and against her husband, Uriah the Hittite. David committed adultery, murder, and deception. Uriah was such a man of integrity that David sent the note sealing his death by means of Uriah's own hands. David thought he had effectively concealed his wickedness, but the Lord had taken note of it—and it displeased the Lord.
- The rebuke from Nathan the prophet is set forth in chapter 12. He began with an allegory about a poor man, a rich man, and a sheep. David was incensed that the rich man would do such a terrible deed, taking the poor man's lone sheep. However, Nathan confronted David, "Thou art the man." There are always consequences to our actions. In this case, David was told that the sword would never depart from his family and that turmoil would haunt his home.
- David broke down, admitting his sin.

- Nathan told David that because the thing gave great occasion to the enemies of the Lord to blaspheme, the child conceived between David and Bath-sheba would die. Indeed, this happened.

- However, God forgave David, blessing their next child, Solomon, with his love and grace. Indeed, Solomon was destined to be the next great king of Israel.

- The consequences of David's sin are recorded in chapters 13 through 20. First, Amnon raped his half sister Tamar, following the bad advice of a friend. He could have married her instead. Second, Absalom avenged Tamar by killing Amnon. Absalom then fled and remained in hiding for three years.

- Joab devised a plot to have David bring Absalom back home (2 Sam 14).

- Absalom asked Joab to arbitrate between him and David, which he did.

- The two finally met again after a separation of about five years—and the king kissed Absalom (2 Sam 14:33).

- The affection did not last long, as Absalom embarked on a campaign to usurp the throne from his father. Absalom was a handsome man who sought to create dissatisfaction among the people of Israel, alleging that he would handle their problems more effectively than David.

- Using political strategy, Absalom stole the hearts of the people. Ahithophel, David's former counselor and Bath-sheba's grandfather, joined the conspiracy against David. David was forced to flee in the face of the rebellion, hearing that Ahithophel was with Absalom; David prayed that God would defeat his counsel. Hushai, David's friend and advisor, returned to Jerusalem and did defeat Ahithophel's counsel.

- Ziba, the servant of Mephibosheth, met David and his traveling company with supplies (2 Sam 16). As they continued their journey, Shimei of the house of Saul encountered them and cursed David.

- Meanwhile, back at Jerusalem, Ahithophel was offering his counsel to Absalom, saying that he wanted to pursue David, kill him, and bring all the people back to serve Absalom. It was a good plan and likely would have succeeded had it not been for Hushai.

- Hushai offered conflicting counsel, warning that David was more dangerous than ever. They should wait. Absalom listened to Hushai. Thus, David was delivered.
- When Ahithophel saw that he would not achieve his vengeance, he went home and hung himself (2 Sam 17:23). It was a brilliant life wasted and ravaged by bitterness.
- Chapter 18 records the battle in the forests of Ephraim between David's forces and those of Absalom. David put his soldiers in three divisions under Joab, Abishai, and Ittai the Hittite.
- Absalom had long hair, and while riding under a low-hanging tree, his hair became tangled in its branches. He was stuck! A messenger told Joab about this. Though David had given explicit orders to deal gently with him, Joab went to the place and fired three spears through Absalom's heart. After Absalom was dead, the insurgency was quickly quelled. News came to David by means of runners, special messengers. When David heard the news, he was crushed.
- Joab reproved David for grieving over the loss of his son/enemy. Thus David addressed his people with thanksgiving. Interestingly, he also stated that he planned to replace Joab with Amasa—Absalom's former general. Others greeted the king, including Shimei, the one who had cursed him earlier, seeking forgiveness and grace from the monarch. Though Abishai wanted to kill him, David forgave him.
- Another revolt under Sheba took place (2 Sam 20). During the campaign to suppress Sheba, Joab murdered Amasa. Joab murdered those who threatened him—Abner and Amasa—and David would never forget these acts of treachery (1 Kgs 2:5).
- Sheba was cornered in a city by Joab and his army. The city was spared because the inhabitants rose up and killed Sheba, decapitating him and throwing his head over the wall to Joab. Thus the rebellion was over.
- A three-year famine came upon the land because of Saul's former violence against the Gibeonites (with whom a covenant had been made in Joshua 9).
- Seven relatives of Saul were to be delivered over to the Gibeonites and hung as a means of restitution. Interestingly, David spared Mephibosheth but offered them the five sons of Adriel, whom Michal had raised. The famine abated.

- More warfare with the Philistines was detailed in 2 Samuel 21:15–22. Four more giants were slain in these encounters; interestingly, David's nephews Abishai and Jonathan slew two of the four. David's courage had no doubt helped to inspire them.
- David offered a beautiful prayer of praise and thanksgiving for God's protection and deliverance in chapter 22.
- In chapter 23, a list of David's mighty men is recorded. Points of interest include the mention of Uriah the Hittite and the exclusion of Joab.
- David's pride urged him to number the soldiers in his kingdom. Joab counseled him against such actions, but David did not listen. Once David received the total, his heart smote him, knowing that he had sinned. Gad the prophet concurred that David had sinned and told him that God offered him three choices. First, seven years of famine, second, three months on the run, and finally, three days of pestilence. David chose the pestilence, and seventy thousand people died.
- Gad directed David to go to the threshing floor of Araunah and offer sacrifices, which he did. Araunah offered to give David the animals for free, but David refused, saying that he would not offer a sacrifice to the Lord that did not cost him anything. So he bought it for fifty shekels of silver. The plague was then quelled.

Key verses: "The LORD is my rock, my fortress and my deliverer; my God is my rock, in whom I take refuge, my shield and the horn of my salvation. He is my stronghold, my refuge and my savior—from violent men you save me" (2 Sam 22:2–3).

The Historical Books (Joshua through Esther)

1 KINGS

The book of 1 Kings chronicles the course of the monarchy in Israel from the death of King David to the death of Ahab king of Israel and Jehoshaphat king of Judah.

- The book opens with an aged King David hovering on the verge of death. His advisors sought out a fair woman to minister to the king, but it did not help. The woman's name was Abishag.
- Meanwhile, Adonijah, David's eldest son, planned to proclaim himself the rightful king. He conspired with Joab and Abiathar the priest, who both pledged their loyalty to Adonijah.
- Nathan the prophet and Bath-sheba both spoke to David, reminding him of his desire that Solomon would be the next king.
- David reaffirmed his choice of Solomon to rule, and Zadok the priest anointed him publicly.
- The people rejoiced at Solomon's inauguration, rejoicing loudly enough to interrupt the clandestine gathering called by Adonijah.
- Those who had gathered in support of Adonijah quickly dispersed, fearing that they would be viewed as guilty of treason. Adonijah fled, grabbing hold of the horns of the altar and asking for mercy. Solomon promised that if he behaved, he would be spared. The transfer of power was seldom peaceful or smooth.
- From his death bed, David charged Solomon to take care of some unfinished business (1 Kgs 2). David remembered Joab's treachery and commissioned Solomon to kill him (1 Kgs 2:5). He also told him to execute Shimei, who cursed David as he fled from Absalom. Furthermore, he reminded Solomon to show kindness to Barzillai, who was kind to David during those distressing times of rebellion. We reap what we sow.
- King David died, having reigned over Israel for forty years, and Solomon his son reigned in his stead (1 Kgs 2:10–12).
- Adonijah devised a cunning plot to create confusion in the monarchy by marrying Abishag (the young woman brought to David as he was dying). He asked Bath-sheba to make the request to Solomon on his behalf.
- In the ancient world, if you took the king's concubine, you were in effect taking his position. Bath-sheba was unaware of Adonijah's ul-

terior motives, but when she asked Solomon, he was very angry. He saw through the ploy, sentencing Adonijah to death. The sentence was carried out by Benaiah.

- Solomon then removed Abiathar from the priesthood, and both Joab and Shimei were executed in turn, as recorded in the remainder of chapter 2. Joab, the ruthless murderer, sought mercy but found none.
- Solomon went to Gibeon to offer burnt sacrifices to the Lord and offered up one thousand offerings upon the altar there. The Lord appeared to Solomon in a dream and told him to make a request.
- Solomon humbled himself before the Lord, acknowledging his inability to rule the nation. Thus, he requested wisdom. This pleased the Lord, who gave Solomon a wise and discerning heart and added all the other blessings besides. God promised to give riches and honor to Solomon above any other king.
- The test of the two harlots, in which each claimed to be the birth mother of one baby, concludes the chapter. Solomon devised a plan to identify the real mother, suggesting they divide the child in half to settle the dispute.
- Of course, he knew that the one who relinquished her claim in order to protect the child from harm was the real mother. She was given full possession of the child. His reputation for issuing wise judgments spread.
- Solomon wisely delegated authority to others to assist him in managing the affairs of the nation. God gave Israel peace during much of Solomon's reign.
- Solomon possessed incredible abundance and great fame. In one day his royal provisions included thirty oxen and one hundred sheep, as well as other commodities. He had forty thousand stalls for horses for his chariots. Solomon wrote songs and proverbs, and royalty from all over the earth came to visit him and hear his great wisdom (1 Kgs 4).
- The king planned to build God a house and made a treaty with Hiram, king of Tyre, who provided him with all the lumber and gold for the project (1 Kgs 5).
- In chapter 6, the construction of the house of the Lord is described. It took seven years to build and was exceedingly beautiful. In chapter 7, the building of Solomon's house, taking thirteen years to construct, is described. Elaborate with gold, ivory, and all manner of precious

stones, both structures spoke to the abundant wealth with which God had blessed Solomon and Israel.

- In chapter 8, the Ark was brought in to the Temple, and the whole house was consecrated with sacrifices that could not be numbered. After the priests placed the Ark in the holy place, the glory of God filled the temple so that the priests could not continue their work.

- At the close of chapter 8, Solomon offered a prayer of thanksgiving and praise to God for his blessings, glory, and greatness. Solomon prayed that his house would provide a place of contact between God and the people. They concluded the dedication by offering twenty-two thousand oxen and one hundred and twenty thousand sheep. Then Solomon held a great feast that lasted fourteen days.

- In chapter 9, God appeared a second time to Solomon, telling him that the house would be hallowed by God and that if Solomon would continue to honor God, he would be blessed. God also issued a warning that if Solomon or his house turned away from God, then Israel would be cut off.

- Solomon's fame continued to spread, and he and Hiram exchanged gifts with one another. Solomon built a navy, and the expedition brought 420 talents of gold back to Solomon.

- The Queen of Sheba visited the king, as recorded in chapter 10. She had heard of his splendor, but as she said, "The half was not told me." His resplendence and wisdom exceeded even the reports she had heard.

- In one year's time, the weight of gold that came to Solomon was 666 talents (1 Kgs 10:14). Remember that one talent weighed about sixty pounds! That's about forty thousand pounds. As one might imagine, Solomon made many objects from pure gold. His splendor was phenomenal.

- Though God had blessed Solomon beyond measure, Solomon forsook the Lord, worshipping other gods. He had seven hundred wives and three hundred concubines who turned his heart away from God to idols.

- Solomon built high places for Chemosh and Molech, among others. The Lord was very angry with Solomon and told him that the kingdom would be rent because of his disobedience. For David's sake, God would not take it from Solomon but from his son, leaving him with one tribe—Judah.

- Though God did not take the kingdom from Solomon, he did stir up trouble against him in the form of opponents—Hadad, Rezon, and Jeroboam.
- Thus Solomon died, having reigned in Jerusalem for forty years, as did his father David.
- Rehoboam, Solomon's son, reigned in his stead
- From about 1050 to 931 BC, Israel was ruled in a united monarchy under Saul, David, and Solomon. That was about to change.
- Rehoboam went to Shechem to be made king. He heeded the counsel of his peers rather than the advice of those who had served his father. Consequently, he dealt roughly with his subjects, seeking to intimidate them into obedience.
- This approach failed. His gruff answer led to a rebellion headed by Jeroboam. Rehoboam gathered all the warriors from Judah and Benjamin to fight against Israel and restore unity. However, Shemaiah told Rehoboam that this division was of the Lord and not to go and fight. Upon hearing this, the army disbanded.
- Jeroboam set up two altars, one in Bethel and the other in Dan, as a guise to keep the people from going to worship in Jerusalem.
- A man of God pronounced judgment against these false altars, incensing Jeroboam, who tried to take hold of him. However, when he stretched forth his hand against the prophet, it withered. The king implored the man of God to pray for restoration, which he did, and his hand was healed.
- This prophet had been told to neither eat bread nor drink water with anyone, and so he headed home. However, another alleged prophet asked him to come and dine with him. This imposter lied, telling the man of God that an angel had reversed the earlier command to abstain.
- So the prophet of God went with him to eat. All this was a lie, and God judged his prophet, slaying him by means of a lion. We should obey the clear teaching of the word of God rather than claims of alleged divine insight that are contrary to Scripture. (But though we, or an angel from heaven, preach any other gospel unto you than that which we have preached unto you, let him be accursed [Gal 1:8].)
- Jeroboam's son Abijah became ill, and Jeroboam's wife went to seek counsel from Ahijah the prophet. He pronounced judgment upon

her and her family because of the evil of Jeroboam. Indeed, the child died as soon as she went back to the city—and some time after, Jeroboam also died. He reined twenty-two years over Israel, and Nadab his son took his place.

- Sadly, Rehoboam led Judah into apostasy as well.
- Two good kings rose up over Judah in chapter 15: Asa and Jehoshaphat. They both followed the Lord and destroyed pagan idols. Asa warred against Baasha, king of Israel, making a league with Ben-hadad, king of Syria, to defeat Baasha. Asa reigned for forty-one years and was succeeded by his son Jehoshaphat.
- Chaos and internal confusion characterized Israel, as chapter 16 makes clear. All of Israel's kings did evil in the sight of the Lord; there was not one righteous king. Hence, Israel was taken in captivity in 722 BC. The worst of the bunch appears in chapter 16—King Ahab who married (the lovable!) Jezebel.
- This national apostasy led to the call of Elijah the prophet, whose ministry is discussed in chapters 17 through 19. Israel had been in continual apostasy for about sixty years by the time Elijah was called.
- A famine was pronounced by Elijah, who took refuge first at the brook, being fed by ravens, and then at Zarephath to a widow who was ready to meet the God of Israel.
- Some of the classic confrontations in the Bible occur in chapter 18—first between Elijah and Ahab and then between Elijah and the prophets of Baal.
- As is frequently the case, the guilty party blamed the innocent for the problem—Ahab blamed Elijah. But Elijah wasn't the problem—he was the solution. Ahab was the problem.
- Elijah challenged the 450 prophets of Baal to a contest in which the true God would become clear. After hours of pleading with Baal, the false prophets gave up in exhaustion.
- Elijah called upon God once, and God answered, totally devouring the sacrifice. Following this, Elijah slew all the false prophets, after which the drought ended.
- Well, from the mountaintop to the valley! Jezebel threatened to kill Elijah, and he fled for his life, plopping down under the juniper tree and asking God to take his life. (Keep in mind that he had raced

Ahab's chariot for some twenty miles.) God told him to take a nap and then eat some snacks—not a bad recipe for recovery.

- God knew that Elijah felt very much alone, so he spoke to him in a still, small voice and assured him that seven thousand others in Israel had not bowed to Baal.
- The call to Elisha was issued in 1 Kings 19:19–21.
- Ahab's first and second Syrian campaigns are discussed in chapter 20. He was victorious in both confrontations.
- Ahab coveted Naboth's vineyard in chapter 21, following the murderous advice of Jezebel in order to attain it. They framed Naboth in order to seize his property.
- God issued a judgment against Ahab and Jezebel for their wicked plotting. Hearing this, Ahab repented in sackcloth and ashes, thus delaying his judgment, but dogs would devour Jezebel.
- Ahab and Jehoshaphat made peace and heard from the prophets regarding the next Syrian campaign. The false prophets predicted a great victory, but Micaiah, the prophet of God, told Ahab the truth—he would be slain in the battle. He was imprisoned for telling the truth. Indeed, Ahab met his doom in the battle even though he had disguised himself.
- So Ahaziah his son reigned in his stead, and Jehoshaphat died too. Jehoram, Jehoshaphat's son, succeeded him, ascending to the throne of Judah. Ahaziah was evil just like his parents, provoking the anger of the Lord, just as his parents had done.

Key verses: "At the time of sacrifice, the prophet Elijah stepped forward and prayed: 'O LORD, God of Abraham, Isaac and Israel, let it be known today that you are God in Israel and that I am your servant ... Answer me, O LORD, answer me, so that these people will know that you, O LORD, are God, and that you are turning their hearts back again'" (1 Kgs 18:36–37).

The Historical Books (Joshua through Esther)

2 KINGS

The book of 2 Kings continues the chronology of the monarchy in both Israel and Judah, including important information on the close of the ministry of Elijah and Elisha.

- The book opens with a serious accident to King Ahaziah. He sent messengers to summon Elijah in order to find out if he would live or die.
- The first two messengers demanded Elijah to come, but they ended up being consumed with fire from heaven. The third one was much more contrite. Elijah then agreed to come to the king. He told the monarch that he would soon die.
- In the following chapter, Elijah was whisked off to heaven via the chariot of fire. Elisha would not leave his side, somehow sensing that such an event was imminent. Since Elisha witnessed the event, he received a double portion of Elijah's spirit.
- Elisha succeeded Elijah, performing two miracles to demonstrate his calling. Irreverent youths were judged for mocking the prophet at the close of the chapter; they were attacked by a bear.
- The book is something of a pendulum swinging back and forth to discuss the kings of Israel and then the kings of Judah, mentioning the work of Elisha intermittently.
- Warfare was a constant—and in chapter 3, Israel and Judah combined their forces to defeat the Moabites. Elisha assisted in the efforts only because of Judah's godly king, Jehoshaphat.
- Sadly, the chapter ends with the king of Moab sacrificing his eldest son as a burnt offering in hopes of achieving victory. It failed to alter the course of events—but it did greatly increase the enmity against the Jews.
- God provided for a faithful widow by causing her cruise of oil to remain full, though she filled many vessels from it. She sold her oil, which was enough to pay her debt and to provide her and her children with a comfortable living.
- Again in chapter 4, Elisha rewarded the Shunammite who provided him with lodging by telling her she would conceive and bear a son. She did have a son and when the baby had grown up, he contracted a fatal illness.

- The woman was greatly grieved and called for Elisha. He came and raised the child from the dead. Elisha also healed a poisoned stew and fed a multitude with minimal food, performing a miracle akin (though on a lesser scale) to the feeding of the five thousand.
- Naaman the Syrian was healed from leprosy by following Elisha's instructions and washing in the Jordan River. Naaman became a believer in the true God. Elisha refused his generous offer of reward.
- But Elisha's servant Gehazi ran after Naaman, fabricating a lie in order to secure some of the reward for himself. Upon returning home, he was questioned by Elisha, who rebuked him for his greed and disciplined him by making him a leper.
- Elisha recovered the lost axe head in chapter 6—a seemingly small miracle but one that indicates how important stewardship was to the Jews.
- Of greater significance, at least militarily, was Elisha's ability to reveal the war plans of the Syrians against Israel. He warned the king every time that Syria moved against them, causing no small amount of frustration among the Syrian forces.
- The king of Syria sent a great host to take Elisha prisoner. However, when his servant (who I assume was still Gehazi) went out that morning, he saw the great Syrian army. But Elisha calmed him by saying there were more with them than with Syria. He prayed that God would open his eyes, and indeed God did so. The servant saw the mountains filled with horses and chariots of fire.
- God smote the Syrians with blindness, and Elisha took them to Samaria. There they found mercy and were given food and water and sent away. One might assume that such a compassionate act would lead to kind reciprocation. However, that was not the case.
- Ben-hadad, king of Syria, attacked Samaria, inciting a terrible famine.
- It was so severe that at least one mother cannibalized her own child.
- Hearing this devastating news, the king of Israel pledged to kill Elisha.
- However, Elisha prophesied that by the very next day the food shortage would come to an abrupt end (2 Kgs 7). Fine flour and barley

The Historical Books (Joshua through Esther)

would be in such abundance that they could be had for a mere shekel.

- In chapter 7, four leprous outcasts decided to enter the camp of the Syrians for food and help, reasoning they would either find relief or be killed.

- Meanwhile, the Lord had made a great noise in the Syrian camp, causing them to believe that the Hittites and Egyptians had invaded them. Thus they fled their camp.

- When the lepers entered the campsite, they discovered it abandoned. It was filled with provisions: food, gold, clothing, etc. After they had their fill, they went and told the king. The king and his servants spoiled the tents of the Syrians, taking all their food and wealth. Indeed, by the following day the cost of food equaled that prophesied by Elijah exactly.

- From chapter 8:16 to 17:41 a discussion of the kings of Israel and Judah to the fall of Samaria is outlined. Every king who ruled over Israel (the ten tribes drawn away by Jeroboam) was evil without exception. Thus they were overtaken by the Assyrians in 722 BC.

- On the contrary, Judah was blessed with a number of godly kings (not perfect by any means, but godly) and were spared God's judgment until 605 BC, when Judah also was taken in captivity to Babylon.

- Notable events in this section include Jehu's judgment over Israel. He was anointed king over Israel by a messenger from Elisha (2 Kgs 9). The two reigning monarchs in Israel and Judah, Joram and Ahaziah, went out to challenge Jehu. However, they proved no match for him, and he slew them both.

- He then went to Jezreel to execute judgment against Jezebel. He ordered some of her associates to throw her out of a high window, which they did. When they went down to bury her, they discovered that the dogs had made a meal of her—precisely as Elijah had prophesied.

- Jehu continued his mighty campaign of judgment against the household of Ahab and all Baal worshippers in chapter 10. He killed Ahab's seventy sons and all their associates.

- He then went to Samaria and pretended to host a feast for all the Baal worshippers of the area, calling them all together at the house of Baal. After conducting a sacrifice for Baal, he ordered his guards to draw their swords and kill everyone who was in the house.

- Though Jehu obeyed the Lord's charge in this matter, he did not walk in the law of the Lord. The days of Israel were now numbered.
- Queen Athaliah killed all the king's sons except Joash who was hidden from her. Her treachery was rewarded with treachery, and Joash was unveiled to her some years later as the rightful king.
- Jehoida the priest had hidden him and secured help from members of the military. When the time came to reveal him, Athaliah was slain and Joash, at the age of seven, began to reign. He reigned forty-one years and followed the Lord all his days. One of his notable acts was to repair the temple and beautify it.
- The death of Elisha is recorded in chapter 13. He died as the Syrians began oppressing Israel mightily.
- More intrigue between the kings of Israel and Judah appears in chapters 14 through 17.
- The culmination is recorded in chapter 17 when Israel was overwhelmed by the Assyrians and deported to Assyria. Furthermore, the Assyrians repopulated Samaria with Babylonians, which led to syncretism throughout the region (2 Kgs 17:6–41).
- Attention then necessarily turned to the kingdom of Judah, describing the reign of Hezekiah to the Babylonian captivity (2 Kgs 18:1—25:30).
- Hezekiah's revival is recorded in chapter 18. He removed all the high places where people offered to pagan gods. He broke Nehushtan into pieces (the bronze serpent of Moses they had lugged around and worshipped for hundreds of years!). He trusted in the Lord with all his heart.
- He experienced early success in defeating the Philistines and the Assyrians. However, he had to pay a ransom later to Assyria, offering them gold from the temple (2 Kgs 18:14–15). In a second campaign, the king of Assyria's representative, Rab-Shakeh, threatened the Jews, warning them to surrender and belittling the God of Israel.
- Hezekiah called upon a trusted associate, the prophet Isaiah, for insight into the situation (2 Kgs 19:1–7).
- Isaiah told the king not to be afraid because God would grant Israel victory. Hezekiah went into the temple and prayed for help. Isaiah reaffirmed God's faithfulness, assuring Hezekiah that God would defend the city.

- Indeed, in one night the angel of the Lord entered the camp of the invading Assyrians and killed one hundred and eighty-five thousand warriors. Upon seeing the devastation of his army, Sennacherib retreated hastily.
- As he was worshipping in the temple of his god Nishroch, two of his own sons assassinated him.
- Hezekiah contracted a fatal illness in chapter 20 and Isaiah went to tell him of his impending death. Hezekiah took the news badly and earnestly prayed that God would heal him. The Lord heard his prayer, and before Isaiah even left the royal vicinity, God commissioned him to go back and tell Hezekiah the good news.
- Indeed, God gave Hezekiah a reprieve from death for fifteen additional years.
- Unfortunately, those years were not well spent. Hezekiah made a fatal mistake, taking the emissaries from Babylon and showing them all the splendor of the temple. Isaiah knew all too well that, having seen the glory, they would be back for it.
- Hezekiah eventually did die and Manasseh, his twelve-year-old son, reigned in his stead.
- He was exceedingly wicked above any that went before him. He committed idolatry, engaged in occultism, committed murder, corrupted the nation, and performed child sacrifice. Though God warned him repeatedly, Manasseh would not listen (though important information about him is included in Chronicles that does not appear in Kings).
- Manasseh died and Amon, his son, became the king. He was evil like his father and was assassinated.
- Josiah reigned thirty-one years in Jerusalem after him and did that which was right. He took power at the young age of eight years old. He spearheaded the temple repairs. While working on the temple, Hilkiah the high priest found the book of the law.
- They took the Scripture to the king, and Shaphan read from it. The king rent his clothes, realizing the great sin of the nation (likely this passage was from Deuteronomy—the Palestinian covenant chapters 28 through 30).
- Huldah the prophetess affirmed that judgment would indeed fall upon Judah. However, because Josiah repented so earnestly, it would not fall in his tenure.

- Josiah then gathered all the elders and people of Judah together and read the words of the book of the covenant to them. And the king made a covenant to walk after the Lord and perform the words of the book—and the people gave their assent too.
- Following this, Josiah got to work and tore down all the pagan altars and destroyed all the pagan images He also slew the false priests and destroyed the house of the sodomites that was beside the temple.
- He also destroyed the high places erected by Solomon for the pagan deities worshipped by his corrupt wives—for Ashtoreth, for Chemosh, and for Milcom. He also reinstituted the Passover, and it was reverent and magnificent. Even with all this zeal, the Lord's anger against Judah was not completely abated.
- Josiah died.
- Nebuchadnezzar arose (2 Kgs 24).
- He began his siege on Jerusalem (2 Kgs 24:10ff).
- The first deportation was recorded (2 Kgs 24:13–16 [605 BC]).
- The second deportation was discussed (2 Kgs 25:1–7 [597 BC]).
- The last deportation is mentioned in 25:8 and following. The temple was destroyed, as well as the king's house, and Jerusalem was burned with fire.

Key verse: "Neither before nor after Josiah was there a king like him who turned to the LORD as he did—with all his heart and with all his soul and with all his strength, in accordance with all the Law of Moses" (2 Kgs 23:25).

The Historical Books (Joshua through Esther)

1 AND 2 CHRONICLES

The books of 1 and 2 Chronicles were originally one book. They are very similar to the books of Samuel and Kings, though there are some notable differences between them. It is to these discrepancies that this survey is principally directed.

- 1 and 2 Chronicles were written much later than 1 and 2 Samuel and 1 and 2 Kings. Samuel has a date of around the tenth century and Kings was written around the sixth century. Chronicles has a date of around the fifth century—probably written during or shortly after the Babylonian captivity. The author is unknown.

- Chapters 1 through 9 contain the most detailed and lengthy genealogy found anywhere in the Bible. Its purpose seems to be to draw the Davidic line together from a number of directions, showing that the line of David is the Messianic, royal line.

- The reign of Saul is considered only briefly in chapter 10. In fact, only the last battle of Saul's life is mentioned. The writer of Chronicles has an aversion to discussing personal failings, as we shall see; they are simply not to his purposes.

- Chapters 11 through 29 deal with the reign of David. The splendor of Solomon is set forth in 2 Chronicles 1 through 9, followed by a history of Judah from the reign of Rehoboam to the destruction of Jerusalem and the Babylonian captivity (2 Chr 10–36).

- The Chronicles deal almost exclusively with Judah, except when mention of the northern kingdom was important to discussing Judah, but Israel remained a decidedly secondary thought to the Chronicler.

- The author was principally concerned with the Davidic Kingdom. Remember that 2 Samuel 7:16-17 recorded a covenant made to David, promising that his seed would be established forever. David's line was through Judah, not Israel (through Solomon and Rehoboam, not Jeroboam). Thus the Chronicler was interested in Judah because it represented the Davidic lineage and hence the line of the Messiah.

- Following the extended discourse on genealogies in 1 through 9, a brief discussion of Saul is included (1 Chr 10). Interestingly, only the final battle of his life is detailed. Nothing is said about his jealousy against David or about his desperate pursuits to kill his young competitor.

- Neither does the author discuss the divided monarchy of David's early days when it was split between David and Ishbosheth. Nor is any mention made of Amasa, the general who led Ishbosheth's forces into battle against David. Joab's treachery against him is also excluded from the account.

- David's personal life is generally ignored. The author made no mention of David's moral failings with Bath-sheba or his attempt to conceal his sin by murdering Uriah, her husband.

- Furthermore, one finds literally no mention of David's troubling family problems; most particularly, the rebellion of Absalom against his father is conspicuous by its absence.

- Interestingly, the Chronicler attributed the numbering of Israel for which David and the people were severely punished to Satan rather than to God, as was the case in 2 Samuel. See 1 Chronicles 21:1 and 2 Samuel 24:1.

- One might harmonize this apparent contradiction by recognizing that all creatures, including Satan, are under God's sovereign control. Satan likely functioned as the immediate agent and God the ultimate agent.

- In general, the Chronicler focused on David's official activity as monarch, most particularly his military affairs and his desire to construct a glorious house for God.

- It concluded with a charge from David stating that Solomon was to be the next king and would build the house of God. In keeping with its character, Chronicles also omits any mention of the attempted coup by Adonijah and Joab as recorded in 1 Kings 1.

- Chronicles also discussed the role of the Levites in worship. Music played an important role in the priestly function. Four thousand Levites were dedicated to the music ministry, praising the Lord with instruments that David either made directly or had made for such purposes.

- First Chronicles concludes with Solomon succeeding David and a brief elegy of David's successful reign in Israel.

- Second Chronicles begins with the reign of Solomon, focusing mostly upon his preparation, construction, and dedication of the Temple.

The Historical Books (Joshua through Esther)

It offers detailed information regarding the size of the temple, its furnishings, its material, and decorative elements.

- The Temple was lavish, being made with only the finest of available materials. Gold was the prominent material. The Temple was ninety feet long and thirty feet wide and divided into two main sections: the main hall or the Holy Place and the Holy of Holies.
- The Bronze Altar and the Bronze Sea, along with two large pillars, were stationed just outside the porch. The porch was about fifteen feet wide and thirty feet long. The Temple was also surrounded by ten bases of bronze each six feet square and four and a half feet tall.
- Inside the main hall were ten tables (five along each wall) upon which rested ten candlesticks of gold. The altar of incense stood directly in front of the entrance to the Holy of Holies. The two sections of the Temple were separated by a veil of blue, purple, and crimson. Two doors also permitted access. They were made of pure gold.
- The Ark of the Covenant stood in the middle of the Most Holy Place. Solomon had two angelic figures placed above the Ark. They turned inward and looked down upon the Mercy Seat (which, as you may recall, was already made of gold for the Tabernacle as discussed in Exod 25). Each of their four wings was five cubits in length and overlaid with pure gold. Within the Holy Place itself Solomon used six hundred talents of fine gold—roughly equivalent to thirty thousand pounds of gold (2 Chr 3:8).
- All the details are set forth in chapters 3 and 4
- The Shekinah glory of God filled the house, affirming God's pleasure with the project.
- Following the dedication and a rehearsal of Solomon's fame, revenue, and splendor, a chronology of the kings of Judah is set forth.
- Chronologically, the kings following Solomon were:
    - Rehoboam (chapters 10 through 12)
    - Abijah (chapters 13 through 14a)
    - Asa (a good king in Judah [chapters 14b through 16], though not without his faults [see 16:7–12])
    - Jehoshaphat (another godly king [17:3–5], though not without his faults [see 20:35–37])
    - Jehoram (chapter 21—was wicked)

- Ahaziah (chapter 22—was wicked)
- Ahaziah's mother Athalia (chapter 22—was a wicked queen)
- Joash (He was greatly influenced by the godly priest Jehoida—but when Jehoida died, Joash took evil counselors and became corrupt himself [24:15-24].)
- Amaziah (a pretty good king [25:2] though not without many faults [25:14ff])
- Uzzah (a good king, though not without his faults [26:16-23])
- Jotham (chapter 27—a good king)
- Ahaz (a wicked king)
- Hezekiah (a godly king who produced many righteous reforms in Judah—see the extended discussion of his reforms in chapters 29 through 32)
- Manasseh, Hezekiah's son and a very evil king, reigned in his stead. Interesting information about him appears only here—33:11-20. God's patience and mercy toward those who turn to him are comforting indeed.
- Amon, Manasseh's son, reigned after him and did evil.
- The seven-year-old boy king Josiah reigned in Amon's stead. He faithfully did that which was right in the eyes of the Lord. He tore down the false idols, repaired the house of God, and honored the newly discovered Word of God found by Hilkiah the priest and Shaphan the scribe (2 Chr 34-35).

- The final chapter focuses upon the Babylonian captivity orchestrated by Nebuchadnezzar, king of the Babylonians. "They set fire to God's temple and broke down the wall of Jerusalem; they burned all the palaces and destroyed everything of value there" (2 Chr 36:19).
- This destruction would eventually be repaired under the leadership of Ezra and Nehemiah. Indeed, the book of Chronicles concludes with the ascension of Cyrus, king of Persia, and his declaration permitting the Jews to return to Jerusalem and rebuild.

Key verse: "For the eyes of the LORD range throughout the earth to strengthen those whose hearts are fully committed to him . . ." (2 Chr 16:9).

EZRA

The book of Ezra is post-exilic, meaning that it examines events following the Babylonian captivity. It focuses on the rebuilding of the Temple, which was destroyed by the Babylonians during their invasion of Judah in 586 BC.

- The book opens in the first year of Cyrus, king of Persia. It is likely that Cyrus was shown the prophecies concerning him in the book of Isaiah and Jeremiah. Cyrus was awed by these prophetic announcements, some of which mentioned him specifically by name, and happily permitted the Jews to return and rebuild the Temple at Jerusalem (Ezra 1:2).
- Cyrus also yielded all the vessels of gold and silver taken by the Babylonians from the house of God. It amounted to five thousand four hundred vessels. The returning Jews brought these items to place in the new temple.
- The first contingent of repatriated Jews was led by Zerubbabel. Chapter 2 names the families of those who chose to leave Babylon and return to Jerusalem. Interestingly, the Jews kept a carefully maintained registry of the priesthood, allowing only those with the right ancestry to fulfill the office of a priest.
- The total number of those who immigrated home was 42,360 (Ezra 2:64). The number of servants they brought with them totaled 7,337. A free will offering was taken to jump start the work and provide necessary living quarters for the new inhabitants.
- After securing housing and other necessities, the people set up a new altar upon which to offer burnt offerings to the Lord. They offered sacrifices every day, most especially because they feared the neighboring inhabitants of the land. Since the walls were destroyed, they remained constantly vulnerable to attack.
- In the second year of their return, they laid the foundation of the new temple. Following the completion of this portion of the work, they convened to celebrate. Ironically, those who had lived through the exile—who had seen Solomon's Temple—wept at the inaugural festivities, while others rejoiced. The shouts of joy and those of weeping intermingled—a bittersweet occasion indeed.
- As always, when the work of God proceeds, adversaries inevitably appear. The enemies of God are never happy to hear that God's work

is advancing. They used a number of tactics (still employed) to try and impede and suspend the work.

- First, they sought to infiltrate the work, asserting that they too sought God. Of course, this was a guise to penetrate and frustrate the rebuilding project. Zerubbabel, however, saw through their plan and refused to allow them to participate. When this ploy did not work, they hired counselors to frustrate progress throughout the entire reign of Cyrus.

- Chapter 4:6–23 is parenthetical and does not follow the chronology of the story. However, it does fit logically as an explanation of how the adversaries continued to plague the work of God for many years.

- King Xerxes (or Ahasuerus) reigned from 485 to 465 BC, and Artaxerxes I reigned from 464 to 424 BC. The antagonists wrote incendiary letters about the Jews, arguing to the king that if the city was rebuilt, the Jews would fail to pay tribute, etc. After checking the book of the records, King Artaxerxes commanded that the work cease—and a pause in the work ensued.

- However, historical documents worked both for and against the Jews. In this case, they appealed to the mandate issued by Cyrus giving them permission to rebuild. God often sends special messengers to encourage his work in the face of opposition. The prophets Haggai and Zachariah both prophesied to encourage the people (Ezra 5:1).

- Tatnai, the governor, confronted the Jews, demanding an explanation for why they were rebuilding. They explained, and Tatnai wrote the letter to Darius noting their explanation. He requested that Darius check the historical records to see if their story fit the facts.

- Indeed, Darius found the pronouncement made by Cyrus to rebuild, and the work was ordered to continue. Moreover, Darius ordered that any supplies needed should be provided free of charge to the Jews, including any animals necessary for their burnt offerings.

- Darius warned Tatnai that if anyone further hindered the Jews, they would be severely punished. Left with no choice, Tatnai commanded that the work resume.

- Encouraged by the exhortation of Haggai and Zechariah, the people finished the work of rebuilding the Temple. They dedicated the house of God with joy and offered up 712 animals as burnt offerings.

- They also reinstituted the Passover (Ezra 6:17–22). The temple took some twenty-one years to complete according to 6:15 (the reign of Darius was from 521 to 486 BC. His sixth year would have been 515 BC). The people initially embarked on the project in about 536 BC.

- About fifty-seven years elapsed between chapters 6 and 7 (it was during this interval that the events of the book of Esther took place).

- Ezra appeared on the scene for the first time in chapter 7. He had found great favor in the eyes of Artaxerxes, the king, who allowed him to return and beautify the house of God.

- Ezra was free to take any silver or gold with him on his return to Jerusalem—anything that had been taken by the Babylonians. Furthermore, anything needed by Ezra was to be immediately provided, including silver, wheat, oil, wine, and anything else deemed necessary. Moreover, Darius exempted the priests from royal taxation (Ezra 7:11–24).

- The chapter ends with Ezra's prayer of thanksgiving for the goodness of God and the kindness of the king.

- Chapter 8 lists those who returned with Ezra. When Ezra discovered that no priests were among those returning, he made special requests to secure some. They entrusted many valuables to the care of the priests, and they weighed them so as to secure against any pilfering. It is always wise to have checks and balances (Ezra 8:24–30).

- Once the people arrived in Jerusalem, the valuables were weighed and measured, so as to secure integrity, and delivered to the temple. All the details were written down.

- Chapters 9 and 10 record Ezra's horror at the failure of the first wave of immigrants to remain separated from the surrounding nations. The habitual problem of intermarrying with the pagan nations round about them had occurred yet again. Thus the people of Israel, including the priests, had engaged in the abominations of their pagan neighbors. Ezra was appalled. When he heard this, he tore his clothes and plucked out the hair of his head and beard, sitting down astonished.

- At the evening sacrifice, Ezra prayed and confessed before the God of heaven. Ezra was ashamed at the sin of his people and blushed. He poured out his soul to God, identifying himself in the sin of the nation. He wondered how God could remain merciful to such a rebellious people. He wept and confessed before the temple.

- Upon seeing this, many people came to the temple, and they too began to weep. Sometimes God sends a messenger to awaken slumbering sinners.

- The repentant Jews were required to divorce their pagan wives. This is the only place in Scripture of which I am aware that divorce was actually commanded. The initial meeting took place in the street during a torrential rainstorm. Those willing to obey needed some time to make appropriate arrangements, so in the process of the next couple of months, many put away their foreign wives.

- The book ends by chronicling the names of those who had transgressed in this way but had also repented of their transgressions. Sin always complicates our lives and creates sorrow. Such was the case as men put away their wives, some of whom had borne them children (Ezra 10:44).

Key verse: "This is what Cyrus king of Persia says: 'The LORD, the God of heaven, has given me all the kingdoms of the earth and he has appointed me to build a temple for him at Jerusalem in Judah. Anyone of his people among you—may his God be with him, and let him go up to Jerusalem in Judah and build the temple of the LORD, the God of Israel, the God who is in Jerusalem'" (Ezra 1:2–3).

NEHEMIAH

Whereas Ezra recounts the rebuilding of the Temple, Nehemiah discusses the rebuilding of the walls around Jerusalem. A city without walls was always vulnerable to easy invasion and represented weakness.

- The book of Nehemiah records the last historical events in the Old Testament, ending about 430 BC. Nehemiah had risen to the position of the king's cupbearer, a position of honor, trust, and responsibility.

- He was conducting his services for King Artaxerxes at Shushan, the ancient capital of Persia. Though he was separated by many miles from Jerusalem, his heart was still burdened for the well-being of his brethren. He inquired of Hanani about the condition of the repatriated Jews. He was informed that the city was in shambles, its walls still in disrepair, standing as a reproach to neighboring peoples.

- Upon hearing this, Nehemiah wept and went to prayer on behalf of his Jewish brethren.

- His prayer was one of confession. He agreed with God regarding the sinfulness of the people, including himself. However, Nehemiah reminded God of his covenant with the Jews and his promise to reward repentance and faithfulness.

- Clearly Nehemiah planned to return and do something because of the way his prayer concluded. He asked God to give him grace in the king's sight, meaning that the king might respond favorably to his request to return home.

- Apparently Nehemiah had a hard time veiling his despair, because in chapter 2 the king confronted him about his depressed appearance. Nehemiah explained the cause of his sadness—that his ancient city was in disarray. The king then asked Nehemiah what he wanted. The text indicates that Nehemiah actually prayed while he answered the king—a brief but powerful missive directed to God. He asked to return home. He had clearly been at work planning his trip, because he knew precisely what letters would be needed and from whom.

- Interestingly, the king's primary concern was how long such a venture would take; doubtless he hated to lose such a faithful servant. Nehemiah was able to give him a time frame (based upon his pre-planning), and the king graciously consented to let him return and rebuild.

- The king not only sent letters with Nehemiah but also captains of the army and cavalry. When Sanballat and Tobiah heard of Nehemiah's return, they were very angry. They did not want the Jews to rebuild. Whenever the work of God moves forward, God's enemies resist.

- Nevertheless, Nehemiah arrived in Jerusalem and spent three days planning the best course of action. Once again, Nehemiah demonstrated the wisdom of planning ahead.

- When Nehemiah was convinced of the best approach to accomplishing the work, he gathered the people together to challenge them to accomplish the task.

- He offered them personal testimony of the good hand of God upon him in causing the king to look upon his request to return and build the walls with favor. When they heard this, the people were strengthened and said, "Let us start rebuilding" (Neh 2:18).

- Once again the enemies of God appeared to discourage the progress. The strategy they employed first was mockery; they laughed and scorned at the plan. But Nehemiah responded to them, saying that the God of heaven would prosper them in the work.

- The key phrase in chapter 3 is "and next to him" or "after him," appearing about thirty-one times. The people needed to be organized. If everyone worked together, the project could be finished fairly easily. God's work often seems insurmountable, until it is arranged into manageable steps.

- Progress was moving forward—much to the chagrin of Sanballat and company. They were exceedingly angry to hear of the early success of the Jews. They gathered enemies together and spent a season mocking the effort of the Jews.

- Nehemiah responded, as usual, through prayer and action. Eleven times in the book Nehemiah is found engaged in prayer. But he combined prayer with action. The classic statement to this effect is found in Nehemiah 4:9: "But we prayed to our God and posted a guard day and night to meet this threat."

- By this time about half of the wall had been rebuilt (Neh 4:6).

- Indeed, Nehemiah and the people preferred to build but were prepared to fight if the need arose. Half of the laborers guarded with their weapons ready while the other half worked on the wall. Peace through strength is an appropriate biblical model.

- Internal problems arose in chapter 5. Some people faced a food shortage (working on the wall impeded their ability to raise crops); others could get grain but had to mortgage their homes to obtain it, still others, not wanting to mortgage their homes, had to borrow money from their Jewish friends (who were charging them interest); and lastly, some were pressed to sell their children to repay their creditors.

- Nehemiah was very angry about these exploitative actions on the part of the lenders. However, he took some time alone to sort things out before responding. He rebuked those who were charging interest in violation of the law of God (Exod 22:25ff) and appealed to their common purpose for showing leniency all around. He also appealed to his own manner of life, in which he refused to exploit the people as governor. He asked that mortgaged fields and homes be returned. The nobles agreed.

- Nonetheless, Nehemiah called the priests as witnesses to their acceptance of his terms. As governor, Nehemiah could have taxed the people and purchased his provisions with this money. But he didn't. Rather, he provided for his needs with his own resources, thus living as an unselfish example to those around him.

- Chapter 6 brought opposition of a different sort from Sanballat and Tobiah. They endeavored to distract Nehemiah from the work by calling for a meeting. They demanded a meeting with him four times, but each time Nehemiah refused, saying, "... I am carrying on a great project and cannot go down. Why should the work stop while I leave it and go down to you" (Neh 6:3).

- Frustrated in their attempts, they sent a servant with a letter accusing the Jews of rebellion against the king. Nehemiah rebuffed their suggestions. They hired a spy—one Shemaiah—who offered to meet with Nehemiah in the Temple privately. But Nehemiah refused his offer saying, "Should a man like me run away?" This, of course, was a conspiracy so that they could have something of which to accuse Nehemiah.

- Nehemiah's determination, grit, and prayer brought the work to completion. As the text states, "So the wall was completed ... in fifty-two days" (Neh 6:15).

- What had lain in waste for generations was repaired in less than two months once proper attention was given to it. Amazing!

- Now built, the city needed protection, and Hanani and Hananiah were put in charge of this need.
- Chapter 7 provides a registry of those who had returned to Jerusalem.
- A great revival under the direction of Ezra is discussed in chapter 8. The word of God was read and explained by Ezra and others as the people gathered together and listened attentively. The teachers encouraged the people to rejoice in the word of God and celebrate having it. They also reinstituted the Feast of Tabernacles, abiding in booths for seven days. Each day the Scripture was read and explained.
- On the twenty-fourth day of this month of renewal, the Jews separated themselves from all strangers and spent a fourth part of the day hearing the word of God and another fourth part confessing their sins. A lengthy history of the nation follows, presented by some of the teachers (Neh 9:4–37).
- In light of the power and mercy of God in his dealings with the nation, they made a covenant with the Lord and signed it. A list of the signatories is set forth in chapter 10, naming some of the most significant people involved. Their promise was to remain unmixed with the people of the land, to pay a yearly tax for the service of the house of God, and to pay the first fruits or the tithe without fail.
- Chapter 11 contains a listing of all those who lived in Jerusalem and those who lived elsewhere in the surrounding vicinity.
- Chapter 12 records the dedication of the wall and of the city to God. They had two choirs march around the wall in different directions and convene together in the temple. Perhaps Nehemiah had them march on the wall as a rebuke to their enemies, who had constantly criticized the strength of the restored walls.
- Nehemiah completed his twelve-year term as governor at the close of chapter 12 (see 13:6). He returned to Artaxerxes and served him in some capacity. However, after a short time, perhaps two or three years, he returned to Jerusalem to inspect progress. Unfortunately, many startling changes had occurred.
- First, the high priest had invited Tobiah to literally come and live in the Temple. From this vantage point, he could constantly frustrate Temple activity.

- Worse yet, the room he occupied was a large storeroom intended to hold grain offerings from the tithe of the people. The Temple storerooms were empty because the people had failed in their promise to bring the tithe into the storehouses. This meant that the Levites had to work the fields, having less time for service in the Temple.
- Nehemiah rebuked those in charge and positioned new leaders to oversee the work of receiving tithes and offerings from the people.
- Furthermore, the people had forsaken the Sabbath and worked upon it as any other day. Once more Nehemiah rebuked the people and called them to obedience.
- Finally, and perhaps most upsetting to Nehemiah, was that intermarriage had already become commonplace once again. Nehemiah was so upset that he actually pulled out some of their beards and smote them, making them swear by God to remain separate.
- Nehemiah appealed to Solomon as a bad example of the influence of pagan women. "If even he became corrupt, what hope is there for you?" Nehemiah reasoned.
- Many of these people were the very ones who had signed the pledge to remain undefiled and to keep the Sabbath and to remember the tithe. Constant vigilance is required. The enemy never rests, and we need to be alert ourselves.
- It is very draining to continue calling people to do the right thing, but Nehemiah was faithful in exhorting the people to obey and follow God.

Key verse: "So the wall was completed on the twenty-fifth of Elul, in fifty-two days" (Neh 6:15).

ESTHER

The book of Esther recounts the deliverance of the Jewish nation from total destruction at the hands of Haman a hater of the Jews. God providentially placed Esther in a position of power and used her to intervene with the king on behalf of her people. Indeed, the book demonstrates God's sovereign protection over his people, though the name of God does not appear in the book.

- Chapter 1 finds King Ahasuerus (Xerxes, who reigned from 484 to 464 BC) convening a royal feast for himself and his people. He displayed his wealth and splendor for 180 days (Esth 1:4). After this, he held a feast for seven days and invited all his subjects to attend.
- On the closing day, the king commanded Vashti, his queen, to come before the king.
- However, she refused his request.
- Amazed at her defiance, the king met with his counselors to consider the appropriate course of action. Memucan, one of his close advisors, suggested that the response of Vashti would cause all women in the kingdom to despise the authority of their husbands. Thus, he argued that the king should deal harshly with the queen, banning her from all royal privileges and replacing her with another queen who would respect the authority of the king.
- As they realized, example is powerful for good or for ill. Indeed, a decree was sent out that the husband of every house should bear rule and receive honor from his wife. This letter was published in many languages and sent to the 127 provinces over which Ahasuerus reigned.
- In chapter 2, a replacement for Vashti was sought. Officers in every province were commissioned to gather together fair young women and send them to Shushan to be considered by the king as his new queen.
- Mordecai the Jew had adopted Esther as his own daughter. (She was the daughter of his uncle, and her mother and father had died.) Hearing the news of the search for a new queen, he sent Esther to Shushan. She was fair and very beautiful.
- The women stayed at the palace in the care of Hegai. Esther found favor in his eyes, and he helped her to prepare—which was no easy

project. The purification process lasted for twelve months! During this time, Mordecai stayed close by the court of the women to see how Esther was doing. Finally it was Esther's turn to go to the king. He fell in love with her and made her his new queen (Esth 2:17–18). A feast was prepared, and the king celebrated her inaugural.

- Now Esther had not revealed her Jewish heritage to anyone. The reason why she failed to do so is unclear, except one might suspect that some underlying prejudice existed.

- Soon after her coronation, Mordecai overheard a murderous plot by two men directed against the king. He exposed their intentions and thus rescued the king. His bravery was recorded in the book of the chronicles of the king (Esth 2:21–23).

- Haman, a proud and arrogant associate of the king, appears in chapter 3. Indeed, he had been promoted to a position of significant power and authority by the king, eclipsing that of other lower rulers. He took great pleasure in receiving reverence from commoners.

- However, Mordecai refused to bow to him. Haman was very angry that Mordecai refused to reverence him. He began planning how to punish him for his insolence—and not him alone, but all the Jews.

- He told the king that a certain people group in the kingdom were rebellious and needed to be exterminated. The king consented and left the matter to Haman. He planned that on one day, the Jewish race would be extinguished.

- He gathered together scribes to write letters for every province informing the officials of the plan. The text reads, "Dispatches were sent by couriers to all the king's provinces with the order to destroy, kill and annihilate all the Jews—young and old, women and little children—on a single day, the thirteenth day of the twelfth month . . ." (Esth 3:13).

- Of course, the reaction of the Jews was one of anguish and despair. Mordecai, upon hearing the news, rent his clothes and covered himself with sackcloth and ashes. There was great sadness among the Jews—weeping, fasting, and mourning.

- The news was communicated to Esther from Mordecai by means of a messenger. Mordecai wanted Esther to talk to the king and discover what had happened. Esther responded by reminding Mordecai that no one was permitted to speak to the king in the inner court unless summoned. It had been thirty days since the king had called for her.

- Nevertheless, Mordecai urged Esther to visit the king, speaking to her perhaps the most famed words of the book, saying, "... And who knows but that you have come to royal position for such a time as this?" (Esth 4:14).
- Esther responded by asking Mordecai and all the Jews in Shushan to fast and pray for her for three days. She and her attendants would do the same. On the third day, she would approach the king.
- She kept her word, and on the third day she entered the inner court of the king. Thankfully, the king was happy to see her, and she obtained favor in his sight. He asked her what she wanted. The king loved Esther and offered to give her up to half of his kingdom if she asked. Esther responded by inviting the king and Haman to a banquet she was preparing for them. The king and his corrupt associate attended the dinner. Still curious, the king inquired again, asking what she wanted. Esther invited them to yet another gathering the following day.
- Haman was absolutely giddy about these invitations, believing that it represented his growing stature. His delight was only abated by his thought of the stubborn Mordecai.
- He told his wife and friends about his feelings, and they suggested that the rebel be hung. So, Haman ordered a gallows to be constructed immediately. He was quite unaware that his devious plan was about to backfire!
- Chapter 6 records a providential case of royal insomnia. The king could not sleep and so decided to do a little historical reading. He ordered that the book of the records of the chronicles be read before him. While listening, he was reminded of the good deed of Mordecai in foiling the assassination attempt recorded in chapter 2. The king wondered what reward had been given to Mordecai for his faithfulness. But nothing had yet been done for him, the king was told.
- Amazingly, God was reminding the king of the faithfulness and character of Mordecai at precisely the moment when such knowledge would be most useful. Humanly speaking, redemptive history hinged upon a case of insomnia. However, the issue was never in doubt, for God was protecting his people and his redemptive program from destruction.
- The king wanted to honor Mordecai, but he was not sure the best way to do so. Haman happened to be in the outer court (perhaps

gloating over his increasing prowess), and the king summoned him. The following section is filled with irony. The king asked Haman what he should do for the man he wanted to honor. Now Haman believed he was the man. So, he told the king to give him royal apparel and the royal horse and parade him about the city proclaiming that this man bore the king's honor.

- The sound of Haman's jaw striking the floor must have been booming indeed when the king announced to him, "... Do just as you have suggested for Mordecai the Jew ..." (Esth 6:10).

- Mordecai was properly arrayed and displayed throughout the city (by Haman!) as a man in whom the king had found great delight.

- Haman was mortified—and began to realize that he might be in serious trouble.

- The king and Haman attended the second banquet of Esther in chapter 7. Here she finally revealed her request—that her people, the Jews, be spared from destruction. The king was incensed that anyone would seek to harm his queen and her people. He demanded to know the identity of the culprit. Esther pointed to Haman, announcing that he was the wicked enemy and adversary of the Jews.

- Haman was in trouble, but what occurred next is comical. The king stormed out of the room for a moment, and Haman approached the queen, seeking clemency. However, he fell on the bed beside her, and when the king reentered the room he concluded the worst. The king ordered that Haman be immediately hung upon the very gallows he had prepared for Mordecai—and so he was hung. Indeed, this represents one of the most vivid illustrations in the Bible of reaping that which we sow.

- Now the pressing order of business was to reverse the earlier decree of the king ordering the execution of the Jews. In another note of irony, Mordecai and Esther were given Haman's house as well. Esther then approached the king asking for a reversal of his decree. The king gave Mordecai the freedom to write the letter and say whatever he wanted to say about the matter, using the king's ring as a seal for all his messengers.

- Mordecai wrote in the king's name and sealed his message with the king's ring and sent the message to all the provinces from India to Ethiopia. The orders allowed all the Jews in every city to band together and oppose anyone who sought their hurt. They needed to be prepared upon the thirteenth day of the twelfth month to defend themselves.

- The posts delivered the message throughout the kingdom. Meanwhile, back at Shushan, Mordecai had assumed the position once occupied by Haman. He was arrayed in royal clothing and had a crown of gold upon his head. Furthermore, the city had become a joyous place again, and most especially there was joy among the Jews. As a matter of fact, many people in the city were converting to Judaism.

- On the appointed day (the thirteenth day of the twelfth month), the Jews were ready. The military aligned with them because they feared Mordecai; his fame had spread throughout the kingdom. In Shushan, the Jews repressed an uprising, killing five hundred men who sought to carry out the initial decree. Among them, the ten sons of Haman were killed. Apparently, they sought to fulfill the evil plan of their father.

- Throughout the entire kingdom, the Jews fought successfully, killing a total of some seventy-five thousand men. On the fifteenth day of that month, the Jews declared a day of feasting and gladness. The coup against them had been thoroughly quelled. They held positions of power and authority in the kingdom and were considered a valiant and noble people. Indeed, the feast of Purim was instituted on the fourteenth and fifteenth days of the month Adar (the last month in the Hebrew calendar, corresponding to February/March).

- The feast was confirmed by letters from the queen and Mordecai to all the Jews in all 127 provinces as a perpetual memorial of God's faithfulness to his people.

- Chapter 10 (all three verses) concludes by honoring the king and Mordecai who, it records, had risen to next in power to the king. He was great indeed among all the Jews, seeking the wealth and peace of Israel.

Key verse: "... And who knows but that you have come to royal position for such a time as this" (Esth 4:14).

3

The Poetical Books
(Job through Song of Solomon)

JOB

The book of Job introduces the poetic/wisdom literature section of the Old Testament. Five books comprise this portion of the Bible: Job, Psalms, Proverbs, Ecclesiastes, and Song of Solomon.

- Hebrew poetry is quite different from English poetry, which is often based on similarity of sound, as in rhymed verse. "Mary had a little lamb, t'was given her to keep, but then it joined the Baptist church and died from lack of sleep!"
- Hebrew poetry is created through the use of parallelism. By means of enforcing, contrasting, or expanding ideas through parallelism, the poets forcefully communicated their message.
- There are three different kinds of parallelism:
    1. Synonymous parallelism: This is the type of parallelism used when the thoughts in the connecting phrases are essentially the same. For instance, "As the deer pants for streams of water, so my soul pants for you, O God. My soul thirsts for God, for the living God . . ." (Ps 42:1–2).
    2. Antithetic Parallelism: This is the kind of parallelism employed when the thoughts in the phrases are contrasting, as in Proverbs 12:24 and 12:27, which read, "Diligent hands will rule, but laziness ends in slave labor," and "The lazy man does not roast his game, but the diligent man prizes his possessions." The use of the adversative "but" is common in antithetic parallelism.

3. Synthetic Parallelism: When the primary thought is expanded from one phrase to the next, it is called synthetic parallelism. An example of this might be found in Psalm 2:1–3 "Why do the nations conspire and the peoples plot in vain? The kings of the earth take their stand and the rulers gather together against the LORD and his Anointed One. 'Let us break their chains,' they say, 'and throw off their fetters.'"

- Certainly not all poetry can be categorized so succinctly. Hebrew poetry is powerfully vivid and makes use of many other devices to communicate thought actively and forcefully. Figures of speech like hyperbole, simile, and metaphor are also frequently employed. However, being aware of the various literary techniques in Hebrew poetry may help the interpreter understand the thought of the writer more clearly.

- The book of Job addresses the age-old question of why the righteous suffer. It is generally considered a very ancient book, written sometime in the patriarchal period. While it fails to mention the Law, Israel, or the Tabernacle, it does speak of God, Satan, righteousness, redemption, and resurrection.

- Job's introduction comes in chapters 1 and 2.

- Here we are introduced to the man from the land of Uz—Job. God had blessed Job greatly; he had seven sons, three daughters, and an abundance of livestock. Indeed, he was immensely wealthy. He was also upright and righteous and one who feared God.

- Satan apparently has limited access to heaven and to God, because on one occasion, he appeared before the Lord. God was proud of Job and asked Satan if he had taken appropriate notice of this godly servant. Satan asserted that the only reason Job feared the Lord was because God had blessed him so greatly. Take the blessings and Job will curse you, argued Satan.

- Thus God gave Satan permission to test Job by removing some of his blessings.

- In rapid succession, Job learned that all his possessions, and most especially his children, were gone—his children were dead and his goods stolen. Job was crushed but continued to trust in the Lord, saying, "... The LORD gave and the LORD has taken away; may the name of the LORD be praised" (Job 1:21).

- Some while later, Satan returned to the gates of heaven from patrolling the earth. Again the Lord praised Job as the most righteous man on earth. But Satan retorted that if his health was taken, then Job would curse God. Therefore, God gave Satan permission again to inflict Job with illness but not to kill him.
- It is comforting to think that the Lord has limits set on what Satan can do to God's people. All of it must pass through God's hands, and he must give approval. Furthermore, it is all done according to his divine plans and purposes—ultimately for God's glory and our good.
- Indeed, Job was afflicted with a horrible illness. Boils covered his body from the soles of his feet to the top of his head.
- Even his wife counseled him "to curse God and die."
- However, Job continued to trust in God.
- Hearing of his desperate condition, three friends of Job came to visit him. They were there for a week before anyone even spoke, seeing that his grief was very great.
- From chapter 3 to chapter 37, we are privy to the running dialogue between Job and his three counselors.
- Chapter 3 records Job's great lament in which he wished he had never been born.
- In chapters 4 and 5, Eliphaz responded to Job's lament, arguing that the innocent do not experience the sort of suffering with which Job was afflicted. However, this assumption was incorrect.
- Job defended himself in chapters 6 and 7, sharing an important thought to keep in mind when seeking to minister to the suffering "A despairing man should have the devotion of his friends . . ." (Job 6:14).
- Bildad spoke as recorded in chapter 8, asserting that Job's problem must be sin. "If you are pure and upright, even now he will rouse himself on your behalf and restore you to your rightful place" (Job 8:6).
- Again Job responded in chapters 9 and 10, agreeing that all men are sinners.
- But Job was confused; he had tried. God is judge, and God will judge the righteous and the wicked.
- In chapter 11, Zophar spoke angrily because Job maintained his innocence of any major failings against God. He accused Job, ". . . Know this: God has even forgotten some of your sin" (Job 11:6).

- Job responded to this accusation in chapters 12 through 14. First, he argued that God does not always punish the wicked immediately for their sins, so his calamity was not proof of any wrongdoing. Job continued to trust in the Lord—"Though he slay me, yet will I hope in him . . ." (Job 13:15). He also rebuked his friends for their pitiful attempts at helping him; they failed miserably because they had the wrong theology. He stated, "You, however, smear me with lies; you are worthless physicians, all of you!" (Job 13:4).

- Eliphaz spoke again in chapter 15, contending that the wicked will not prosper, implying that Job was lying. Again Job responded in chapters 16 and 17, first affirming that collectively they were "miserable comforters" (Job 16:2). What Job really wanted them to do was pray for him (Job 16:21).

- Bildad countered in chapter 18 through a series of proverbs that amounted to saying the evildoer was deceitful and unwilling to confront his own sin—another accusation.

- In chapter 19, Job responded by again asserting his trust in the Lord, saying, "I know that my Redeemer lives, and that in the end he will stand upon the earth. And after my skin has been destroyed, yet in my flesh I will see God" (Job 19:25–26).

- The final speech of Zophar is recorded in chapter 20. It is once again filled with false doctrine. His basic assumption is that only the wicked suffer like Job.

- Job insightfully corrected his confused friends in chapter 21.

- This bantering characterizes the book from chapters 22 to 37: Eliphaz responded in chapter 22, followed by a response from Job in chapters 23 and 24. Bildad offered his final appeal in chapter 25, and Job continued to maintain his righteousness in a lengthy reply recorded in chapters 27 through 31.

- A young associate, Elihu, offered a monologue from chapter 32 to chapter 37 in which he sought to explain the matter. He charged Job with folly for seeking to justify himself before God (Job 34:36–37; 35:16) and endeavored to defend God's actions as being inexplicable but not arbitrary, due to God's integrity, greatness, and power.

- God's wisdom is far above human wisdom, Elihu argued, as evidenced by the entire created order. Therefore, it was unwise to seek to explain all of God's dealings, since they eclipse human comprehension.

- Finally, God intervened into the discussion, appearing to Job. He asked Job a series of questions designed to demonstrate God's glory, wisdom, and power and Job's frailty and weakness. By implication, these questions were intended to remind Job of God's surpassing wisdom and power.
- Remember, God had showcased Job to the enemy, revealing both his pride in and pleasure over Job. Job's calamity was not caused by his sin but by his righteousness.
- Surely God can be trusted to do what is right. It is impossible for human beings to pinpoint the causes of human suffering, because much activity related to it is imperceptible to human senses.
- A faulty theology of prosperity led Job's friends to conclude the worst, but they concluded wrongly. God was pleased with Job, not angry with him. Sometimes the most righteous people suffer unto the glory of God. We must always be slow to judge the sufferer.
- Once Job encountered the glorious God, he humbled himself and confessed his haste in trying to understand his plight. He was brought to the absolute end of himself, repenting in dust and ashes.
- God turned to Eliphaz and his two colleagues and ordered them to offer sacrifices for their sin in judging Job falsely. They offered the sacrifices, and God relented of his anger after Job prayed for his friends.
- Moreover, the time of testing ended. God blessed Job again with good health and a robust family and many possessions. Indeed, Job's brothers and sisters came to visit and comfort him, bringing him money and earrings of gold.
- Job became twice as wealthy as he had been at the time of his testing—and most especially, Job had seven more sons and three more daughters. Job lived 140 years after his calamity and enjoyed his prosperity, watching his grandchildren grow up and multiply unto the fourth generation "And so he died, old and full of years" (Job 42:17).

Key verses: "Then Job replied to the LORD: 'I know that you can do all things; no plan of yours can be thwarted. You asked, "Who is this that obscures my counsel without knowledge?" Surely I spoke of things I did not understand, things too wonderful for me to know'" (Job 42:1–3).

PSALMS

This book takes its name from the Greek "Psalmoi" or "Psalmos," which signifies music accompanied by instruments. The Hebrew title means "Book of Praises." Thus the Psalter served as the hymnbook for the Jews in their Temple worship and private meditations.

- The Bible tells us that David was a composer and singer of songs, as well as the chief architect of musical worship (1 Chr 13:8; 15:16–17; 16:4ff; 23:5).
- Many of the psalms are anonymous, but ninety psalms designate an author. King David wrote seventy-three of these psalms. Asaph also contributed to the Psalter and served as one of the chief musicians in worship under King David (1 Chr 15:17; 16:5).
- Asaph produced Psalms 73 through 83 and Psalm 50. Heman, the son of Joel, who served in the music ministry together with Asaph, wrote Psalm 88. King Solomon is said to have authored Psalms 72 and 127, and Ethan, another Levite musician, composed Psalm 89.
- Lastly, it is said that Moses wrote Psalm 90. Furthermore, some psalms were clearly post-exilic, as they discussed events pertaining to the exile. Thus we can see that the book of Psalms was compiled over time—a time span covering a substantial period. Certainly editors at various points included psalms as they were being produced across time.
- Since the writing of the psalms occurred over extended time periods, one concludes that it changed over time, becoming increasingly developed. Indeed, David probably served as the principal organizer of the Jewish hymnal. However, the Bible tells us that other kings were also involved in this endeavor.
- Solomon had a part in organizing temple worship, according to 2 Chronicles 5:11–14, 7:6, and 9:11.
- Jehoshaphat and Jehoiada also participated in various revisions and expansions of worship (2 Chr 20:21–22; 23:18), and Hezekiah reformed the music ministry by instructing the Levites to lead music using the psalms of David and Asaph (2 Chr 29:30).
- There is no powerfully cohesive structure to the book of Psalms, making it easy to pick up and begin reading anywhere. In this way,

The Poetical Books (Job through Song of Solomon)

the poetry literature differs significantly from the didactic or teaching books.

- However, tradition has organized the book into five sections. Book I is made up of Psalms 1 through 41; Book II contains Psalms 42 through 72; Book III is Psalms 73 through 89; Book IV includes Psalms 90 through 106; and finally, Book V runs from Psalm 107 to Psalm 150. Each of these five books concludes with a doxology, and the entire composition ends with a grand doxology in Psalm 150.
- This five-fold division is attested to by the Qumran literature dating from about the first century.
- There are various kinds of psalms:

A. Personal Laments—These psalms correspond to personal prayers or cries for help and deliverance. No book of the Bible is as deeply personal and as openly honest regarding the feelings of the composer as is the book of Psalms.

- o The basic pattern is something like this: an opening cry to God, an elaboration of the lamentable situation, a confession of trust in God, and a prayer for help, concluding with a statement of praise and/or thanksgiving.
- o It is a great encouragement in times of distress or trouble to read the psalms. The psalmist expressed his emotions vividly, making it is easy to identify with him. It is impressive to see the transparency with which the writers presented their individual cases to God. We really can be honest with God about how we are feeling and doing. (Remember, he knows about it anyway.)

B. National Laments—These psalms are quite similar to the personal laments, only directed toward national concerns. The nation is faced with some peril, and the psalmist is ushering the people collectively before God, asking for divine intervention on their behalf.

C. Psalms of Thanksgiving—Psalms under this broad category focus on praise to God for his wonderful works and provisions. It is instructive to consider how frequently the psalmist is found thanking and praising God.

D. Messianic Psalms—Some aspect of the work or person of Messiah is identified prophetically in these psalms. For instance, Psalm 2 reveals the exalted Son ruling over his rebellious enemies at a future date. One of the greatest Messianic psalms is Psalm 22, which speaks directly to the suffering of the Messiah. Psalm 22:12–18 sounds almost as though one is reading directly from the gospels. In such psalms, the writer goes beyond his own experience, speaking words that become literally true in the person of Jesus.

E. Imprecatory Psalms—These psalms call for justice and deliverance from enemies. Examples of this sort of psalm are abundant, most especially in the Psalms of David. (See, for example, Ps 3:7; 5:9–10; 6:10; 35:4–8; 40:14–15.)

- Question: How might one harmonize the imprecatory psalms with a forgiving and merciful spirit?

F. Penitential Psalms—The psalmists are frequently found confessing their sins and shortcomings before God, laying before us a good reminder of the importance of regular confession. Perhaps the best-know penitential psalm is Psalm 51, which records David's confession of his sin with Bath-sheba.

H. Psalms in praise of the word of God—These are probably best illustrated by the majestic psalm praising God's word—Psalm 119.

- This psalm is 176 verses long and is carefully organized as an acrostic (alphabetically arranged) psalm. Each paragraph (comprised of eight verses each) begins with the corresponding next letter of the Hebrew alphabet.
- There are twenty-two letters in the Jewish alphabet, and twenty-two times eight equals 176 verses. In other words, verses 1 through 8 of this psalm begin with the first letter of the Jewish alphabet, verses 9 through 16 begin with the second letter, and so on throughout the psalm.
- The word of God was referred to by ten different synonyms in this psalm: law, word, saying, commandment, statute, judgment, precept, testimony, way, and path.
- In expressing his feelings and responses to God and his word, the psalmist employed a number of words: delight, love, obey, and meditate.
- The expectation of the psalmist was that the word of God would both "renew" him and "preserve" him from evil.

The Poetical Books (Job through Song of Solomon)

- The book of Psalms scales the height and depth of human emotion, indicating that our God knows us altogether and accepts us when we come to him in any season or circumstance in life.

Key verse: "Oh, how I love your law! I meditate on it all day long" (Ps 119:97).

PROVERBS

Proverbs is a book of wisdom written by a father (Solomon) to his son. Wisdom might be defined as the practical application of knowledge. Indeed, wisdom is of the utmost value. However, wisdom alone without commensurate action fails to suffice. Solomon, the wisest man who ever lived, apart from Jesus, failed to apply many of his own admonitions. Indeed, he seems to have violated much of his own wise advice.

- As with the book of Psalms, Proverbs is not constructed around an argument, so classifying or outlining it is difficult. However, in general, chapters 1 through 9 are fatherly instructions to a son; chapters 10 through 24 contrast the way of wisdom with the way of foolishness; chapters 25 through 29 are proverbs of Solomon edited and included by the servants of Hezekiah; and the last two chapters are supplemental addendums by Agur and Lemuel.

- Chapter 1 introduces the author (Solomon), the intended audience (his son [Prov 1:8, 10]), and the purpose (to give prudence, knowledge, and discretion to the simple).

- The fear of the Lord is a regular theme throughout Proverbs (Prov 1:7; 8:13; 16:6). A respect for God and an awareness of our accountability to him is the beginning of the quest for wisdom. It also causes us to hate or oppose evil and motivates us to depart from it.

- Solomon exhorted his son to listen to him. Indeed, one of the rudimentary traits of a wise person is a willingness to be taught (Prov 1:8). Conversely, one of the chief attributes of the fool and scorner is stubbornness and a refusal to hear instruction.

- Solomon also expressed concern that his son might forge alliances with evil people, being acutely aware that bad company corrupts good morals. This thought occupied him from 1:10 to 1:19 (and elsewhere).

- Wisdom invites all to learn from her, but many chose to live in ignorance. She cries to the simple, the scorner, and the fool (Prov 1:21–23). If received, her reproof and counsel is able to help them all. But because she does reprove people, many turn a deaf ear. Those who do so suffer the consequences, for, "Since they would not accept my advice and spurned my rebuke, they will eat the fruit of their ways..." (Prov 1:30–31).

- Wisdom must be pursued. In Proverbs 2:1–4, Solomon used eight verbs of action to describe the right attitude toward wisdom: accept, store up, turn to, apply, call out, cry aloud, look for, and search. As with most precious commodities, it is not acquired without effort.
- Two important benefits of wisdom are emphasized in chapter 2—discretion will protect you from "the ways of wicked men" and from "the adulteress."
- Again we see that our associations are critical. The paths we choose determine in many respects the lives that we lead: "Thus you will walk in the ways of good men and keep to the paths of the righteous" (Prov 2:20).
- Various admonitions appear in chapter 3. Cling to mercy and truth, and trust firmly in the Lord, Solomon exhorted his son. Interestingly, one can be both truthful and merciful. We tend to think that people are either one or the other—but not both. But Jesus was full of grace *and* truth.
- We honor the Lord by offering him the first fruits of our resources—not the leftovers. Solomon asserted that the Lord also honors those who honor him (Prov 3:10).
- Neither should we grow weary with the correction of the Lord, for every father corrects the son in whom he delights.
- Happy is the person who finds and retains wisdom, for, "She is more precious than rubies; nothing you desire can compare with her" (Prov 3:15).
- The praise of wisdom's value continues in chapter 4. Solomon argued that "Wisdom is supreme; therefore get wisdom. Though it cost all you have, get understanding. Esteem her, and she will exalt you; embrace her, and she will honor you" (Prov 4:7–8).
- The decisions we make regarding the paths we tread are discussed in the close of chapter 4. The words "path" and "step" and "way" occur almost one hundred times in Proverbs, indicating their importance. We are exhorted to "Make level paths for your feet and take only ways that are firm. Do not swerve to the right or to the left; keep your foot from evil" (Prov 4:26–27).
- Chapter 5 discuses the temptations and dangers associated with immorality. Indeed, the adulteress is portrayed using her basic strategy of flattery and seduction. Behind the appearance of pleasure lurks the dead. The end result is bitterness. "Keep to a path far from her,

do not go near the door of her house" (Prov 5:8). Sexually transmitted diseases were common and one of the terrible consequences of immorality (Prov 5:11).

- The chapter concludes by reminding the listener that the ways of man are in full view of the Lord, and that he examines all his paths. Nothing is done in secret. Once again we see that the consequences of one's actions are often the greatest punishment.

- Solomon concluded the chapter by saying, "The evil deeds of a wicked man ensnare him; the cords of his sin hold him fast. He will die for lack of discipline, led astray by his own great folly" (Prov 5:22–23).

- The virtues of hard work and the dangers of debt are outlined in 6:1–11.

- Be careful of co-signing loans—becoming "security" for a friend. Often this provides a means to the end of the friendship.

- Instead of borrowing, we are encouraged to work hard—"Go to the ant, you sluggard; consider its ways and be wise! It has no commander, no overseer or no ruler, yet it stores its provisions in summer and gathers its food at harvest" (Prov 6:6–8).

- Seven things the Lord hates are specifically outlined in 6:16–19: haughty eyes, a lying tongue, the shedding of innocent blood, wicked schemes, a readiness to engage in evil, a false witness, and one who stirs up dissension among brethren.

- Again the issue of immorality and harlotry is discussed from 6:24 to 7:27. It is the reproof and instruction of the word of God that leads to the abundant life and protects us against the lying flatteries of the immoral (Prov 6:23; 7:1–5).

- Those who succumb to the way of immorality are likened to an ox being led away to the slaughter. The harlot is depicted as hunting for the precious life. Indeed, "Many are the victims she has brought down; her slain are a mighty throng. Her house is a highway to the grave, leading down to the chambers of death" (Prov 7:26–27).

- Chapter 8 is in praise of wisdom. Once again, wisdom is found crying out in the high places and in the city gates. This imagery is intended to convey her willingness to share her insight with all in the city—if only we are willing.

- But now she is crying out to only the simple and the foolish—the scorners have rejected her. As we shall see, in chapter 9 her invitation is then only to the simple. The fools have also forsaken her (Prov 9:4). It is important to note that she has not refused them; they have refused her.

- Wisdom declares, "I love those who love me, and those who seek me find me. With me are riches and honor, enduring wealth and prosperity" (Prov 8:17–18). We are exhorted to hear her words and embrace her teachings, for they are the paths of peace, prosperity, and favor with the Lord.

- Chapter 9 concludes the first main section. In chapter 1 we saw wisdom crying out to the simple, the scorner, and the fool (Prov 1:22). In chapter 8, she was found addressing only the simple and the fool—the scorner has departed (Prov 8:5). Finally, in chapter 9 her voice is aimed at only the simple, for the fool too has forsaken her counsel (Prov 9:4).

- In fact, she now enjoins the simple to forsake the foolish and live (Prov 9:6). Wisdom expounds on the basic malady of both the fool and the scorner—they will not listen to reproof and correction. Instead of heeding wise counsel, they become angry and defiant in their sin.

- What a different attitude is found in the wise person. The wise are not perfect—far from it—but they realize it and desire to grow and change. They welcome constructive criticism as a gift, not an intrusion. As the text states, "Do not rebuke a mocker or he will hate you; rebuke a wise man and he will love you. Instruct a wise man and he will be wiser still; teach a righteous man and he will add to his learning" (Prov 9:8–9).

- The key difference between the wise and the foolish has little to do with intelligence. It involves one's attitude. The wise listen intently to wisdom's voice and are moldable in the hands of God. The foolish are intractable and stubborn, refusing to listen or change.

- Chapter 9 concludes with a final warning against immorality.

- Proverbs chapters 10 through 31: This section contrasts the differences between the wise person and the foolish one. Many important topics help differentiate between those with discretion and those without it: wealth, words, work, child-rearing, self-control, and giving, among others.

- The passage begins with a potent truth—wise children make parents happy, and foolish ones bring sadness. Indeed, parents are so connected to their children and invest so deeply in them that they are generally greatly influenced by their children's actions—thus the many admonitions to instruct and discipline children.

- Integrity is of greater value than riches because wealth is fleeting.
- However, those with character and industry may acquire riches as well.
- An idea closely associated with the accumulation of wealth and success is a willingness to be a lifelong learner. "He who ignores discipline comes to poverty and shame, but whoever heeds correction is honored" (Prov 13:18).
- Another significant theme pertains to our speech. In general, the mouth of the just dispenses knowledge, wisdom, encouragement, strength, peace, and sometimes—at appropriate moments—silence. In contrast, the fool slanders others, gossips incessantly, lies, rarely shows discretion or tact, pours out foolishness, destroys reputations, and is generally debased (Prov 16:23–24; 18:7; 18:21).
- The gossip incites trouble—often for the teller's own amusement or benefit. "As charcoal to embers and wood to fire, so is a quarrelsome man for kindling strife. The words of a gossip are like choice morsels; they go down to a man's inmost parts.... A lying tongue hates those it hurts, and a flattering mouth works ruin" (Prov 26:21–22, 28).
- Scripture endorses a strong work ethic. Laziness is consistently rebuked and industry just as consistently applauded. Honest hard work is one of the key moral virtues established in the book. The slothful are a constant source of irritation to the diligent. "As vinegar to the teeth and smoke to the eyes, so is a sluggard to those who send him" (Prov 10:26).
- In contrast, the industrious person refuses to make excuses or procrastinate, nor does he permit unfavorable circumstances to dissuade him from completing his tasks. He is a good steward over his resources, caring diligently for them.
- Indeed, there is a great chasm between the indolent and the industrious. "The sluggard says, 'There is a lion outside!' or, 'I will be murdered in the streets!'" (Prov 22:13). Lazy people always have a "good excuse" to leave things undone or ignore their responsibilities.
- In general, diligent people are promoted to positions of authority while the lazy end up as servants to the wise. "Diligent hands will rule, but laziness ends in slave labor" (Prov 12:24).

The Poetical Books (Job through Song of Solomon)

- Self-control is another trait that Solomon praised, most especially the ability to control one's anger. "Better a patient man than a warrior, a man who controls his temper than one who takes a city" (Prov 16:32). "A man's wisdom gives him patience; it is to his glory to overlook an offense" (Prov 19:11).

- The next generation concerned Solomon greatly. He offered guidance and counsel to parents. His insights are superior to many modern-day "experts" who counsel parents to indulge disobedience and tolerate disrespect.

- Obviously, children must know that they are loved and cherished, but part of love is providing appropriate discipline, guidance, and correction. Children need to learn self-control if they are to experience happiness. They also must learn to submit to appropriate authority and to respect it.

- Solomon had several things to say about training up children. "The rod of correction imparts wisdom, but a child left to himself disgraces his mother" (Prov 29:15). "Folly is bound up in the heart of a child, but the rod of discipline will drive it far from him" (Prov 22:15). "Train a child in the way he should go, and when he is old he will not turn from it" (Prov 22:6).

- Generosity is one of the characteristics of the wise. They realize God is pleased with sacrificial giving—and they practice it. The greedy man constantly hoards up, yet remains unsatisfied. The generous giver is rewarded time and again for his benevolence. "One man gives freely, yet gains even more; another withholds unduly, but comes to poverty. A generous man will prosper; he who refreshes others will himself be refreshed" (Prov 11:24–25).

- The book concludes with an ode to the virtuous woman (Prov 31:10–31). One notices several features about her. She is valuable, loyal, and industrious in providing for her family and for the needy. She also possesses a high degree of business skill, buying and selling real estate, and her abilities allow her husband to achieve success. Her speech is wise and kind. Because of this, her family praises her. Indeed, her works will also praise her in the end.

- The book of Proverbs is filled with wisdom—for those who are willing to listen.

Key verse: "Wisdom is supreme; therefore get wisdom. Though it cost you all you have, get understanding" (Prov 4:7).

ECCLESIASTES/SONG OF SOLOMON

Ecclesiastes takes its name from the Greek translation of the Hebrew title "koheleth," which means "Preacher." It is an autobiographical account of life rendered by an aged Solomon, "son of David, King in Israel."

- The general tenor of the book is one of sadness. All the accomplishments of man had failed to fulfill the great monarch. Sadly, Solomon drifted away from the Lord in his latter life (1 Kgs 11:1-9; Neh 13:26). The book testifies to the futility of living apart from God, revealing that even in great success and splendor, life is empty apart from communion with the Most High.

- The word "vanity" or "meaninglessness" occurs throughout the text, meaning futility or emptiness. "Meaningless! Meaningless!" says the teacher. ". . . Utterly meaningless! Everything is meaningless" (Eccl 1:2).

- Each succeeding generation has its moment in history and then fades away, forgotten or misunderstood by the next generation. Life for the preacher was an endless cycle of monotony (Eccl 1:4-11).

- Solomon tried everything to fill the void that he experienced in his heart—from pursuing knowledge and wisdom to succumbing to folly and madness. Yet, he found no sense of wholeness. He discovered that knowledge apart from the Lord only produced greater grief and sorrow (Eccl 1:18).

- Solomon tried a number of other world philosophies to satisfy him, as recorded in chapter 2. He turned to sensuality (2:1-3), philanthropy (2:4-6), materialism (2:7-8), and scholarship (2:9). Whatever interested him, he pursued to the fullest. "I denied myself nothing my eyes desired; I refused my heart no pleasure . . ." (Eccl 2:10).

- However, these too failed to produce lasting contentment. Even though Solomon acknowledged that wisdom far exceeded folly, one thing haunted him throughout the book. The inescapability of death plagued the elder statesman.

- "For the wise man, like the fool, will not be long remembered; in days to come both will be forgotten. Like the fool, the wise man too must die!" (Eccl 2:16).

- Indeed, the author of the book of Hebrews was in complete accord with Solomon, asserting that through the fear of death people are kept in bondage all their lives. How wonderful that Jesus Christ came to deliver us from that bondage—". . . so that by his death he might destroy him who holds the power of death—that is, the devil—and free those who all their lives were held in slavery by their fear of death" (Heb 2:14–15).

- Solomon wrote, "Man's fate is like that of the animals; the same fate awaits them both: As one dies, so dies the other . . ." (Eccl 3:19). "No man has power over the wind to contain it; so no one has power over the day of his death . . ." (Eccl 8:8). "This is the evil in everything that happens under the sun . . . they join the dead" (Eccl 9:3).

- Solomon rightly perceived that there is a time for every purpose under heaven; indeed, one key to living well is to know what time it is.

- In the midst of life's oppressions and problems, it is important to have friends who will assist us in our journey. In the welfare state in which we live, it is easy to forget how stark life was for millions of impoverished people throughout history. ". . . A cord of three strands is not quickly broken" (Eccl 4:12).

- Solomon prohibited rash speech in chapter 5. It is better to refrain from making a vow to God rather than making one and breaking it.

- Riches are incapable of satisfying the soul. How much money does a greedy man want? Just a little bit more!

- Enjoying the fruit of one's labor, however, is the apex of human experience, apart from an eternal expectation. Solomon stated, ". . . It is good and proper for a man to eat and drink, and to find satisfaction in his toilsome labor under the sun . . . this is a gift of God" (Eccl 5:18–19). We are thankful that God has provided yet another gift—the gift of eternal life through Jesus Christ.

- Mirth is fleeting, and Solomon knew it from experience. He stated, "Like the crackling of thorns under the pot, so is the laughter of fools. This too is meaningless" (Eccl 7:6).

- Solomon offered us an important piece of theological insight in the book stating, "There is not a righteous man on earth who does what is right and never sins" (Eccl 7:20). This sounds a good bit like Paul writing in Romans 3:23, "For all have sinned and fall short of the glory of God."

- Both wisdom and money are a defense against life's exigencies, but wisdom is better, because it gives life (Eccl 7:12).

- Chapter 8 points out that the evil and ignorant forget the coming judgment and thus are often caught unawares (Eccl 8:11).
- Life contains much contingency, even for those who live wisely and in a way that honors the Lord. Our full reward is never realized in this world. Some of the most faithful people fail to receive a just recompense in this life.
- The words of the wise are often not remembered. Sometimes they are not even heard—spoken to empty chairs and vacant rooms (Eccl 9:15–17).
- Chapter 10 is proverbial in nature, sounding a good bit like the book of Proverbs. A little folly can sour an entire life. Leadership has far-reaching effects, making life either good for the citizens or evil. "Blessed are you, O land whose king is of noble birth and whose princes eat at a proper time—for strength and not for drunkenness" (Eccl 10:17).
- Solomon exhorted young people to order their lives in a way that pleases God before they get old and lose their capacity to make wise decisions. Live today in light of God's judgment, he urged (Eccl 11:8).
- Solomon employed some penetrating imagery about the aging process. Get right with God and stay right with God, he enjoined his listeners, before the "keepers of the house tremble" (the hands), "the grinders cease because they are few" (the teeth), "the windows grow dim" (the eyes fail), "the almond tree blossoms" (whose flowers were white, probably representing the gray hair of the elderly), etc.
- The end of the matter as Solomon viewed things was, "Fear God and keep his commandments for this is the whole duty of man." His rationale for this path is that all the living stand in anticipation of the judgment of God (Eccl 12:14).
- Indeed, from the merely human vantage point, the case is depressing. Thank God for Jesus Christ, who gives us the victory over death and judgment—"Therefore, there is now no condemnation for those who are in Christ Jesus" (Rom 8:1), and "When the perishable has been clothed with the imperishable, and the mortal with immortality, then the saying that is written will come true: 'Death is swallowed up in victory.'... But thanks be to God! He gives us the victory through our Lord Jesus Christ" (1 Cor 15:54, 57).

Key verse: ". . . Fear God and keep his commandments, for this is the whole duty of man" (Eccl 12:13).

- **The Song of Solomon:** This book was written by the king at an earlier stage of life. Indeed, the order of the books seems inverted, since the Song expresses the optimism of youth. Indeed, no other book more thoroughly celebrates the happiness associated with marital love as does the Song. It is literally a love song between Solomon and the Shulamite. It is also likely a figurative description for God's love toward his people Israel, as well as a picture of Christ's love for his bride, the Church.

4

The Prophetical Books
(Isaiah through Malachi)

ISAIAH

Isaiah was the greatest of all the writing prophets, prophesying during the reign of four kings: Uzziah, Jotham, Ahaz, and Hezekiah (Isa 1:1). He likely began his ministry sometime during the reign of Uzziah and continued until shortly after the reign of Hezekiah, dying as a martyr at the hands of Manasseh. No other prophet writing under the dispensation of law was privy to such a clear vision of grace. Indeed, this grace was revealed through the Servant of the Lord, Messiah, who would die as a sacrifice for the sins of his people and redeem them back to God. The invitation of Isaiah, offered early in the book, governs much of the content and direction: "'Come now, let us reason together,' says the LORD. 'Though your sins are like scarlet, they shall be as white as snow; though they are red as crimson, they shall be like wool'" (Isa 1:18).

The book may be briefly outlined in the following manner:

I. **Prophecies concerning the judgment against both Judah and Israel (Isa 1—12)**
- This section is mostly concerned with the approaching judgment of the northern kingdom by Assyria and the Babylonian captivity, into which Judah would later fall. God employed these pagan nations as a vehicle of punishment toward his idolatrous, stubborn, and wayward people.
- "In that day" is a recurring phrase throughout the first half of the book, referring primarily to the "Day of the Lord," which day is a day

of vengeance and retribution exacted by the Lord against those who have rebelled against him.

- "'Woe to the Assyrian, the rod of my anger, in whose hand is the club of my wrath! I send him against a godless nation, I dispatch him against a people who anger me, to seize loot and snatch plunder, and to trample them down like mud in the streets'" (Isa 10:5-6).
- Near the close of each major section of the book there is a glimpse of the millennial kingdom and sometimes the eternal state—the new heavens and the new earth.
- This is the case in chapters 11 and 12. The prophet zooms in and out from the present to the near future to the distant future. Of the millennial reign the prophet states, "The wolf will live with the lamb, the leopard will lie down with the goat, the calf and the lion and the yearling together; and a little child will lead them" (Isa 11:6).
- Though God used the pagan nations as his tools of judgment, this did not excuse them from their actions. God would still judge them for their deeds (Isa 10:12-16).

II. Prophecies regarding the future judgment of the Gentile nations (Isa 13—27).

- Once again the prophet transitions from near to distant judgment, focusing on Babylon (Isa 13:1—14:23), Assyria (Isa 14:24-32), Moab (Isa 15—16), Syria (Isa 17), Ethiopia (Isa 18), and Egypt (Isa 19:1-15).
- Yet, people from both Egypt and Assyria will be present in the millennial kingdom, as suggested by Isaiah 19:16-25.
- God also punished the Egyptians at the hands of the Assyrians, according to chapter 20.
- The fall of Babylon is prophesied in chapter 21 and will be discussed again with even greater precision, ". . . Babylon has fallen, has fallen! All the images of its gods lie shattered on the ground" (Isa 21:9). Amazingly, Babylon had not yet even established itself as a world power.
- Other impending judgments are mentioned involving Jerusalem and Tyre (Isa 22—23).
- In the midst of the other judgments of God, the Tribulation judgment is mentioned in chapter 24. Isaiah wrote, "The earth reels like a

drunkard, it sways like a hut in the wind; so heavy upon it is the guilt of its rebellion that it falls—never to rise again" (Isa 24:20).

- The end-time reign of Christ is suggested at the conclusion of this section on judgment (25—27). Death shall also be judged, and life will prevail, "He will swallow up death forever; the Sovereign LORD will wipe away the tears from all faces ..." (Isa 25:8). "But your dead will live; their bodies will rise. You who dwell in the dust, wake up and shout for joy ..." (Isa 26:19).

III. Warning of the Impending Judgment against Ephraim (another name for Israel), Ariel (Jerusalem), and Judah (Isa 28—39).

- The Assyrian invasion, which would bring the northern kingdom into exile, is predicted in chapter 28.
- The Babylonian captivity is suggested as a judgment against Judah in chapter 29.
- No alliance with any foreign power will deliver Israel from God's judgment. In this case, Isaiah warned them not to forge an alliance with Egypt because it would prove futile.
- Isaiah then pictured the eventual rescue of Jerusalem by the Lord himself.
- A picture of the coming deliverer is offered in chapters 32 and 33. Interestingly, all the branches of government are perfectly fulfilled in him, "For the LORD is our judge, the LORD is our lawgiver, and the LORD is our king; it is he who will save us" (Isa 33:22). The reign of Messiah encompasses the judicial, legislative, and executive branches of government. He does not need the checks and balances of mixed government.
- Chapters 34 and 35 foreshadow the future tribulation period and the kingdom age.
- The Lord will gather the pagan armies of the world together for the onslaught. "The LORD is angry with all nations; his wrath is upon all their armies. He will totally destroy them, he will give them over to slaughter" (Isa 34:2).
- That day will be a day of God's vengeance—when the time has come, judgment will fall. "All the stars of the heavens will be dissolved and the sky rolled up like a scroll; ... For the LORD has a day of vengeance, a year of retribution, to uphold Zion's cause" (Isa 34:4, 8).

- But for those who are redeemed, the kingdom will be a place of unspeakable joy, "And the ransomed of the LORD will return. They will enter Zion with singing; everlasting joy will crown their heads. Gladness and joy will overtake them, and sorrow and sighing will flee away "(Isa 35:10).
- In chapters 36 through 39, events during the reign of Hezekiah are outlined, leading up to the Babylonian captivity. However, first God rescued them from the hand of the Assyrians (Isa 36—37).

In one night, the Angel of the Lord slew one hundred eighty-five thousand Assyrian troops. Indeed, the Lord is a mighty warrior. Seeing this destruction, Sennacherib retreated, seeking asylum in the house of his god, Nisroch. However, his own sons assassinated him in his house of worship (Isa 37:36–38).

- Hezekiah received divine healing in chapter 38. Unfortunately, he exercised poor judgment in his remaining years by welcoming emissaries from Babylon to tour the glory of the Temple and palace. Isaiah prophesied that having seen the glory, they would return and plunder it, thus predicting the Babylonian siege (Isa 39:3–7).

IV. The greatness of God, the work of the suffering Servant, and future prophecies of the coming kingdom and the eternal state (Isa 40—66)

- Following the prediction of exile, God offered comfort to his people. The eternality of God was contrasted with the brevity of mankind.
- John the Baptist was foreshadowed as well in 40:3.
- The Servant of the Lord, the Christ, appears frequently in this final third of the book. Indeed, he is the one who will rescue sinners from the judgments so often described in the book (Isa 42:1).
- The foolishness of idolatry is also explicitly stated many times throughout the book; the absurdity of worshipping that which one made with one's own hands is repeatedly expressed (Isa 44; 46). Idols are incapable of offering any real help. Absence of peace is the reward of those who commit idolatry.
- Isaiah prophesied that God would deliver Judah from the Babylonians by the Medo-Persians, and specifically by the hand of Cyrus (Isa 44:28; 45:1–4). Incredibly, this prophecy was made about 150 years before Cyrus was born and about one hundred years before Judah

went into captivity. Only God can predict the future with precision and specificity.

- Isaiah offered the clearest prophetic statements about the Servant of the Lord, including his virgin birth (Isa 7:14), his deity (Isa 9:6–7), his atoning ministry and sacrificial death (Isa 42:1–7; 52:1—53:12), and his future reign (Isa 61; 63—64; 66).
- Sin is the problem and the cause for God's judgment, and the Servant is the solution.
- He is the one who intervenes on behalf of the guilty and becomes the means of rescue and forgiveness.
- Isaiah predicted Jesus's suffering and atoning work more fully than any other writing prophet. The work of Jesus Christ is clearly in view throughout Isaiah 53: "But he was pierced for our transgressions, he was crushed for our iniquities; the punishment that brought us peace was upon him, and by his wounds we are healed. We all, like sheep, have gone astray, each of us has turned to his own way; and the LORD has laid on him the iniquity of us all" (Isa 53:5–6). Isaiah continued describing in vivid detail the work of the Servant throughout the remainder of the chapter.
- The Servant solved the sin problem by becoming a sacrifice—a substitute for the guilty, one who fully satisfies the righteous indignation of God against sin.
- If he does not remove our sins by bearing them upon himself, then we must be judged for them—a grim prospect indeed.
- God mercifully invites sinners to return to him and find mercy and forgiveness (Isa 57:15).
- Our sin separates us from God (Isa 59:2, 12).
- An amazing statement occurs regarding the first and second advents of Christ in Isaiah 61:1–2: "The Spirit of the Sovereign LORD is on me, because the LORD has anointed me to preach good news to the poor. He has sent me to bind up the brokenhearted, to proclaim freedom for the captives and release from darkness for the prisoners, to proclaim the year of the LORD's favor, and the day of vengeance of our God . . ."
- Jesus quoted this very passage in the Temple as recorded in Luke 4:16–21, applying it directly to himself. But he stopped the quotation

The Prophetical Books (Isaiah through Malachi)

in the middle of verse 2, after, "to proclaim the year of the LORD's favor." The day of vengeance will occur at the second advent of Christ.

- Thankfully, we are still in the acceptable year of the Lord. Messiah's vengeance against the world was expressed vividly in chapter 63. Those who refuse him will be judged by him.
- The creation of the new heavens and new earth and the exaltation of Israel, and most especially Jerusalem, are expressed in 65:17–66.
- In the newly created order, devoid of any curse, "The wolf and the lamb will feed together, and the lion will eat straw like the ox ... They will neither harm nor destroy on all my holy mountain" (Isa 65:25).

Key verse: "'Come now, let us reason together,' says the LORD. 'Though your sins are like scarlet, they shall be white as snow; though they are red as crimson, they shall be like wool'" (Isa 1:18).

JEREMIAH/LAMENTATIONS

Jeremiah, often referred to as the weeping prophet, composed this letter under the direction of the Lord, whose word came to him initially during the thirteenth year of King Josiah. He was the son of a righteous priest named Hilkiah, the same Hilkiah who recovered the lost book of the Law of Moses in the Temple of the Lord as recorded in 2 Chronicles 34:14–15. Essentially, the book is a message of the impending judgment of God against his stubborn and rebellious people, using the Babylonians as his instrument of chastisement. Unless they repented, Jerusalem would be utterly destroyed. Habakkuk and Zephaniah presented a parallel message during their early ministries. However, the message of captivity was not without hope. God promised to restore the people in their homeland after a season of discipline.

I. The Call of Jeremiah: Chapter 1

- God commissioned Jeremiah before birth (Jer 1:5). Jeremiah responded to this privilege in a manner reminiscent of Moses, asserting that he was unable to fulfill his calling due to his innate limitations.

- However, God rebuked him, promising to be with the reluctant prophet. God commanded him to speak God's word to the nation. Prophetic preaching does a number of things: (1) it uproots, (2) it tears down, (3) it destroys, (4) it throws down, (5) it builds, and (6) it plants (Jer 1:10).

- God strengthened Jeremiah for his task, knowing that the people would despise him and his message. Indeed, that was the general response of the rebellious nation throughout the book. Preaching the word of God does not always draw crowds. The problem is not necessarily with the seed or with the sower but with the recipients.

II. Prophecies of Judgment against Judah and Other Nations: Jeremiah 2 through 52

A. Impending judgment and its causes: Jeremiah 2 through 6

- Jeremiah literally wandered around Jerusalem pronouncing impending judgment upon the idolatrous nation. Two great offenses were described, "My people have committed two sins: They have forsaken me, the spring of living water, and have dug their own cisterns, broken cisterns that cannot hold water" (Jer 2:13).

- The latter imagery referred to the Israelites' unceasing propensity to engage in idolatry—making their own idols and worshipping them. God considered this spiritual adultery, and it was detestable in his eyes. As such, God justly divorced Israel, giving her a bill of divorcement (Jer 3:8).
- The entire nation had become depraved: idolatrous, adulterous, covetous, proud, and stubborn. Having itching ears, they devoured the true prophets of God and turned themselves to fables and lies. This corruption included not only the people but also the prophets and priests and princes and kings (Jer 5:1, 29–31).
- Eventually this national sin brought judgment. It would be administered by a pagan nation, "This is what the LORD says: 'Look, an army is coming from the land of the north; a great nation is being stirred up from the ends of the earth. They are armed with bow and spear; they are cruel and show no mercy. They sound like the roaring sea as they ride on their horses; they come like men in battle formation to attack you, O Daughter of Zion'" (Jer 6:22–23; see also Jer 5:15–16).
- However, a message of hope was attached to even this harsh message of judgment, "'Yet even in those days,' declares the LORD, 'I will not destroy you completely.'" (Jer 5:18). God will always retain a remnant.

B. The message at the Temple Gate—Jeremiah 7 through 10

- God directed Jeremiah to stand in the Temple Gate and announce another message.
- The people had retained a semblance of religion but had lost the heart of worship.
- They still attended "church," but they were far from God. Syncretism was rampant; they worshipped the Lord, but not exclusively. Of particular concern to Jeremiah was the worship of the false "queen of heaven," who is mentioned frequently in this missive (Jer 7:15; 44:15–30). They practiced thievery, adultery, murder, lying, and idolatry, yet felt no compunction to repent (Jer 7:9–10).
- Furthermore, and of particular repulsion to God, they worshipped false gods in the valley of Hinnom, sacrificing their children to pagan gods (Jer 7:30–31).
- They had become so callused to their sins that they experienced no shame at all in committing them (Jer 8:12).

- The time for judgment had arrived, and God forbade Jeremiah from praying for the rebellious people (Jer 7:16; 11:14; 14:10).

C. Warnings based on the Palestinian Covenant—Jeremiah 11 and 12.

- God means what he says. He had warned the people of the consequences of turning away from him. Treachery, idolatry, and rebellion would bring his curse upon the nation, and this curse was about to be experienced (Jer 11:3-4).
- Yet, even in judgment, God would show compassion and maintain his remnant (Jer 12:15).

D. The sign of the girdle and the coming drought—Jeremiah 13 through 15.

- God ordered Jeremiah to bury a linen girdle at the Euphrates River. After a period of time, he was to dig it up. It was marred and good for nothing. God told the prophet that he was going to mar the pride of Judah and Jerusalem (Jer 13:9). God also sent a drought as a preliminary judgment upon the people, which was discussed in chapter 14.
- One of the major problems in Judah pertained to self-proclaimed prophets who prophesied lies to the people (Jer 14:14). In contrast, Jeremiah prophesied the true message of God and was hated because of it.

E. The sign of celibacy, the depths of Judah's sin, the sign of the potter's house, and the broken flask—Jeremiah 16 through 20.

- The impending judgment would be so severe that God told Jeremiah not to marry and have children (Jer 16:2).
- Judgment would surely fall because the sin of Judah was etched upon their hearts: "Judah's sin is engraved with an iron tool, inscribed with a flint point, on the tablets of their hearts . . ." (Jer 17:1).
- This thought led Jeremiah to declare, "The heart is deceitful above all things and beyond cure. Who can understand it?" The answer, of course, is, "I the LORD search the heart" (Jer 17:9-10a).
- Jeremiah stood at the gate of the city and railed against the king—but no one would listen (Jer 17:19-23).
- He went to a potter's house and watched him work at the wheel. A vessel in process became ruined, and the potter remade it. God asked,

"O house of Israel, can I not do with you as this potter does? . . ." (Jer 18:6).

- While Jeremiah warned the nation, they devised schemes against him (Jer 18:18).
- He next took a potter's flask and marched into the valley of Hinnom, announcing God's wrath against the nation for their deplorable practice of child sacrifice. Indeed, Jeremiah declared God would make Judah and Jerusalem desolate, and having said this, he broke the flask in the presence of those watching (Jer 19:5–10).

F. Further judgments issued against the nation, the rebellious response of the people, and Jeremiah's unrelenting faithfulness to the message of God—Jeremiah 20 through 39.

- Jeremiah was thrown into the stocks by Pashur, ruler in the house of the Lord. Nevertheless, Jeremiah reiterated his prophecy that the nation would be punished by the Babylonians in a season of captivity.
- Messages against Judah's last four kings—Zedekiah, Shallum (Jehoahaz), Jehoiakim, and Jehoiachin—were announced.
- A prophecy was made about Messiah, the righteous Branch, in whose days Judah and Israel would be saved (Jer 23:5–8).
- A lament over false prophets who had misled the nation appears (Jer 23: 9–40).
- The sign of the two baskets of figs—one good and one evil—was mentioned. God told the people to submit to the Babylonians and accept their punishment. If they did, he would bring them back again. If they refused, he would destroy them. Those who went into exile represented the good figs; those who refused were likened to the evil figs.
- The seventy-year captivity was prophesied in chapter 25. However, when the seventy years were accomplished, God would punish Babylon for their wickedness too (Jer 25:12).
- Jeremiah proclaimed God's message at the Temple Court. God warned his prophet not to diminish his message by so much as a single word (Jer 26:2). Even up to this point, God gave the people time to repent, but they refused to listen (Jer 26:8ff).
- The sign of the yoke was given to the surrounding nations. Jeremiah placed a yoke and bonds on his own body (Jer 27:2). The Lord then instructed him to send them to various pagan kings round about.

Those who accepted the domination of the Babylonians would be permitted to survive, but those who fought against them would be conquered (Jer 27:11–12).

- The false prophecy of Hananiah that Judah would be kept safe from Babylon was popular but incorrect. Popular messages are not always true.
- Again, God told the Jews to submit to Babylon and even pray for the peace of their city (Jer 29:7–10).
- A foreshadowing of the tribulation period occurs in chapter 30 (Jer 30:7ff). Yet even here, God will save his remnant.
- Chapter 31 looks forward to the millennial reign and the making of a new covenant with Israel (Jer 31:31–34).
- In chapter 32, Jeremiah was imprisoned by Zedekiah, king of Judah. Jeremiah bought the field of Hanameel as a sign of a future return to the land.
- In chapter 33, a prophecy of the ultimate deliverance of the nation by the Branch and the establishment of the Davidic Kingdom forever was revealed (Jer 33:15–17).
- Jeremiah delivered another message to Zedekiah that captivity was unavoidable (Jer 34). Of course, this was an unpopular, yes, even unpatriotic, message, leading to a lot of anger among his fellow Jews. Jehoiakim was so incensed that he destroyed the writings of Jeremiah. However, Baruch the scribe was commissioned to write them again from the mouth of Jeremiah (Jer 36:1ff).
- Indeed, in a reconnaissance mission, the Babylonians did retreat for fear of Pharaoh's army, leading to outrage at Jeremiah's prophecies of inevitable captivity (Jer 37:11). The princes of Jerusalem thus had Jeremiah imprisoned after beating him for his "false" prophecies of impending judgment (Jer 38:6–7).
- Jeremiah was delivered by the Ethiopian Ebed-Melech at the command of King Zedekiah, who wanted to hear more prophecies from Jeremiah.
- Jeremiah told him that if he submitted to the Babylonians, the city would be spared, but if not, it would be destroyed (Jer 38:17–18).

G. Jerusalem fell to the Babylonians, and Jeremiah was exiled to Egypt—Jeremiah 39 through 44

H. Judgment against the surrounding nations by Babylon was announced—Jeremiah 45 through 50

I. Judgment against Babylon was assured following the seventy-year captivity—Jeremiah 51

J. Final summary of the historical events leading to the captivity—Jeremiah 52

Key verse: "'Although you wash yourself with soda and use an abundance of soap, the stain of your guilt is still before me,' declares the Sovereign LORD" (Jer 2:22).

- **Lamentations**: The reason Lamentations is placed among the Major Prophets is because it is seen as something of an appendix to the book of Jeremiah. In its relatively brief five chapters, the author, who was undoubtedly Jeremiah, lamented the desolation of his homeland under the judgment of God against Judah. The book concludes with Jeremiah asking God to remember his people and return them to the land. Though Jeremiah likely never witnessed this, his prayer was eventually answered seventy years later—just as God promised.

EZEKIEL

Ezekiel prophesied during the Babylonian exile, warning the generation born in exile of the national sins that led to their overthrow and encouraging them with the hope of national restitution and eventual millennial glory. Ezekiel's visions are described in great detail, offering us insight into the glory of God.

- Chapters 1 through 3 describe God's call to Ezekiel. God sent angelic visitors to introduce the prophecies to Ezekiel. While Ezekiel was surrounded by paganism, God offered him a comforting glimpse of the incomparable glory of heaven. Four living creatures emerged out of a heavenly brilliance and fire that appeared to Ezekiel.

- They each had four faces; some commentators think each face was symbolic of the way in which Christ would reveal himself to the world in the incarnation. They had the face of a man, an ox (symbolizing a servant), a lion (symbolizing his kingship), and an eagle (symbolizing his deity) (Ezek 1:5–11). They appeared suddenly, like lightning.

- A throne stationed above the angelic visitors appeared to Ezekiel. Its appearance was as a sapphire stone, and the one upon it was brilliant, like a flame of fire and amber—a deep yellow like fine gold. The one seated on the throne directed Ezekiel to speak (Ezek 1:26–28).

- God gave Ezekiel a scroll upon which was written his word. He ordered Ezekiel to eat the scroll; God wants his word in us. God commanded Ezekiel to speak his word of warning to the house of Israel, but God told him that they would not listen to him, because they would not listen to God. Ezekiel served as a watchman warning Israel—though often being opposed by them (Ezek 3:7, 14, 17). Doing God's work is rarely easy and often unappreciated—yet we are called to obey.

- The outline of the book aligns closely with Isaiah and Jeremiah over the next many chapters. First, the prophet pronounced various judgments against God's people (Ezek 4—24), and then turned to a pronouncement of God's judgment upon pagan nations, some of whom God employed as his instruments of wrath against the Jews (Ezek 25—32).

- God explained to Ezekiel the reason for the captivity and the destruction of Jerusalem. In chapter 8, Ezekiel was brought into the

The Prophetical Books (Isaiah through Malachi)

Temple and there observed groups of men and women worshipping various false gods, like Tammuz and the sun.

- Israel's constant rebellion and idolatry had finally resulted in God's judgment (Ezek 8:9-18). They had turned the house of God into a den of paganism. Because of this, the glory of the Lord departed from the Temple in 586 BC (Ezek 9:3; 10) and will not return until the millennial reign of which Ezekiel spoke (Ezek 43:2-5).

- God is patient, but stubborn resistance produces his anger and chastisement. He pledged to fulfill his discipline against his erring people, refusing to relent until they had experienced his wrath (Ezek 8:18, 9:9-10).

- Indeed, even if ". . . Noah, Daniel, and Job—were in it, they could save only themselves . . ." (Ezek 14:14, 20). In other words, there was no diverting the anger of the Lord against his rebellious people. This does suggest that the presence of godly people in society acts as a preservative against the wrath of God. No wonder that during the tribulation period his anger will be felt so forcefully, since the church will be raptured.

- One of the horrific practices of which Ezekiel spoke repeatedly was child sacrifice performed by the Israelites (Ezek 16:20-21; 20:31; 23:37). Indeed, the nation had become entirely debased.

- The sins that are specifically named included both spiritual and physical adultery and lewdness, the shedding of innocent blood, lying prophets and false prophecies, violating the sacred character of the Temple, sacrificing children to idols, turning from the true God, and oppressing strangers, widows, and orphans (see especially Ezek 22; 23:36ff).

- Judgment started with the leaders and the lying prophets who told people what they wanted to hear instead of the word of God—a continuing problem today (Ezek 11:1-13; 13).

- The terrors of the Babylonian invasion are discussed at various points throughout (see Ezek 23:25-30).

- Ezekiel also informs us that no Davidic king would reign again over Israel until the promised Messiah would come and fulfill the Davidic covenant (Ezek 21:25-27).

- However, even in his pronouncement of justice, God promised to retain a remnant and provide future glory for his people (Ezek 11:16-20; 16:60-63; 36:26-38; Jer 32:39). God takes no pleasure in punishing the wicked; his holiness demands retribution against evil (Ezek 18:32). How wonderful that Jesus was willing to stand in our place and be punished as our substitute and sacrifice for sins (2 Cor 5:21).

- Thus, even in his fury God promised Ezekiel that a remnant would be spared and that the nation would yet enjoy the promised land and future glory.

- Chapters 25 through 32 contain a series of prophetic judgments against Gentile nations. Coming destruction against the Ammonites (Ezek 25:1-7), the Moabites (Ezek 25:8-11), the Edomites (Ezek 25:9-14), the Philistines (Ezek 25:15-17), Tyre (Ezek 26—28), and Egypt (Ezek 29—32) are mentioned specifically.

- It is sobering to discover that the unseen king of Tyre was Satan, and demonic powers unquestionably rule over various regions of the globe (Ezek 28:11-19; Dan 10:10-13). This harmonizes with New Testament teaching, which asserts that Satan is the god of this world and has set it on its course—a collision course with God (Eph 2:2; 6:12). Let us be faithful in sharing the way of escape (Eph. 2:3-8 et. al).

- In chapter 33, Ezekiel was likened to a city watchman who sees an approaching army. If he sounded the warning, he was absolved from his responsibilities. But if he remained silent, he shared the culpability. That is good to remember the next time God opens a door of witnessing opportunity. We are not responsible for the choices of other people, but we are commissioned to give them a warning of the coming judgment. That is never popular, but it is often precisely what God wants us to do.

- Prophecies concerning the unfaithful shepherds of Israel, the future restoration of Israel, the battle of Armageddon, and the millennial reign are offered in chapters 34 through 39. The worthless shepherds failed to protect, feed, and guard the flock, therefore God was against them. But in the end, one faithful shepherd will lead them (Ezek 34:23).

- Israel will literally possess the promised land one day (Ezek 36). In that day, God will make a new covenant with them in which their hearts will be changed from stubborn to receptive (Ezek 36:26-28).

- The vision of the valley of dry bones appears in chapter 37. The dry bones were made to live once again in dramatic fashion and are illustrative of the new life awaiting Israel under the new covenant. The future union of Judah and Israel was signified by the vision of the two sticks that merged into one (Ezek 37:15ff).

- A future invasion of Palestine by Gog, a northern confederacy, is discussed in chapters 38 and 39. Indeed, this is likely the tribulation battle of Armageddon. The invaders came against the Jews only to discover that God was fighting with his people (Ezek 8:15–16; 39:1–5).

- This section culminates in a furious destruction in which Gog was utterly crushed. According to the prophecy, it would take seven months to bury the dead (Ezek 39:12), and the fowl of the sky were invited to partake in the feast provided by the fallen warriors of Gog, sounding very much like Revelation 19:17–19.

- Chapters 40 through 48 of Ezekiel discuss the Millennial Temple and various activities in the thousand-year reign.

- Chapters 40 through 42 offer great detail on the measurement of the Temple and its surrounding court. A special messenger with measuring tools met Ezekiel and gave him precise specifications about its dimensions.

- The culmination is the return of the glory of the Lord within the Temple. Apparently it rises up from the east with a great sound and moves to the Temple, filling it with splendor and glory—"it filled the House" (Ezek 43:1–5).

- Sacrifices will be offered in the Temple during the millennial kingdom. This raises a question about death: won't it be abolished?

- Scripture is precise. A careful perusal of Revelation indicates that death will finally be completely abolished when the new heavens and new earth are created, after the thousand-year reign (Rev 21:1–4). This clearly takes place after the great white throne judgment following the millennium. But why are the sacrifices still offered? It would seem that they are sacrificed as a memorial of the great work of Christ. They seem to replace the Lord's Supper as a remembrance of the great work on the cross of the Messiah.

- Interestingly, the Prince will worship together with the people. There will be a priesthood assigned to preparing the offerings taken from among the nation of Israel. There will be various kinds of offerings: the burnt offering and the meat offering, along with the peace offerings.

- These sacrifices could never take away sins in the Old Testament, nor are they capable of doing so in the Kingdom. However, in the Old Testament they looked ahead to the work of Messiah, and in the Kingdom they will look back upon his great work. Can you imagine remembering with the risen Christ present and among us? How awesome!

Key verse: "But the house of Israel is not willing to listen to you because they are not willing to listen to me, for the whole house of Israel is hardened and obstinate" (Ezek 3:7).

DANIEL

The book of Daniel is the Old Testament equivalent to the book of Revelation in the New Testament. It contains some of the most specific and startling prophecies in all of Scripture. Indeed, Daniel is a key in understanding God's prophetic plan for the world and the consummation of the Kingdom of God. We will focus mainly on the contents of this book, but we will also consider its amazing prophecies.

- Chapter 1 deals with the first deportation by the Babylonians in 605 BC. At this time, choice young men like Daniel, Hananiah, Mishael, and Azariah (whose names were later changed) were transported to Babylon to be trained and assimilated into Babylonian society and culture.

- However, Daniel purposed in his heart not to sin against God by consuming prohibited food or drink. The king's guard allowed Daniel to try eating vegetables and drinking water to see how they compared to others who ate the meat and wine of the king. After ten days, Daniel and his friends appeared more robust than the others, so they were allowed to continue honoring God in their dietary consumption.

- Once brought before the king, these four youths eclipsed all the others and found great favor in the eyes of king, Nebuchadnezzar.

- In chapter 2, Nebuchadnezzar had a dream that deeply troubled him. He demanded that his magicians and wise men come to the palace and clear up the matter. He mandated that they not only interpret the dream but also first tell him what he had dreamt. Of course, that was a much more difficult challenge (Dan 2:5–6). However, if they failed to do so, the king planned to kill all the wise men in Babylon.

- Arioch, one of the king's captains, arrested Daniel and told him what was happening. Daniel responded by assuring him that God would reveal the matter if given time. The king agreed to give Daniel a reprieve. The secret was then revealed to Daniel in a night vision (Dan 2:19).

- The dream was of a great image. Its head was gold, its chest and arms of silver, its stomach and thighs of brass, its legs of iron, and its feet partly of iron and partly of clay (Dan 2:32–33). A little stone struck the image on the feet, causing it to collapse. It was then blown away like chaff by the wind and the little stone mushroomed into a great mountain that filled the whole earth (Dan 2:35).

- Daniel then interpreted the dream. The precious metals represented four different kingdoms. Nebuchadnezzar was the head of gold; the Medo-Persian Empire was the second; Greece was the third; and Rome the fourth. Notice that Rome was divided by the legs, representing an Eastern and Western empire. It would be subdivided still further into a future coalition consisting of ten kings—often thought of as a European association of world powers.

- The ten toes represented ten still future kings, out of which the anti-Christ shall come. The little stone shall establish an everlasting kingdom after destroying these future kings.

- Daniel was describing the "times of the Gentiles" as defined by Christ in Luke 21:24.

- Daniel was quick to offer all the glory to God for granting him this amazing insight. After revealing this to the king, Daniel was elevated to a position of great authority and honor. He asked the king to allow his friends, Shadrach, Meshach, and Abednego, to rule alongside him. This request was honored, but Daniel retained the greatest position (Dan 2:48–49).

- Nebuchadnezzar made an image nearly one hundred feet tall that all the subjects of the realm were required to worship whenever musicians played a certain sound. The image was of gold, and one is left to assume that it likely represented the king.

- However, not all the royal subjects responded in obedience to the mandate. Shadrach, Meshach, and Abednego refused to bow down to the image. Clearly, neither did Daniel, but he did not get caught. The three young men were brought to the king and ordered to submit (Dan 3:15–18). However, they refused. They knew that God was able to deliver them from the king's punishment, but even if he did not, they resolved to worship God alone.

- The king was furious at the young men and ordered that the furnace be heated seven times hotter than normal. The heat was so severe that those who threw the young men into the furnace died—but not Shadrach, Meshach, or Abednego.

- Indeed, one like the Son of God met them in the furnace and protected them from all harm. They were unhurt, their clothing was not singed, and neither did they smell like smoke (Dan 3:27). Of course,

The Prophetical Books (Isaiah through Malachi)

this caused Nebuchadnezzar to have a change of mind about his law. He released the young men and praised their God, decreeing that anyone who spoke anything against their God should be severely punished (Dan 3:29). He then promoted them.

- Nebuchadnezzar was humbled in chapter 4, being struck dumb for a time. He was made to live like an ox or some other field beast until he came to realize that God rules in the affairs of men. Thus God judged the pride of the king and then restored him for a period of time (Dan 4:28–32). This concludes the narrative about Nebuchadnezzar.

- Chapter 5 opens with Belshazzar, the king's son, ruling in Babylon. We are nearing the collapse of the Babylonian Empire. The king and his friends were using the vessels stolen from the Temple in Jerusalem to drink wine and to toast to their pagan gods (Dan 5:4). Suddenly, a hand appeared, etching something on the wall. The king was horrified and sought someone to decipher the writing.

- Scripture is reliable, even in minor details; the reward promised that any translator would be promoted to the third ruler in the realm (Dan 5:7). The book of Daniel does not explain this "third ruler" reward, but secular history does.

- We know from profane history that Nabonidus was the king over Babylon and that Belshazzar was a co-regent with the king, ruling in Babylon. So the person next in line after Belshazzar would in fact have been the third ruler.

- Daniel was brought in (remember that by this time he was about eighty-five years old). He interpreted the writing to mean that the kingdom would swiftly be rent from Belshazzar. Daniel specifically named the conquerors, the Medes and the Persians (Dan 5:28).

- Secular history confirms Daniel's prophecy. The Medes and Persians overwhelmed Babylon in one night, invading via the main water source of the city, taking all the guards completely by surprise.

- In chapter 6, Darius, the new leader over Babylon, is introduced. He elevated Daniel to second in command over Babylon to provide oversight (Dan 6:2–3). The other leaders resented this and concocted a plan to get Daniel out of the way.

- They tricked the king into issuing a decree that no one could make a request of anyone but the king for thirty days (Dan 6:7). Anyone who violated this decree would be thrown into a den of lions.

- Though Daniel knew about this, he did not hesitate to pray three times a day with his windows wide open. Of course, the conspirators watched him and told the king of his disobedience. The king was very sad, because he loved and respected Daniel, but to accommodate his edict, he had Daniel thrown to the lions (Dan 6:16).

- As we know, in the morning when the king hurried to the den, he found Daniel alive and well. An angel had miraculously shut the lions' mouths. The king was delighted, and he commanded that the men who had accused Daniel should be thrown into the den. Indeed, they and their families perished among the savage beasts (Dan 6:24).

- Chapters 7 through 12 describe a series of visions afforded to Daniel in which God revealed to him coming Gentile empires, the antichrist, the Great Tribulation, and the glorious reign of Messiah the Prince. It is worth noting that God only dealt with those pagan empires who would deal specifically and closely with his chosen people, Israel.

- Chapter 7 describes four beasts: a lion, a bear, a leopard, and a devouring beast with ten horns (Dan 7:4-7). Daniel was greatly troubled by his vision, but an angel revealed its interpretation to him (Dan 7:17ff). The four beasts represented four kings or kingdoms. From the fourth beast (Rome) would arise ten kings, of which three would be destroyed, and one would be the antichrist (Dan 7:23-25). He will suffer defeat, and the saints will receive an everlasting kingdom.

- Chapter 8 offers an amazing prophecy regarding two of the kings and kingdoms: the Medo-Persian Empire and Greece (Dan 8:20-22). The former is represented by a ram with two horns (one larger than the other) and the latter by a he goat with one great horn (Alexander the Great).

- They collided, and the goat destroyed the ram. The great horn was broken, and from it arose four other horns. Indeed, upon the death of Alexander, his four generals took control of the massive realm; Ptolemy in Egypt, Seleucus in Babylon, and Lysimachus and Cassander in Macedonia and Greece respectively.

- A later king is described in verses 9 through 12—perhaps referring to Antiochus Epiphanes, who in 170 to 168 BC besieged Jerusalem, subjecting it to prolonged massacre and converting the holy sanctuary into a pagan temple. In 165 BC, after much conflict, Judas Maccabaeus rededicated the Temple to the worship of God, an event celebrated as Hanukkah by the Jews ever since.

- Chapter 9 contains Daniel's prophecy of the seventy weeks. Knowing from Jeremiah's report that the captivity must be nearing its end (Dan 9:2; Jer 25:11–12; 29:10), Daniel went to prayer, hoping to discover what would transpire following the exile (Dan 9:3–19).
- The angel Gabriel appeared to Daniel in a vision to explain future events regarding Israel. This is the only prophecy that specifically identifies the moment in history when Messiah would accomplish his work.
- Seventy weeks (seventy weeks of years or seventy units of seven or 490 years) are accomplished before everlasting righteousness will prevail. Please note that the prophecy concerns "thy people" the Jews. The Church Age is omitted entirely. The prophecy became increasingly specific. From the commandment to rebuild Jerusalem until Messiah the Prince would be sixty-nine weeks of years, or 483 years (Dan 9:25–27).
- Several observations should be made.
- The Jewish calendar operated by a 360-day per year reckoning—twelve thirty-day months
- There are three periods of time given: seven units of seven years, sixty-two units of seven years, and one unit of seven years. Likely it required some forty-nine years to remove all the debris in Jerusalem, reconstructing all the palaces, houses, roads, etc. The seven units of seven and the sixty-two units of seven are viewed collectively (434 years plus 49 years), amounting to 483 years.
- Thus, 483 years of 360 days amounted to 173,880 days.
- Notice that the Messiah is not cut off in the seventieth week but after the sixty-ninth week, indicating an interval of time between the sixty-ninth and the seventieth week. We are currently in this interval, a time when the nation of Israel has been set aside and God is working with the Church. After the rapture, God will once again turn to the Jews, and the seventieth week of Daniel will commence with the Tribulation period.
- An important question: When was the decree to restore and rebuild Jerusalem given?
- The decree of Cyrus in 538 BC was very specifically addressed to the Jews in captivity to return and rebuild the Temple (Ezra 1:1–4 and 5:13). So that was not the decree mentioned here.

- However, King Artaxerxes gave permission to Nehemiah to begin the rebuilding process for the city in 444 BC (in March of that year—Neh 2:1–8). It appears highly likely that this is the decree of which Daniel spoke.
- Taking into account leap years and including some days in March, 173,880 days from that decree would lead one to a date of around March 30 A.D. 33, in which Messiah the Prince was cut off.
- Admittedly, it is difficult to calculate this time precisely, but it is clear that this prophecy harmonizes amazingly with the crucifixion of Christ.
- In the final week of years (seven years), the future prince of evil will confirm a covenant with Israel, making peace. However, in the middle of that time, he will cause all sacrifices to stop and essentially establish himself as deity (Dan 9:27). This is the abomination of desolation to which Jesus referred in Matt 24:4–31.
- Chapters 10 through 12 record Daniel's final vision of the consummation and the glory of God
- Chapter 10 records the sobering reality of spiritual warfare taking place over regions of the globe (Dan 10:13)
- Chapter 11 discusses menacing kings who will threaten and harm Israel, most especially Antiochus Epiphanes and the future willful king in the Tribulation.
- Chapter 12 closes the book with a glimpse of the Tribulation warfare and the glorious resurrection of believers.

Key verse: "Those who are wise will shine like the brightness of the heavens, and those who lead many to righteousness, like the stars for ever and ever" (Dan 12:3).

Special thanks to J. Dwight Pentecost for harmonizing the 483 years in the Jewish calendar and the Gregorian calendar in Daniel's prophecy of the seventy weeks. For a fuller discussion see: J. Dwight Pentecost, "Daniel," in *The Bible Knowledge Commentary,* eds. John F. Walvoord and Roy B. Zuck (Wheaton: Victor Books, 1986) 1363.

The Prophetical Books (Isaiah through Malachi)

MINOR PROPHETS

There are twelve books that constitute the Minor Prophets: Hosea, Joel, Amos, Obadiah, Jonah, Micah, Nahum, Habakkuk, Zephaniah, Haggai, Zechariah, and Malachi. They are best understood and organized juxtaposed to the Babylonian Captivity. We refer to them as either pre-exilic prophets, exilic prophets, or post-exilic prophets.

- The pre-exilic prophets were: Isaiah and Jeremiah among the Major Prophets and Hosea, Joel, Amos, Jonah, Micah, Nahum, Habakkuk, and Zephaniah.
- The prophets who ministered during the exile were: Daniel, Ezekiel, and Obadiah
- Lastly, three prophets were commissioned to speak to the nation after the Babylonian exile: Haggai, Zechariah, and Malachi. You may recall reading about the ministry of Haggai and Zechariah in the book of Ezra as they exhorted the returning Jews to complete the rebuilding of the Temple (Ezra 5:1).
- The delineation of these prophets as major and minor is based on the length of the books and has nothing to do with their chronology or the importance of their message, though the Major Prophets are generally much more comprehensive.
- The book of Hosea is fourteen chapters in length. Hosea was a contemporary of Isaiah and Micah in Judah and of Amos in Israel, prophesying in the eighth century. Hosea's own marriage became an allegory of God's deteriorating relationship with his spiritually unfaithful people, Israel.
- Indeed, Gomer played the harlot against Hosea. Yet, God told him to go and buy her back to himself. Hosea purchased his wife for fifteen pieces of silver and a homer and a half of barley, serving as a vivid picture of redemption. Upon doing so, he told her she must not play the harlot again but remain true to him.
- God has bought us back to himself, not with corruptible things like silver or gold, but with the precious blood of Christ as of a lamb without blemish and without spot (1 Pet 1:18–19).
- This then became the picture of God's relationship with Israel. The nation had betrayed him by worshipping other gods. Though they would suffer his chastisement for their disloyalty, he would never

fully forsake his covenant people. Instead he would buy them back to himself as well, for his love is steadfast and enduring.

- The book of Joel is three chapters in length. It uses an invasion of locusts to teach greater truths about the future. The locust invasion was a foreshadowing of future invasions of human warriors. Joel promised a future deliverance for God's people on the Day of the Lord when God will judge the Gentile nations and bring blessings to Israel. Wonderfully, God is able to restore the years the locusts have eaten.
- The book of Amos is nine chapters in length. Amos was incensed at the abuse of justice that was occurring in Israel. God's holiness demands a human corollary of social righteousness.
- In the first four chapters, God declared his impending judgment. In chapter 5, he pled with his people to repent of their sin. God is far more interested in our heart attitude than in our external rituals, as we see in 5:21–27. Captivity was promised for continual rebellion.
- The book ends with a promise of a future deliverance and restoration for the people as they dwell securely in the promised land—a place of perfect harmony and justice (Amos 9:13–15).
- The book of Obadiah is just one chapter. It deals with the judgment of Edom, the descendants of Esau. They had constructed their capital city in a great rock cliff that they considered impregnable (Obad 3–4).
- However, God prophesied that he would destroy them, and he did. The ruins of this great city cut out of solid cliffs south of the Dead Sea were discovered in 1812 and stand as a silent tribute to the fulfillment of prophecy, the truth of Scripture, and the power of God.
- The book of Jonah is certainly one of the best-known Minor Prophets. Written in the eighth century, Jonah deals with God's mercy toward Nineveh. Of course, Jonah was less than merciful himself and sought desperately to thwart God's plan by running in precisely the opposite direction.
- While attempting to run from God via ship, a great storm arose. Jonah accepted the blame for it and was cast overboard, subsequently becoming a meal for the great fish. It took three days in the bowels of the fish before Jonah repented and prayed for deliverance (Jonah 1:17—2). God did show Nineveh mercy—just as Jonah feared!

The Prophetical Books (Isaiah through Malachi)

- The fish expelled Jonah, and he went to Nineveh—a several-hundred-mile trip. Nineveh was a great city that required three days to travel its full extent. Jonah, a man lacking compassion, preached the greatest revival message in history. It was short: "... Forty more days and Nineveh will be overturned" (Jonah 3:4).

- The king decreed that the whole city should repent and cry out to God for mercy. God spared the city, but Jonah was very angry. God loves people and is merciful to those who call upon him. The book ends with Jonah stubbornly defiant. Judgment would eventually fall upon Nineveh, but this was the message of Nahum.

- Micah, a contemporary of Isaiah, prophesied around 740 BC. His book is seven chapters long. He directed his message at Israel and Judah, and especially the chief cities of influence, Jerusalem and Samaria.

- He warned of a coming captivity and of Assyria as God's rod of chastening. (Remember that Israel fell to the Assyrians in 722 BC, and Judah was taken into captivity by the Babylonians in 605 BC).

- As the other prophets, Micah concluded with an assurance of the mercy of God and a future restoration under Messiah. "Who is a God like you, who pardons sin and forgives the transgression of the remnant of his inheritance? You do not stay angry forever but delight to show mercy. You will again have compassion on us; you will tread our sins underfoot and hurl all our iniquities into the depths of the sea" (Mic 7:18–19).

- Nahum prophesied about 150 years after Jonah. The time for mercy toward Nineveh had passed; their repentance had long since been forgotten, and they had resumed their evil ways. Thus God's once-delayed judgment would soon fall upon them. In his short three-chapter prophecy, Nahum tells of God's judgment upon Nineveh, giving both the details of it (chapter 2) and the cause for it (chapter 3). As Nineveh sowed evil, so would it reap judgment. Thus Nahum forms the sequel to the book of Jonah. Indeed, Nineveh was destroyed by the Babylonians in 612 BC.

- Habakkuk prophesied from about 630 to 620 BC. We are not surprised that his short, three-chapter message is concerned with the coming Babylonian captivity. He was perplexed by the problem of evil and most especially by the use of the Babylonians for chastening. Habakkuk 2:4 is quoted in Romans, "The just shall live by faith." Sin invariably results in judgment and faith in life. God appeared to

Habakkuk in chapter 3, assuring the prophet of his sovereign control even in bewildering circumstances.

- Zephaniah probably prophesied during the reign of Josiah, around 630 BC. He glimpsed the future fall of Jerusalem and God's judgment against the Gentile nations. He also was encouraged with a vision of the Kingdom blessings to come in the future under the Messiah.
- He spoke frequently of the Day of the Lord (Zeph 1:14–18); it will be a day of great judgment and wrath. He urged Judah to seek the Lord that they might escape the Day of the Lord's anger (Zeph 2:3). Zephaniah was likely the great, great grandson of Hezekiah.
- The Post-Exilic prophets were Haggai, Zechariah, and Malachi.
- Both Haggai and Zechariah prophesied during the rebuilding of the Temple under Zerubbabel. One reads of their ministry of encouragement and exhortation in Ezra 5:1 and elsewhere. They both prophesied of a coming glorious kingdom. In his brief two chapters, Haggai most especially focused on the glory of the future Temple in the millennial reign. Zechariah is fourteen chapters in length and is considered difficult to understand principally because of the series of visions from chapters 1 to 6. However, Zechariah speaks with amazing clarity and precision regarding the Messiah.
- He identified the Messiah's entrance into Jerusalem on Palm Sunday riding upon a young donkey (Zech 9:9), his betrayal for thirty pieces of silver (Zech 11:12–14), and his crucifixion and glorious return (Zech 12:10).
- Zechariah concluded with a depiction of the bodily return of Messiah to earth, setting down on the Mount of Olives (Zech 14:4), and the establishment of his Kingdom on earth.
- A great plague will afflict all those who oppose Messiah (Zech 4:12–13), but those who are with him will enter the Kingdom. It seems that saved human beings who endure the tribulation successfully will enter the Kingdom as human beings and continue to marry and have children. Some of their offspring will eventually rebel against Christ and join Satan in the final conflict discussed in Revelation 20:7–10.
- The last book in the Old Testament is the book of Malachi. He addressed his prophecy to the inhabitants now returned from the exile.
- Sadly, the people had fallen into some of the same sins that led to their initial displacement. They were offering God animals that were blind or lame; in other words, the ones they didn't want. The priest-

hood had once again become corrupt, saying that evil was good and good evil. The people had turned to intermarrying with their pagan neighbors. As always, this led to idolatry (Mal 2:11).

- The people had also forsaken the giving of the tithe and other offerings. In this way, Malachi stated, they were robbing God. The people acted surprised or confused, but God knew better. God issued them a challenge to test him by giving him the tithe.

- "'Bring the whole tithe into the storehouse, that there may be food in my house. Test me in this,' says the LORD Almighty, 'and see if I will not throw open the floodgates of heaven and pour out so much blessing that you will not have room enough for it'" (Mal 3:10). This is the only place of which I am aware where God tells us to test him.

- Some repented and turned to the Lord. Chapter 4 concludes with a brief glimpse of the coming Day of the Lord and the return of Christ. A prophecy of John the Baptist is offered in 4:5. John's work would partly include turning the hearts of the fathers to the children and the hearts of the children to the fathers (Mal 4:6).

Thus ends the Old Testament. Four hundred years of silence would ensue before the revelatory curtain of God opened again with the coming of the Promised One, Messiah the Prince, the Lamb of God.

5

The Gospels and Acts

THE SYNOPTIC GOSPELS

Since the first three gospels contain so much similar information, though presented differently by the respective authors, they are often referred to as the Synoptic Gospels. Matthew, Mark, and Luke share parallel information roughly 90 percent of the time. However, they do present the same scenario from varying vantage points. This is not surprising, considering each one was writing with a specific purpose in mind. Matthew presents Jesus as the King, Mark as the Servant, and Luke as the Son of Man. Furthermore, Matthew was writing principally to the Jews, while Mark was addressing the Romans, and Luke was writing to the Greeks. The gospel of John is very different, presenting unique material roughly 90 percent of the time.

- Even so, all the gospels share some things in common: (1) they all present Jesus as the Christ, the Promised Messiah from God; (2) they all record the feeding of the five thousand; (3) they all discuss the betrayal by Judas and the failing of Peter; (4) they all record the events of the trial and crucifixion; (5) all record the glorious bodily resurrection; (6) all speak to the post-resurrection ministry of Christ; and (7) all point forward to his bodily return in the future.

- The divine intention throughout the gospels was to clearly present Jesus as the Savior of the world, the Messiah, the Promised One from God who would take away the sins of the world. They were not intended to present a biography of Jesus. Indeed, other than the birth narratives, the silence of the early life of Jesus is only interrupted once by Luke (Luke 2:40–52).

- John told his readers that his gospel was not comprehensive, noting, "Jesus did many other things as well. If every one of them were written down, I suppose that even the whole world would not have room for the books that would be written" (John 21:25).
- But John revealed the specific purpose of his letter: "But these are written that you may believe that Jesus is the Christ, the Son of God, and that by believing you may have life in his name" (John 20:31). Thus we see that each author selected material under the guidance of the Holy Spirit to accomplish his own writing mission.
- Each of the synoptic gospels has unique aspects.
- While Matthew and Luke began their letters by describing the miraculous birth of Jesus and providing genealogies endorsing his right to rule through the Davidic Covenant, Mark, writing to the Romans, began his letter immediately with the baptism of Jesus.
- The Romans placed great value on action, thus the key word in the gospel of Mark is the word "immediately," occurring over forty times in the book.
- Matthew, also called Levi, was one of the twelve apostles. He was a tax gatherer for the Romans and thus an object of scorn among the patriotic Jews like Simon the zealot (another one of the twelve).
- As the gospel of the King, Matthew used the term "Kingdom" more than fifty times in the book and the unique term "kingdom of heaven," which occurs nowhere else in the New Testament, about thirty times. Because he was writing to the Jews, Matthew spoke of the actions of Christ as fulfilling Old-Testament prophecy more than any other gospel writer (see 1:22; 2:15, 17, 23; 4:14; 12:17; 13:14; 21:4; 26:54, 56; 27:9; 35). It is important to keep one's audience in mind.
- He also included an extensive genealogy, extending from Abraham to David and then from David to Christ. His purpose was to demonstrate that Jesus fit the qualifications to rule as King. Scripture is amazingly incisive. One finds the common term "begat" or "the father of" used throughout the genealogy record until one reaches Joseph. At this point it simply says, "... Joseph, the husband of Mary, of whom was born Jesus, who is called Christ" (Matt 1:16).
- That Jesus was the adopted son of Joseph was vitally important for two reasons. First, Jesus was divine and had no human father—this the language of the text makes plain. Furthermore, Jechoniah (Matt 1:11) or Coniah, as he is called in Jeremiah, was cursed with a curse

that included all his progeny. None of his natural descendants could reign on the throne of David, according to Jeremiah 22:24–30.

- Thus, if Jesus had been a natural descendant of Joseph, he would have been disqualified from the throne. That Jesus came through Mary's line, as detailed by Luke (3:23–38), protected him from this curse. Jesus had a legal right to the throne through his adopted father Joseph, but he was not marred by the curse as a natural descendant.

- The gospel of Mark was written by John Mark, the nephew of Barnabas who accompanied Paul and Barnabas on the very first missionary journey. His initial foray into service ended badly. He deserted the tiny company soon after he had begun (Acts 13:5–13). Paul clearly considered him a failure, refusing to permit him to accompany them again on the second journey.

- The contention was so severe that Paul and Barnabas parted company from each other (Acts 15:36–41). However, Mark demonstrated that early failures need not be the final word in one's life.

- Barnabas refused to give up on him, and Mark became one of the great leaders of the early church. Even Paul came to realize his mistake in judging the young man too harshly. In his last letter, Paul commented to Timothy, "... Get Mark and bring him with you, because he is helpful to me in my ministry" (2 Tim 4:11). Of course, his inclusion as one of the gospel writers also indicates that God never gave up on Mark either. We are all thankful for God's grace, mercy, and patience.

- Mark wrote to the Romans, for whom action was preeminent. Therefore, it is more a book of actions than it is of words, being by far the shortest gospel. It contains no lengthy discourses and only a few parables. Special emphasis is placed upon miracles and miraculous healings.

- Luke is the longest gospel, written by the beloved physician. Luke is in many ways the gospel of compassion. He stressed the Lord's concern for the lost, broken-hearted, and lonely. Luke alone records the well-known parables of the lost coin, the lost sheep, and the lost son (15:3–32).

- While the Sermon on the Mount occurs in only Matthew (5—7) and Luke (6:20–49), the Olivet Discourse appears in all three gospel accounts. It occurs in Matthew 24—25, Mark 13, and Luke 21. Just days before his sacrificial offering of himself for the sins of the world,

Jesus sat upon the Mount of Olives and was asked by the disciples about the end times.

- Jesus appealed to Daniel's seventieth week of years to frame his answer. He told them that when they saw the abomination of desolation (the antichrist setting himself up as God in the newly constructed temple) that the Great Tribulation had finally begun. Jesus would return to bring a close to these tumultuous days, visibly returning to earth to establish his glorious reign. "For as lightning that comes from the east is visible even in the west, so will be the coming of the Son of Man" (Matt 24:27).

- All the synoptic writers detail the last week of the earthly ministry of Jesus. They all include his participation at the last supper, the last Passover, because Jesus would offer himself as the perfect Passover Lamb. They all record the betrayal by Judas and the denial by Peter. They all address the agony and loneliness of Jesus in the Garden of Gethsemane. All record the arrest of Jesus and the subsequent trial, particularly at the hands of Pilate.

- Each writer discussed the questioning before Pilate and the offer to release either Jesus or Barabbas. Of course, the divine plan would not permit Jesus to be rescued or delivered from the cross, for that was the very reason why he had come. His abuse at the hands of the Roman soldiers was also mentioned by all the gospel writers. The grim details of the crucifixion were also outlined by each one. All record the death of Jesus at the cross and his burial. We are so happy that the story does not end here!

- All the gospel writers also attest to the glorious resurrection of Jesus from the dead. Indeed, only the resurrection rationally explains the transformation among his disciples following his brutal crucifixion. Every skeptic must explain, at least to him or herself, the amazing events subsequent to the crucifixion of Jesus, which is the best-attested event in all of antiquity.

- All the gospel writers tell us that the risen Christ was seen by a wide variety of people, that the tomb was really empty, and that the living Christ had commissioned his followers to take the message of hope and eternal life through him to the entire world. This order they explicitly obeyed, even unto death.

- Thus all the gospel writers end their message with a clear affirmation of the bodily resurrection of Jesus Christ and the command by Christ to carry out the Great Commission of making disciples.

Key verses: The call of Matthew is probably the most familiar, "All authority in heaven and on earth has been given to me. Therefore go and make disciples of all nations, baptizing them in the name of the Father and of the Son and of the Holy Spirit, and teaching them to obey everything I have commanded you. And surely I am with you always, to the very end of the age" (Matt 28:18–20).

THE GOSPEL OF JOHN

John was the son of Zebedee and the brother of James, who was also an apostle of Christ. Jesus nicknamed these two brothers "Boanerges" or "The sons of thunder," according to Mark 3:17. This seems an appropriate title, since on at least one occasion they were prepared to call fire down from heaven to devour those who did not respond favorably to Christ (Luke 9:54). John and James, along with the impetuous Peter, formed the inner circle, a small group of apostles who had an especially close friendship with Jesus.

- While Matthew and Luke began their gospels with the birth of Christ and Mark with his baptism, John opened his gospel in eternity past, in the beginning, offering the reader one of clearest assertions of the deity of Christ in the Bible. "In the beginning was the Word, and the Word was with God, and the Word was God" (John 1:1).
- The identity of the Word is clearly revealed later in the same chapter, "The Word became flesh and made his dwelling among us . . ." (John 1: 14).
- John the Baptist was also introduced in chapter 1, serving as the forerunner to the Messiah, announcing his arrival. John served principally as a witness to the light, announcing the coming of the Promised One.
- Chapter 1 also includes the call of some early disciples—Andrew and Simon, his brother, and Philip and Nathanael, his brother. Both Andrew and Philip first introduced Jesus to their siblings. Witnessing often begins with those closest to us.
- The first miracle of turning water into wine occurred in chapter 2.
- Jesus was incensed at the transformation of the temple into a marketplace, driving the money changers from it (John 2:13–17).
- Jesus also claimed to have power to raise the temple in three days. The religious leaders misunderstood him, thinking that he spoke of the actual temple, when in fact he spoke of the temple of his body, referring to the resurrection (John 2:18–25).
- A Pharisee by the name of Nicodemus met with Jesus by night in chapter 3. He came to see Jesus secretly because of the peer pressure of his colleagues among the religious elite. Jesus claimed that a man must be born again in order to enter the Kingdom of God.

Confused, Nicodemus wondered how a person could possibly return to the womb and be reborn.

- Jesus was frequently misunderstood throughout the gospel of John. He explained to Nicodemus that he was not speaking of a second physical birth but of a spiritual birth. The mechanism that produces this birth is faith in Jesus as our Savior (John 3:15–18). The term "believe" is used about one hundred times in the gospel and is the key issue set forth by John. Indeed, John wrote his gospel for a precise purpose: "But these are written, that ye might believe that Jesus is the Christ, the Son of God, and that by believing you may have life in his name" (John 20:31).

- Chapters 4 through 11 recount the public ministry of Jesus, most especially his miraculous work. In chapter 4, Jesus spoke with the Samaritan woman, offering her living water. However, just as in the case of the Pharisees and Nicodemus, she misunderstood him, thinking that he spoke of actual water from a well. However, he was alluding to himself and the eternal life he offered. He then gently confronted her about her sin and called her to repent.

- He then healed a nobleman's son (John 4:46–54).

- Jesus continued his miraculous ministry in chapter 5, healing a man crippled for thirty-eight years. The calloused religious leaders were greatly displeased by this healing, allegedly because it was performed on the Sabbath day. Most likely they were especially unhappy because it drew great attention to Jesus.

- The chapter concludes with a probing assessment of the religious leaders by Christ. He stated, "You diligently study the Scriptures because you think that by them you possess eternal life. These are the Scriptures which testify about me, yet you refuse to come to me to have life" (John 5:39–40).

- Studying the Bible does not give us eternal life (nor does any good work); the Scriptures teach us the way to have eternal life—by trusting in Christ. Even very religious, pious Bible readers may fail to go to heaven. Trusting in Jesus Christ is the way to heaven.

- Jesus performed the great miracle of the feeding of the five thousand in chapter 6. He used the donation of a young boy (of five barley loaves and two small fish) to accomplish this miracle. After feeding this great multitude, they still had twelve baskets of food left. Jesus can make much out of little.

- The account of Jesus walking on the water is recorded in 6:15–21.
- Jesus used the occasion of the miracle of the bread and fish to identify himself as the Bread of Life. Many people followed Jesus out of curiosity or because he satisfied their physical needs. However, Jesus wanted them to understand that he offered much more than this. Three times in this chapter Jesus made it clear that eternal life is the result of faith in him (John 6:29, 40, 47).
- Once again, many people misunderstood Jesus about being the bread of heaven. He was clearly speaking metaphorically, but just as the Pharisees, Nicodemus, and the Samaritan woman, those following him took his spiritual message and applied it strictly to the physical world. This is a recurring pattern in the book to this point. Therefore, many followers left him, being confused and unable to grasp his true message.
- Jesus, seeing this mass exodus, asked his disciples if they too would leave him. Peter then offered his great confession: "Lord, to whom shall we go? You have the words of eternal life. We believe and know that you are the Holy One of God" (John 6:68–69).
- In chapter 7, we learn of divided opinion over Jesus, some thinking that he was the Christ and others contending that he was a deceiver. The Pharisees wanted to arrest him and get rid of him, but others were becoming convinced of his legitimacy.
- At the close of the chapter, Nicodemus defended Jesus before members of the Sanhedrin, reminding them that they should not condemn people before hearing them out. After this, people disbanded and went to their homes; each left to contemplate the person of Christ.
- The account of the woman taken in adultery appears in chapter 8. The religious leaders were more than ready to stone this woman, but Jesus stopped them. He probed into their own lives, asking that the one without sin cast the first stone. Gradually, all left the scene. Jesus did not condemn her but did exhort her to change her lifestyle.
- The great joust between Jesus and the Pharisees unfolded in the rest of chapter 8. The argument swung back and forth—they accusing and Jesus declaring. It ends with our Lord's assertion, ". . . Before Abraham was born, I Am!" (John 8:58). The Pharisees knew precisely what Jesus was claiming—He was claiming to be the great "I Am." We know this because they then picked up stones to stone him for blasphemy, but he escaped.

- Jesus healed a blind man in chapter 9, inciting yet another confrontation with the religious leaders. The Pharisees interrogated the healed man and his parents, wanting to know how this miracle happened. Again there was a division between them, some believing and others accusing Jesus of deceit. Interestingly, they did not deny the miracle—only its source.

- Jesus set himself forth as the Good Shepherd who would give his life for the sheep in chapter 10. The division between the Jews regarding Jesus was growing deeper. Now his opponents accused him of demonic activity or insanity. Jesus claimed equality with the Father—a claim to deity. The Jews certainly understood him to be doing so, because once again they sought to stone him for blasphemy (John 10:30–33).

- In chapter 11, Jesus raised Lazarus from the dead—amazing. He used this occasion to assert that he was the resurrection and the life—and who could refute that after what had just happened! Following this event, many of the Jews believed on Jesus. But others tattled about it to the Pharisees, who had a different and less-flattering explanation. After this, the chief priests and Pharisees determined to kill Jesus. Now the Passover was drawing nigh (John 11:55-57).

- Mary anointed Jesus with costly ointment in chapter 12. Judas complained that the money was wasted and could have been used more wisely for the poor—yes, poor Judas. He was the apostolic treasurer who pilfered money from the bag. He didn't care about the poor. Jesus saw through his hypocrisy and rebuked him, saying that Mary had anointed him for burial.

- His entry into Jerusalem on Palm Sunday is recorded in 12:12–50. The people praised and honored him on that day. Sadly, many of these same people would be shouting for his death just a few short days later.

- The Pharisees knew something drastic needed to be done because, as they said, "... The whole world has gone after him" (John 12:19). Even some of the religious elite believed on Jesus, but they failed to confess him, loving the praise of men more than the praise of God (John 12:42–43).

- Chapters 13 through 17 offer a detailed description of the events surrounding the last supper. John is the only gospel writer to provide such a penetrating glimpse into those last hours.

- In chapter 13, Jesus washed the feet of the disciples, taking the opportunity to teach them about service. It was after supper that he did so (John 13:2), and all of the disciples had ample opportunity to do what should have been done when they first entered the room.
- It was here that Jesus gave a new commandment—"Love one another. As I have loved you, so you must love one another" (John 13:34). Peter made his rash vow at the close of chapter 13.
- In chapter 14, Jesus sought to encourage his disciples against the sad news of his impending death. Indeed, the crucifixion would not mark the end of their relationship but establish it eternally. He told them to simply trust him.
- He promised them that he would send them another Comforter—the Holy Spirit. Jesus offered them peace—a peace that the world could not comprehend. As he continued talking with them, he reminded them that he was the source of their strength, as the vine is to the branches (John 15:1–2). His hope was that every believer would draw upon his power and bear fruit—indeed, much fruit (John 15:8).
- After iterating the new commandment to love one another, Jesus solemnly warned his disciples not to flag in the face of animosity, stating, "If the world hates you, keep in mind that it hated me first" (John 15:18).
- Jesus warned the disciples that persecution would follow but that the Holy Spirit would assist them (John 16:1–11). He revealed his death once again but assured his friends that joy was not far off.
- The high priestly prayer of Jesus Christ is recorded in chapter 17. He prayed for the disciples and for those who would believe on him through their witness. Unity was a major component of his prayer. Jesus also prayed that those who believe on him might be with him and behold his eternal glory (John 17:21–24).
- The scene then shifts to the Garden of Gethsemane. John omitted the agonizing prayer of Jesus uttered in the garden, moving swiftly instead to the betrayal by Judas.
- Jesus was arrested by the guards. However, Peter drew his sword and cut off the ear of Malchus, the high priest's servant. Such courage would soon dissipate in the face of the angry mob. Jesus was then escorted to the high priest. Meanwhile, Peter followed from a distance.
- The three denials of Peter are recorded in John 18:15–27.

- Jesus was then led from Caiaphas to Pilate, where the trial was resumed. Jesus stated directly to Pilate that the cross was the purpose for his coming, "... For this reason I was born, and for this I came into the world ..." (John 18:37).
- Chapter 19 describes the suffering of Jesus.
- First he was scourged, and then he was forced to wear the crown of thorns. The Romans taunted him in mockery while punching and striking him. Pilate declared to the mob that he found no fault in Jesus, but this incited a frenzy in which the people cried to crucify him. Under intense pressure from the crowd, Pilate delivered Jesus to be crucified (John 19:12116). They led him to Golgotha, and there they crucified him between two criminals.
- Several prophecies were fulfilled at this troubling hour—the soldiers cast lots for his clothes (Ps 22:18), no bone was broken (Ps 34:20), and Messiah died by the piercing nails and spear (Zech 12:10 and Rev 1:7).
- It is from the cross that Jesus told John to take good care of Mary as her own son. Jesus suffered horrible thirst, of which he spoke in John 19:28.
- He expired with the words, "It is finished." This was a shout of victory, for the word literally means "the debt is paid in full." The atoning, sacrificial work of Christ had now been accomplished. Joseph and Nicodemus took the body of Jesus and prepared it for burial, wrapping it in linen and spices. They laid him in the tomb.
- Chapter 20 recounts the joyful discovery of the resurrection. Mary Magdalene was the first to discover the missing body, and she quickly went to inform Peter and John. They both ran with great haste to the tomb, where they found the linen garments and the face cloth neatly wrapped in a place by itself. The mystery was left unsolved at this time.
- Mary then saw two angels in the tomb. Jesus called to Mary but did not reveal himself for a moment—then he called her by name, and she knew it was the risen Lord. We can only imagine the relief and delight that gripped her. She could not touch him yet, for he had not yet ascended to the Father.
- That same evening Jesus appeared to the disciples. Thomas was not present at this meeting, and upon hearing the news, refused to believe it.

- After eight days, Jesus appeared to the disciples again, only this time Thomas was present. Jesus permitted Thomas to examine his wounds carefully and exhorted him to believe. Thomas fell down and worshiped before the risen Christ. Jesus indicated that there will be a special blessing for those who believe but have not seen.
- It is here that John stated his purpose directly: "But these are written that you might believe that Jesus is the Christ, the Son of God, and that by believing you may have life in his name" (John 20:31). John had compiled an impressive body of evidence pointing undeniably to Jesus as the Christ. He urged his readers to trust in Jesus as their Savior.
- In chapter 21, Jesus appeared to some of his friends again while they were fishing. He told them to cast their nets to the side and they would find fish. Indeed, they did find fish—153 of them (John 21:11). Even with so great a catch, the nets did not break.
- They came to shore to discover a fire and fish laid upon the coals and bread. Jesus invited them to eat, and he ate with them (John 21:15).
- This was the public restoration of Peter. Peter had denied the Lord three times, and here he was given the opportunity to pledge his devotion to the risen Christ three times.
- Jesus then warned Peter about the kind of death he would suffer for the cause. Tradition indicates that Peter was crucified upside down. Peter then asked Jesus what was going to happen to John, and Jesus told him not to worry about John—just take care of Peter.
- John concluded with a sense of wonder and awe, writing, "Jesus did many other things as well. If every one of them were written down, I suppose that even the whole world would not have room for the books that would be written" (John 21:25).
- Thus the gospel record concluded. The major purpose of the gospel historians was to present Jesus as the Messiah, the Promised One from God, the Savior of the world.

Key verse: "But these are written that you may believe that Jesus is the Christ, the Son of God, and that by believing you may have life in his name" (John 20:31).

ACTS

The book of Acts, written by Luke, is a historical account of the propagation of the gospel in the first century, and more specifically shortly after the resurrection of Jesus Christ from the dead. Indeed, nothing else but the resurrection adequately explains the boldness and temerity that gripped these first-century disciples, causing them to risk ridicule and death repeatedly for the cause of the gospel. Luke wrote both the gospel that bears his name and the book of Acts.

- The treatise is written to "Theophilus" or to the "lover of God." Whether this was a specific person is disputed, but surely all those who love God in earnest will be encouraged by the account of these early witnesses.

- The book opens with a direct claim to the reliability of the resurrection of Christ, with Luke stating that many persons had actually seen the risen Christ, most especially the apostles. "After his suffering, he showed himself to these men [the apostles] and gave many convincing proofs that he was alive ..." (Acts 1:3).

- The key verse of the book occurs in Acts 1:8, which states, "But you will receive power when the Holy Spirit comes on you; and you will be my witnesses in Jerusalem, and in all Judea and Samaria, and to the ends of the earth." The rest of the book is an exposition of the literal historicity of this verse in the early church.

- Chapters 1 through 7 recount the early witness of the Church in Jerusalem, while chapters 8 through 14 discuss its witness in Judea and Samaria, followed by the Jerusalem Council in chapter 15, and finally focusing upon the witness of the gospel to the ends of the earth in chapters 16 through 28.

- In this case, "the ends of the earth" refer to Paul's missionary endeavors in Greece and finally to Rome, where he remained under house arrest for two years. However, during that time Paul had great freedom to receive visitors and share the gospel freely.

- The words of Acts 1:8 were the last recorded words of Jesus on earth before ascending to the Father. They represented his last wish and command for his disciples to testify on his behalf throughout the world, proclaiming the gospel. Indeed, this is one of the key texts endorsing support of local and world missions by all believers.

- Chapter 1 also recorded the addition of Matthias as one of the twelve apostles, taking the place of the traitor, Judas. The apostles placed two prerequisites upon possible candidates for this office—that they had been with Jesus from the beginning of his ministry and that they had been witnesses of the resurrection of Christ (Acts 1:21–22). Clearly, there is no one who qualifies for apostleship today. Indeed, the Scripture indicates that apostle was a foundational gift that passed away in the first century (Eph 2:20).

- Chapter 2 records the beginning of the Church Age, accompanied by the permanent indwelling ministry of the Holy Spirit, occurring on the day of Pentecost. This initial filling was accompanied by the miraculous ability to speak in tongues. The language of the passage indicates very clearly that this gift was the ability to speak in a previously unlearned foreign language (Acts 2:6, 8, 11).

- This gift was evangelistic in orientation and was intended to be used in the initial stages of missionary outreach. Indeed, the ability to speak a previously unlearned foreign language is truly miraculous (as anyone who has studied a foreign language can testify!), but speaking in unintelligible garble is not.

- While some argue that tongues was an unintelligible angel language based upon 1 Corinthians 13:1–3, such an appeal seems unsustainable, since that passage is clearly a hyperbole.

- Tongues was also a sign that the Gentiles as well as the Jews were invited into the church on the same basis—faith in Jesus Christ for salvation (see Acts 10:44–46).

- The key sign of being filled by the Holy Spirit was courage to witness, not speaking in tongues (Acts 4:31). On this occasion, Peter spoke to the crowds that had gathered.

- Appealing to Joel and Psalms, Peter asserted that God had made Jesus, whom they had crucified, both Lord and Christ (Acts 2:36). This was very convicting, but those who believed were baptized that same day, numbering about three thousand souls. These new converts needed to be taught, and so many opened their homes, and the disciples began an intensive teaching ministry.

- It was through the apostles that many miracles and signs were performed (Acts 2:43).

- Sharing was spontaneous and based upon the exigencies of the moment. The response of the church to this mass influx of new believers does not endorse socialism or communism. It is descriptive in nature, not prescriptive.

- They enjoyed worshipping together and praising God. Wonderfully, God added new converts to the church each day (Acts 2:47).
- Chapter 3 records the first specific healing work through the apostles. As Peter and John went to the temple to assemble with others for a season of prayer (apparently a daily ritual), they encountered a crippled beggar asking for money.
- In the name of Jesus Christ of Nazareth, Peter commanded the cripple to stand up. Instantly the man was healed. It is interesting that no faith on the part of this man was required to perform the miracle. He had no idea what Peter had in mind.
- Peter used this opportunity to preach yet another message. Once again a huge number of converts believed (Acts 4:4—about five thousand men). However, the adversaries also responded. The Sadducees (who denied the resurrection) brought Peter and John to the Sanhedrin. They were unhappy about the miraculous activities and demanded to know in what name or by what power they performed these wonders (Acts 4:7).
- Peter and John declared that their power came from Jesus Christ who was crucified and who rose from the dead. One of the great declarations of the exclusive nature of salvation is stated in Acts 4:12: "Salvation is found in no one else, for there is no other name under heaven given to men by which we must be saved."
- The religious elite were amazed at the eloquence and boldness of these unlearned men and commanded them to stop teaching in his name. Civil disobedience is sometimes required when the law demands us to sin—in this case to stop witnessing, which was contrary to the direct command of Christ. So they answered that they must obey God rather than men.
- They were released after this warning and returned to the other disciples praising God and were once again filled with the Holy Spirit, speaking the word of God with boldness (Acts 4:31).
- A man named Joses sold land and gave the money to the apostles to assist in this time of need. His name was changed to Barnabas—the son of encouragement.
- In chapter 5, we discover Ananias and Sapphira yearning for the same sort of glory without the same level of sacrifice. They too sold

some property and acted as though they had given the total amount to the apostles. They were struck dead in their lie.

- Their sin was not in keeping some of the money but in lying in order to be honored. We're glad that God does not act so decisively with every offense. As a new era begins, we often find God responding with swift judgment in order to communicate his perspective.
- Once again it is stated directly that the apostles served as the primary wonder workers in the early church (Acts 5:12, 15).
- The religious elite became increasingly angry and determined to stop the witness of the disciples (Acts 5). They imprisoned at least some, if not all, of the apostles (Acts 5:18). However, an angel released them from bondage at night.
- When their escape was discovered, the religious elite sent officers to apprehend them and bring them in to be questioned. The religious leaders were very angry because they had commanded the apostles to stop teaching in the name of Jesus. Peter responded with boldness, asserting that God had raised up Jesus "... Whom you had killed by hanging him on a tree" (Acts 5:30).
- This infuriated the leaders, implicating them in a terrible crime. Gamaliel, one of the chief leaders, counseled restraint in dealing with the apostles. He argued that if the current turmoil was of men, it would soon enough die down, but if it was of God, they surely did not wish to find themselves fighting him. So, they beat the apostles and thrust them out, commanding them to stop preaching in the name of Jesus (Acts 5:40)
- The apostles left, rejoicing that they were counted worthy to suffer for his sake.
- They continued worshipping in the temple and from house to house and in fact did not cease to teach and preach in the name of Jesus (Acts 5:42).
- The first deacons appeared on the scene in chapter 6; necessity is the mother of invention. There were Hellenistic widows who were overlooked in the daily rationing of food. This problem evoked bitterness and anger among the Greeks. The response of the apostles is instructive. They unapologetically refused to be the solution to the problem. Their priority was the word of God.
- However, they did suggest a remedy. They encouraged the brethren to select seven men of good report who could be trusted to make

sure that everyone was treated fairly. The congregation selected seven people, and the apostles appointed them to the task of meeting the needs of these widows. Thus the first group of deacons began serving the church. The apostles realized they could not do everything, but they tried to make sure everything was done—a good pattern for leaders today.

- Stephen, the first man selected, was indeed a man full of faith, and along with the apostles, he worked miracles too (Acts 6:8).

- The third persecution against the church focused on Stephen, who disputed with some of the religious authorities. They set him up by employing false witnesses against him who testified that Stephen blasphemed against the temple and the law. While they were staring at him, they saw his appearance glorified. Stephen then preached a penetrating sermon, starting at Abraham and working his way all the way through Moses and even to Solomon.

- His conclusion was very pointed and convicting. He stated, "You stiff-necked people, with uncircumcised hearts and ears! You are just like your fathers: You always resist the Holy Spirit! Was there ever a prophet your fathers did not persecute? They even killed those who predicted the coming of the Righteous One. And now you have betrayed and murdered him" (Acts 7:51–52).

- As one might imagine, the religious leaders were furious at this convicting summary. When they heard this indictment, they attacked Stephen, pummeling him. However, he was full of the Holy Spirit and gazed up into heaven, where he saw the glory of God and Jesus standing at the right hand of God (Acts 7:55).

- Stephen testified to what he saw, which only infuriated the crowd. They stopped their ears, refusing to listen, and they ran upon him. They took him outside the city and stoned him with stones. Kneeling down under the blows, Stephen asked the Lord not to count their sin against them. He then died (Acts 7:60). Thus Stephen became the first martyr of the Christian Church.

- Those who actually hurled the stones at Stephen left their outer garments in the care of a young Pharisee who watched the stoning with approval—his name was Saul. He was the same Saul who would shortly be converted himself on the Damascus road and become a great witness for Christ to the Gentiles—the apostle Paul.

- Chapter 8 begins with the burial of Stephen and the aggression of Saul against the church. He was thoroughly committed to destroying the new sect and went about his mission with gusto. This led to the dispersion of the church from Jerusalem into the outer regions (i.e., Judea and Samaria). Interestingly, those who went out witnessing were the newly saved converts, not the apostles (Acts 8:4).

- The ministry of Philip is discussed in the rest of chapter 8, most especially his work with the Ethiopian eunuch. He was obviously a seeker, because he was reading Isaiah 53 and wondering of whom the prophet spoke.

- Philip offered his services in explaining the passage to this man and was invited to join him in his chariot. The Ethiopian became a believer and wanted to be baptized. Philip responded saying that if he believed with all his heart, he could be. The Ethiopian went on his way rejoicing and no doubt took the gospel into Africa with him—another way of reaching the ends of the earth.

- Chapter 9 records the glorious conversion of Saul, meeting Jesus on the Damascus road. An error in the text has been imagined by some critics between Acts 9:7, 22:9, and 26:14. The passages can be harmonized by understanding that those with Saul saw a light but no person and heard a sound but not articulate speech. Alleged errors such as this always yield to a careful assessment.

- But Saul saw the Lord and heard his voice. The visitor told Saul, "I am Jesus whom you are persecuting" (Acts 9:5). Saul humbly submitted. He was struck with blindness and instructed to wait for Ananias to come and explain things further.

- Ananias went to Saul, with some concern, and laid hands on him. At this point Saul's sight was restored and he was filled by the Spirit. Immediately after, Saul was baptized and began his preaching ministry for Christ. What an incredible transformation!

- Of course, a lot of people were unhappy about Saul's change of heart. The Jews sought to kill him as a traitor (Acts 9:23). He escaped and was introduced to the church leadership by an encouraging disciple by the name of Barnabas (Acts 9:27).

- Already churches had been established in Judea and Samaria as well as Galilee (Acts 9:31). Saul went to Tarsus, and the believers were filled with wonder that this enemy had now become a friend and fellow worker.

- Peter became the central focus of the story from 9:32 to chapter 12. In chapter 10, Peter was sent to the Gentiles (quite against his will) and the household of Cornelius. He was a centurion and a God-fearer. The Lord knows those who are seeking him.

- Following the vision of the sheets, Peter went to the home of Cornelius and found a very receptive audience for the gospel. An angel had prepared Cornelius for Peter's arrival, and thus he had invited many of his friends to come and listen.

- Peter preached the gospel, asserting that Jesus had died and rose again from the dead and that all who believe on him shall receive forgiveness for their sins. While Peter spoke, the Holy Spirit fell upon the group (obviously in response to their belief). They spoke in tongues as well (as a sign that the Gentiles received the Holy spirit just like the Jews. Many years later, Peter appealed to this event as proof that the Gentiles could be saved without first becoming Jews, making it obvious that this was an extraordinary event).

- In chapter 11, Peter defended his ministry to the Gentiles before legalistic Jews. The Jews responded with amazement that God had granted "repentance unto life" to the Gentiles too (Acts 11:18).

- The church of Antioch was established in chapter 11, and it was there that believers were first called Christians (Acts 11:26).

- Persecution against the church broke out again in chapter 12, this time under the hand of Herod the king. He executed James, the brother of John, and seeing that this pleased the Jews, he arrested Peter also. The church then made fervent prayer for Peter, and he was miraculously released by an angel.

- Herod was filled with pride, and arrayed in royal apparel, he made a grand oration. The people attributed his eloquence to a god, and Herod did not offer any corrections. It was then that the angel smote him with a fatal illness. In contrast, the word of God spread and multiplied.

- The very first missionary journey appears in chapters 13 and 14. Here the Holy Spirit called out Barnabas and Saul for service. These two men had served the church at Antioch faithfully, and indeed, it was while they were serving that their call came. God often calls those already active to become even more active, but he rarely calls people on the sidelines to full-time ministry.

- Satan opposed the spread of the gospel from the very beginning, confronting Barnabas, Paul, and John Mark nearly immediately in the person of a sorcerer by the name of Elymas. Paul won this confrontation, but John Mark was terribly shaken by it, leaving the others to return home (Acts 13:13). They continued on through Antioch, Iconium, Derbe, and Lystra, preaching Jesus and the justification that comes about by faith in him (Acts 13:39).
- Paul was hotly persecuted at Lystra, where he was stoned and left for dead. However, he revived and amazingly went back into the city to continue his preaching ministry. Concerned that these fledgling churches would not founder, they ordained elders in all of them. Following this, they returned to Antioch and reported to the sending church all that God had done.
- The Jerusalem Council was recorded in chapter 15. Here a division among the Jews arose over the inclusion of the Gentiles into the church without them first converting to Judaism.
- Peter testified that "a good while ago" (when he preached to Cornelius) God gave them the Holy Spirit as he had the Jews. Once more this allusion to a long-past event makes it clear that this did not occur regularly.
- Paul and Barnabas also testified for the Gentiles and their receptivity to the gospel, and James rendered the final verdict. He argued that there was no reason to force a Jewish conversion on them. He only asked that they refrain from meats offered to idols, fornication, and things strangled and from blood. The findings of this council were sent via letter to the Gentile churches with Barnabas and Paul, among others.
- The second missionary journey appears in 15:36 through 18:22. Here we discover Paul and Barnabas at loggerheads as to what to do with John Mark. Barnabas wanted to take Mark along, but Paul refused, arguing that he could not be trusted. The contention was so severe between them that they parted company from one another (Acts 15:37–39). Sometimes godly leaders disagree.
- So Barnabas took Mark and sailed to Cyprus, and Paul took Silas and departed through Syria. From the text it appears that the church commended Paul and not Barnabas. This is the last mention of Barnabas in Acts.

- Paul and Silas also received a young man named Timothy to go along and help them. He had a good reputation and was ready to sacrifice for the cause (Acts 16:1–4).

- While heading to Troas, a man appeared to Paul in a vision and requested that they come to Macedonia and help them. This then began the movement of the gospel into Greece.

- We read of the conversion of Lydia, the first convert in Greece, who invited the small company to stay with her. The owners of a young woman possessed by a demon were greatly displeased after Paul healed her. They beat Paul and Silas and cast them in prison. At midnight, as Paul and Silas sang hymns of praise to God, an angel opened the prison doors by means of an earthquake. The jailer entered their cell, asking what he had to do to be saved. Their response was, "Believe in the Lord Jesus, and you will be saved—you and your household" (Acts 16:31).

- The jailer took them to his home and bandaged their wounds. He and his family were baptized. They then ate a joyful meal together. Paul and Silas then must have returned to the jail, for the next day the magistrates sent to release them. Paul appealed to his Roman citizenship, asking for a public apology. The leaders were clearly shaken by this and came to appeal to Paul to forgive them, which he did.

- They continued their journey through Thessalonica, Berea, and Athens, as told in Acts 17:1–34. As usual, Paul and his team were challenged and harangued by opponents, mostly from among the legalistic Jews. They created riots and falsely accused them (17:5–15). It was principally envy that motivated them to do so (Acts 17:5).

- Clearly Paul had some facility with Greek philosophy, as he preached to the Athenians on Mars Hill. As usual, some mocked and others believed (Acts 17:32, 34).

- The church of Corinth was established in chapter 18. Paul ended up staying with Aquila and Priscilla, who became life-long friends and associates. He stayed there for a year and a half teaching the word of God (Acts 18:11).

- He made a brief stop in Ephesus before heading back to the church in Jerusalem (Acts 18:19–21).

- After going to Jerusalem and then to Antioch, Paul set out on the third missionary journey, as recorded in chapters 18:23—21:14.

- Paul went back to Ephesus and stayed for three years, teaching them. As was his custom, he went into the synagogue and witnessed to the Jews.

- God wrought special miracles through Paul so that even his clothing had efficacious effects on the sick. Seeing his popularity, the seven sons of Sceva tried to duplicate the miracles. I love the response from the dark side, ". . . Jesus I know, and I know about Paul, but who are you?" (Acts 19:15). The possessed man beat the tar out of these sons of Sceva so that they fled for their lives.

- Paul moved out to other outposts in Greece, including Troas and Miletus.

- A touching farewell to the Ephesian elders is recorded in 20:17–38. Paul exhorted the elders to protect the church of God, which Christ purchased with his own blood. He knew wolves would seek to ravage the flock, as they always do. Danger lurked from without and from within. Charging them to be responsible with their leadership, Paul bid them farewell, saying it was unlikely that he would ever see them again.

- Paul and his company sailed to Miletus and then to Tyre and finally to Jerusalem. Some mistakenly thought Paul had violated the temple by bringing Gentiles into it, and a riot broke out. They began beating Paul until a contingent of military police of Rome came to the scene.

- The rest of the book is a record of Paul's defense against the accusations of the Jews. It led him all the way to Rome.

- In summary, Paul defended himself before the initial mob (Acts 22:1–30); before the Sanhedrin (Acts 22:30—23:11); a conspiracy to kill Paul erupted Acts 23:12–22; Paul was rescued by night and moved to Caesarea; he then defended himself before the Governor Felix (Acts 24:1–23); before Festus (Acts 25:1–9); and eventually appealed to go to Caesar. Before being sent to Rome, he also defended himself to King Agrippa (Acts 25:13—26:32).

- Finally, he was sent to Rome by ship (Acts 27:1–13). The company encountered a terrible storm, which destroyed their craft and left them stranded on the island of Miletus or Malta—south of Sicily.

- As they were making a fire by which to warm themselves, Paul was bitten by a highly venomous snake. Yet, no harm came to him (Acts 28:1–6). Others on the island experienced healing at the hands of

- Paul, among them the father of Publius, the leader of the island. In gratitude, they helped the company leave the island, giving them many gifts.
- Once in Rome, Paul was placed under house arrest. He was guarded by a Roman soldier and was free to receive anyone who wanted to visit him. Paul summoned the leaders of the Jews to come and meet with him and boldly testified to them of Jesus—the hope of Israel.
- They did come, and Paul spoke to them of Jesus out of the Law of Moses and the prophets from morning till evening (Acts 28:23). Some believed, and some did not believe. Paul stayed in Rome for two years in his own house. "Boldly and without hindrance he preached the kingdom of God and taught about the Lord Jesus Christ" (Acts 28:31).

Key verse: "But you will receive power when the Holy Spirit comes on you; and you will be my witnesses in Jerusalem, and in all Judea and Samaria, and to the ends of the earth" (Acts 1:8).

6

The Pauline Literature (Romans through Philemon)

ROMANS

The book of Romans begins the Church letters, books that were written directly to the saints in the Church Age. Thus they speak with specificity and clarity to all Christians. Furthermore, Romans stands first among the Pauline literature, which it introduces, being by far the most comprehensive treatment of the Christian faith. There are thirteen letters written by Paul arranged together, beginning with Romans and concluding with Philemon. These thirteen books are followed by Hebrews, James, 1 and 2 Peter, 1, 2, and 3 John, Jude, and Revelation. Collectively, these books are critical to the development of right doctrine and practice for the Church.

- The book of Romans may be briefly outlined as follows:
    - Chapters 1 to 3: The universal need for the gospel—the whole world is lost
    - Chapters 4 and 5: The principle of the gospel illustrated by Abraham, David, and Adam
    - Chapters 6 through 8: The gospel lived out, not by excess liberty or legalism but by the Spirit
    - Chapters 9 through 11: But what about Israel? The temporary rejection of the Jews due to their rejection of the gospel
    - Chapters 12 through 16: Practical applications of the gospel

- In chapter 1, Paul greeted the saints at Rome, affirming his earnest desire to come and visit them. Part of his desire was so that he could preach the gospel in the great city. The key verse for Romans appears early on in chapter 1, "I am not ashamed of the gospel, because it is the power of God for the salvation of everyone who believes: first for the Jew, then for the Gentile" (Rom 1:16).

- Indeed, Paul was not ashamed of the message of the gospel because he knew it was God's power for saving the lost. The gospel is powerful either to save or condemn. We can all take courage in sharing it because God uses it for his purposes and because it is the sole remedy of mankind's greatest problem—the problem of separation from God because of our sin.

- The rest of chapter 1 focuses on the lostness of the Gentile world. Scripture tells us that the creation is an undeniable witness to the existence of God, but the people refused to recognize that fact and fashioned idols by their own hands to worship.

- The rejection of God and the practice of idolatry led invariably to all kinds of immoral practices, as described in verses 24–32, most especially the practice of homosexuality, which Paul clearly condemned as reprehensible to God.

- Paul's main point, of course, was that the Gentiles were in desperate need of the gospel.

- However, it was not only the Gentiles who needed the gospel. Paul's argument continued in chapter 2, this time implicating the Jews. They knew the Scripture, but they could not keep it perfectly and thus had become guilty before God. Even deeply religious people are in dire need of the gospel of grace.

- In chapter 3, Paul conceded that there were important advantages religiously for the Jews, most particularly that they had the word of God. Indeed, Scripture is a lamp and a light—a word from God. But it is through the Scripture that one realizes one's sinful condition before God—and the way of deliverance.

- Now to both Jew and Gentile Paul offered a litany of shortcomings inherent in the human condition: "... There is no one righteous, not even one; there is no one who understands, no one who seeks God" (Rom 3:10–11); "Therefore no one will be declared righteous in his sight by observing the law; rather, through the law we become conscious of sin" (Rom 3:20).

The Pauline Literature (Romans through Philemon)

- Most people think that the law was given to make people righteous, but this is not the case. While it did provide a legal and ceremonial framework for Jewish society, no one could ever really keep it all. Paul affirmed the same principle in Galatians 3:22 and 24. The real purpose of the law was to reveal our sinfulness and drive us to the Savior Jesus Christ. "So the law was put in charge to lead us to Christ that we might be justified by faith" (Gal 3:24).

- Paul affirmed the universal need of the human race, writing, "For all have sinned and fall short of the glory of God" (Rom 3:23). Some people are very good and some people are very bad, humanly speaking. But everyone has sinned and missed the mark of perfection established by God as a condition of eternal fellowship.

- The only way to have this standing is through Christ, who died for our sins and rose again, making all who believe the sons and daughters of God. At the moment of faith in Christ, all our sins are justly forgiven, having been transferred to the cross, while the righteousness of Christ is also credited to our account. How marvelous!

- There could scarcely be a clearer and more direct statement of this principle than that which Paul provided, "... Justified freely by his grace through the redemption that came by Christ Jesus. God presented him as a sacrifice of atonement, through faith in his blood ... For we maintain that a man is justified by faith apart from observing the law" (Rom 3:24, 25, 28).

- No Christian can boast, for we have all been rescued in the same wonderful manner, through the gift of God—the sacrifice of the Servant, the Messiah, the Promised One from God who died as a sacrifice for our sins.

- Those who trust in Jesus are redeemed and justified, being declared not guilty. The substitutionary death of Christ has fully satisfied the righteous indignation of God against sin—so that those who accept Christ as Savior are forgiven (Rom 3:26).

- In chapters 4 and 5, the gospel is illustrated by three people: Abraham, David, and Adam.

- Paul argued that Abraham was justified by faith. Of course, the law could not possibly have been responsible for his righteousness, since he predated the law by many hundreds of years.

- Nor was obedience the condition of his righteousness, though faith was made visible by his obedience. (This is the point that James stressed in his book—that true faith will express itself in action.) But faith in God is that which activated God's gracious mercy, ". . . Abraham believed God and it was credited to him as righteousness" (Rom 4:3).

- This word "credited" is the Greek word "logizomai," and it occurs eleven times in this chapter. It means to place on someone's account. God credited Abraham with righteousness because of his faith.

- David pronounced the person who is forgiven as blessed. Indeed, David declared, "Blessed is the man whose sin the Lord will never count against him" (Rom 4:8).

- Neither is any religious ritual able to save us. The Jews placed great confidence in their sign of circumcision to make them acceptable to God. However, Paul cogently argued that this had no efficacy, since Abraham was justified before the rite of circumcision was instituted (Rom 4:10).

- The importance of the concept of imputation was carried forward into chapter 5 with Adam.

- One of the most powerful and beautiful verses in Romans opens the fifth chapter. Here Paul wrote, "Therefore, since we have been justified through faith, we have peace with God through our Lord Jesus Christ" (Rom 5:1). It is certainly a great thing to be at peace with God.

- Paul then explained that imputation is neither irrational nor isolated. Indeed, Adam's sin was imputed to the entire human family, making all of us victims of death (Rom 5:12). Adam served as our representative, sometimes referred to as the Federal Headship theory.

- His disobedience resulted in the infection of sin spreading to the whole race through the principle of imputation. "Therefore, just as sin entered the world through one man, and death through sin, and in this way death came to all men, because all sinned" (Rom 5:12).

- However, just as the moral ruin of the race resulted from Adam's sin, the rescue of all who believe is the result of the work of Christ for us—through imputation.

- This is precisely what Paul had in mind when he wrote, "For if, by the trespass of one man, death reigned through that one man, how much more will those who receive God's abundant provision of grace and of the gift of righteousness reign in life through the one man, Jesus Christ" (Rom 5:17).

- Having asserted that righteousness (salvation and eternal life) is the imputed gift of God to those who receive Christ by faith, Paul clarified the way to appropriately live out this faith.

- He realized that some confusion was nearly inevitable. On one hand, some might be tempted to abuse grace, the libertines, and on the other hand, there might be those who would try to legislate righteousness—the legalists. Paul offered a corrective to both sides and explained the way to live out our faith—the Spirit-led life.

- He addressed the libertines in chapter 6, the legalists in chapter 7, and offered his own inspired guidance in chapter 8.

- Some people believed (and some still do believe) that being under grace permits them to continue to live sinful lives without guilt. They feel that this only accentuates the grace of God. However, this is incorrect.

- Those who are saved by grace should strive to please God and live for him—not in order to earn or even to maintain our salvation, but because we already have it and are thankful. Paul had strong words of correction for the libertines, "What shall we say, then? Shall we go on sinning that grace may increase? By no means! . . ." (Rom 6:1–2).

- Paul argued that since we have been identified with Christ by faith in his death burial and resurrection, we should die to self and sin and seek to live the resurrected life right now (Rom 6:4). The love, mercy, and grace of God should act as a magnet, not a repellent.

- Living a life of obedience is difficult, as we all know. How do we do it? We are to "count" ourselves dead to sin but alive to God and actively enlist for God's service throughout the day (Rom 6:11–13). Though we sometimes fail, this is an effective path to spiritual growth.

- When a Jew was saved, it was often terribly difficult to let go of the law. Though the intention of the law was to lead a person to Christ, they often felt frustrated without a list of religious rituals to keep. Now there is nothing wrong with having strong convictions—quite the contrary, we should have them. But the list does not necessarily make one spiritual.

- We all need to be open to the word of God and the Spirit of God to lead and change us. That was the problem addressed here by Paul—many religious Jews simply continued to rigidly follow the law instead of listening to the promptings of the Spirit. No law can communicate all the subtle nuances of a relationship.

- Paul used the illustration of marriage to try to communicate that idea to his readers (Rom 7:3b–4).
- In chapter 8, Paul explained the appropriate way to live out our faith. He began by reminding us of the completed work of redemption through Christ stating, "Therefore, there is now no condemnation for those who are in Christ Jesus" (Rom 8:1). What a glorious thought! Thankfulness, not fearfulness, should serve as our motivation for living for Christ.
- Paul spoke of the work of the Holy Spirit in our lives nineteen times in this chapter. We are called to walk after the Spirit, not the flesh (Rom 8:4, 14)—to allow the Spirit to be our governing force. This affects our minds (Rom 8:5), our actions (Rom 8:13), and our readiness to suffer for Christ (Rom 8:17, 18).
- The Spirit ministers to believers, testifying of our part in God's family and praying for us (Rom 8:16, 26–27). The chapter concludes with the great promise that all things work together for good for God's people (Rom 8:28) and that nothing can separate us from the love of God that is in Christ Jesus (Rom 8:35–39). Amen.
- Like Elijah, we need to listen to the still, small voice in our hearts, prodding and prompting us in accord with the word of God.
- Paul wrote about the universal need of the gospel in chapters 1 through 3; he illustrated the principle of the gospel in chapters 4 and 5; and he discussed the right balance in living out the gospel in chapters 6 through 8.
- Then he turned to a logical question some of his readers would surely have been thinking—what about Israel? He addressed that question in chapters 9 through 11. Chapter 9 considers Israel's past election, chapter 10 discusses their current rejection, and chapter 11 focuses on their future restoration.
- Chapter 9 begins with Paul expressing his great desire that Israel might know the truth, suggesting that he would be willing to endure the curse of God if only they would respond correctly (Rom 9:1–4).
- He noted the great advantages that God has bestowed upon them, principally that they received the word of God (Rom 9:4–9). He noted that it is not the physical descendents of Abraham who are just before God but the spiritual ones. Messiah would come through Israel, but many in Israel disregarded him. He offered a discussion on election, using Jacob and Esau as the examples.

- It is important to note that this election concerned who would be the heir of Messiah. Since both could not be, one was chosen. It had nothing to do with salvation or with establishing a relationship with God. When the text notes "Esau I hated," it does not mean that God detested Esau, but rather concerns his sovereign choice of Jacob as the heir.

- Paul discussed Pharaoh and his hardness of heart, asserting that God hardened his heart. Again, one must keep in mind that Pharaoh had many opportunities to hear of the true God from the enslaved Israelites. Constant rejection is dangerous indeed, for God turns people over to their own desires. On some occasions the text says God hardened his heart and on other occasions it tells us that Pharaoh hardened his own heart.

- The rest of the chapter details God's plan to work with the Gentiles because of Israel's refusal to accept God's way to righteousness. (See Rom 10:20–21.)

- Israel constantly stumbled over the grace of God, instead trying to establish their own righteousness by law keeping, which, as we have seen, does not work (Rom 9:30–33).

- In chapter 10, we learn that very religious people can be terribly lost. Israel had great zeal for God (Rom 10:2), but not according to knowledge. They tried to earn their way to heaven through religious obedience, and they were damned because of it.

- Paul makes the way of salvation abundantly clear. God's plan is to save those who believe on his Son and the Son's great redeeming work—"for, 'Everyone who calls on the name of the Lord will be saved'" (Rom 10:13).

- Verses 14 through 17 emphasize the need for faithful witness on the part of the church. People can only believe if they have heard, and they can only hear if someone tells them, and they will only be told if someone is sent. (The progression in reverse is (1) call, (2) believe, (3) hear, (4) preach, (5) go.)

- The chapter closes with a description of God's patience in calling upon Israel and their refusal to listen (Rom 10:21).

- Chapter 11 deals with the eventual restoration of Israel after the rapture of the church. Paul reminded his readers that God will always have a remnant in Israel that believes. He used the illustration of

Elijah, who felt terribly alone. However, God told him that he had seven thousand souls who believed (Rom 11:1–5).

- Today many Jews believe on Jesus as their Messiah, for which we rejoice. However, the nation in general is blinded to this truth. Because of this, God turned to the Gentiles. This resulted in the formation of the Church. As we saw from Acts, this confused many Jews (note the Jerusalem Council), because God had worked with and through Israel for many hundreds of years. Part of the reason that God turned to the Gentiles was to provoke Israel to jealousy (Rom. 11:11, 14).

- God will graft the Jews back in during the Tribulation Period, when they will witness for their Messiah with great zeal (Rom 11:25). Then God will turn back to the Jews, and they will respond in faith. The chapter concludes with a doxology of the great wisdom and knowledge of God—indeed, God's ways are mysterious and awesome and far above our own.

- Having addressed the question of Israel in her past, present, and future, Paul returned to the Church and discussed many practical applications of the faith. He began this section of exhortation and instruction with an appeal to the great mercy of God as the motivation for obedience (Rom. 12:1).

- Paul called Christians to make good use of our spiritual gifts, serving regularly and enthusiastically (Rom 12:3–8).

- A series of proverbial instructions are set forth in verses 9 through 17, among them to love in sincerity, to work with industry, to wait patiently, to give generously, and to do good even to our enemies.

- As much as it depends on us, we should live peaceably with all men (though sometimes others make it impossible). We should avoid personal vengeance, trusting God to make things right (Rom 12:19–21). Instead of seeking vengeance, we should do good to our enemies. Passages such as this indicate that love is principally an action, not a feeling, for we certainly have no feelings for our enemies, but we can do them good.

- In chapter 13, Paul exhorted Christians to honor those in authority over us, most especially those in government. He offered two reasons for this: (1) the rulers that exist are ordained of God (Rom 13:1), and (2) if you disobey them, you will be punished (Rom 13:2).

The Pauline Literature (Romans through Philemon)

- In general, Christians should live as obedient and faithful citizens of society. The only reason for civil disobedience is if a government commands us to sin. In that case, we must obey God rather than men.
- Capital punishment is clearly endorsed by Paul as the power of a government to punish those who commit capital crimes (Rom 13:4).
- The chapter concludes with an exhortation to allow love to govern our relationships. (Rom 13:8).
- Chapter 14:1 through 15:3 is an important section on getting along together in spite of our differences. The church is filled with people who differ in many ways. Our backgrounds and prior experiences will invariably color the way we view certain practices to which Scripture does not speak specifically. Paul identified three commonly debated practices in the ancient church over which believers often disagreed—and disagreed disagreeably.
- First, he mentioned the issue of dietary restrictions; second, he talked about special days; and finally, he mentioned the manner in which servants were treated (Rom 14:1-4).
- He warned against two universal tendencies expressed against people with whom we differ: judging them or disdaining them. Those with liberty tend to disdain those without it, and those without liberty tend to judge those with it. Of course, this can lead to turmoil in the church and deep division, leading to the loss of mission and purpose to which we have been called.
- So Paul spent quite a bit of time correcting such attitudes. He called the church to recognize that differences of opinion over gray areas were inevitable. He further urged those with liberty to restrict it for the sake of the weaker brother (Rom 14:15, 20-21; 15:1-3).
- This does not mean that we can never practice our liberty, but that when with those who are offended, we should refrain. For instance, some Christians consider a deck of cards as an unpleasant symbol of drinking and gambling, while for others it is a happy reminder of family table game nights. We need to be sensitive to the feelings of others but need not be held captive when in the company of those who share our liberty.
- The great rationale for refusing to judge or disdain others in these areas is the Judgment Seat of Christ before which all believers will

stand (Rom 14:10–12). At this great judgment, Jesus will assess each of us and render his judgment of our works perfectly.

- He knows our history and our background entirely and will take all the appropriate factors into consideration. We don't. Sometimes we think we do, but we don't. That is why it is better not to spend time judging or disdaining people regarding gray areas.
- In the remainder of chapter 15, Paul defended his ministry, and most especially his mission to the Gentiles. He concluded this section by requesting prayer of the church at Rome, that he might be kept safe from the unbelievers and that his service might be acceptable to the saints at Jerusalem (Rom 15:30–32).
- The book concludes in chapter 16, with Paul greeting many of his friends and associates in the gospel. The value of teamwork is clearly evident in this passage. Many of those Paul greeted served the Lord with great zeal and effectiveness, perhaps most especially Aquila and Priscilla, who became life-long friends of Paul after their initial meeting in Corinth (Acts 18).
- He also warned his friends to identify those who caused division among them and avoid them. Discernment is a necessary ingredient for God's people, and we must be on guard against those who seek to deceive us for their own purposes.
- He offered an encouraging word of our eventual victory over the dark side, noting, "The God of peace will soon crush Satan under your feet ..." (Rom 16:20).
- Paul concluded his letter with a doxology of the glory of the gospel and the wisdom of God (Rom 16:27).

Key verse: "I am not ashamed of the gospel, because it is the power of God for the salvation of everyone who believes: first for the Jew, then for the Gentile" (Rom 1:16).

The Pauline Literature (Romans through Philemon)

1 CORINTHIANS

The first letter to the Corinthians was written by Paul as his three-year stay in Ephesus was drawing to a close (1 Cor 16:5-8). While among the most gifted of churches (1 Cor 1:7), this was a troubled congregation. Paul wrote to correct a number of moral, ethical, and doctrinal problems that had arisen in the Church at Corinth. They were torn by internal strife and division (1 Cor 1:11-12), plagued by carnality among the membership (1 Cor 3:1-4), infiltrated by immorality (1 Cor 5:1), and given to lawsuits (1 Cor 6:1-7). They also were confused over marital issues (1 Cor 7) and the exercise of Christian liberty (1 Cor 8).

Furthermore, they were participating in the Lord's Table irreverently, causing many problems among the people, including sickness and death. Some employed their spiritual gifts selfishly, disrupting the church services and clamoring for attention and praise (1 Cor 12—14). Most especially, Paul offered an important corrective to the use of tongues in this section. Doctrinal error had spread concerning the resurrection of the body, to which issue Paul turned in chapter 15.

- Even with all these problems, Paul considered them saints, part of the company of the redeemed, addressing them as "the church of God in Corinth, to those sanctified in Christ Jesus..." (1 Cor 1:2).

- Indeed, the church at Corinth underscores the old adage that Christians are not perfect, but we are forgiven.

- After offering them a warm greeting, Paul moved directly to problem number one—divisions in the church. Some were declaring themselves followers of Paul, others of Apollos, and still others of Cephas. The very spiritual asserted that they followed Christ! Such assertions apparently simply veiled their desire to be combative over various issues. In the end, Paul argued we are all followers of Christ and should remain supportive of leaders pointing us in that direction.

- Paul offered a crucial statement on baptism in this section, making it clear that it has no saving power. Paul stated, "For Christ did not send me to baptize, but to preach the gospel..." (1 Cor 1:17). Baptism is a step of obedience for the saved; it has no power to redeem. Only the gospel can do that.

- From 1:18 to 2:16 Paul discussed the greatness of God's wisdom as juxtaposed with man's wisdom. Indeed, God calls the lowly, not many mighty, not many noble, not many wise after the flesh (1 Cor 1:26). The reason is that God confounds the world with his own glorious wisdom.

- The Jews seek signs, and the Greeks seek wisdom; to both groups the preaching of the cross is foolishness. But to those being saved, the cross represents Christ, who is the power and wisdom of God (1 Cor 1:24).
- Paul spoke the word of God and trusted it to have its proper effect. Paul's message was Jesus Christ and him crucified for the forgiveness of sins (1 Cor 2:2).
- Paul was not impressive physically and was filled with fear and trembling, but this did not dissuade him from the mission upon which Christ sent him (1 Cor 2:3-5).
- Part of the problem with the Corinthian church was carnality. Many of the members of this church acted like they did before they were saved, and this was preventing their growth and inciting problems.
- Paul redressed the divisions mentioned in chapter 1 again in chapter 3, attributing the problem to carnality among the group. Paul reminded the people that the messengers of the gospel are only ministers or servants through whom people believe. The object of our faith, Jesus Christ, is to have dominion over us. United together in our common mission and purpose, we should move forward together harmoniously.
- This topic led to another for Paul—the Judgment Seat of Christ. We are all fellow laborers for God, and Christ is the one who will render the final assessment of our work.
- At the "Bema Seat Judgment," Christ will evaluate the works and service of every Christian. This judgment has nothing to do with the eternal destiny of those involved, since everyone present will be saved. Thus, it must be differentiated from the Great White Throne Judgment—which is a judgment reserved for the lost.
- At the Judgment Seat of Christ or the Bema Seat Judgment, Jesus Christ will assess the works of individual Christians—not our sins (they have been forgiven), but our service for Christ.
- Some, who have served honorably and sacrificially, will be rewarded, and others will not be rewarded. But each person present will be saved—some yet as by fire. This formal meeting with Christ has eternal consequences. It is wise to live in light of it (1 Cor 3:10-15).

- Paul continued this theme into the fourth chapter, asserting that his main concern in life and service was the opinion of Christ. He noted, "I care very little if I am judged by you or by any human court; indeed, I do not even judge myself. My conscience is clear, but that does not make me innocent. It is the Lord who judges me" (1 Cor 4:3–4). That is a good rule of thumb—assessing our lives in terms of what Jesus would think.

- The problem of immorality was addressed next by Paul in chapter 5. A man was living with his father's wife—his step-mother. The church, rather than being concerned about this relationship, embraced it (1 Cor 5:2). However, Paul was very upset and admonished the church to exercise discipline against the erring participants.

- Obviously, not all sins deserve church discipline; the vast majority should be dealt with personally and privately. When a sin is public, blatant, and persistent, it may become a matter of church discipline. Paul told the church to remove these people from the fellowship. (In 2 Corinthians, we discover that the man repented and Paul urged the church to restore him).

- Paul's disciplinary prescription was to put these people out of the church (1 Cor 5:9–11). This is unpopular, but is an important principle to follow, keeping the church clear on appropriate behavior. Of course, discipline is also intended to have remedial consequences, causing the individual to reconsider his or her course of action. The church should be ready to readmit the repentant, though not necessarily to positions of leadership.

- Paul prohibited taking fellow believers into court in chapter 6. First, believers should be able to resolve their differences reasonably. Second, if not, it is better to be defrauded than become a spectacle to the world. Christian arbitration is a good middle ground for believers today who need help settling their differences.

- A special appeal against fornication is offered at the close of chapter 6. This sin, Paul asserted, is especially detrimental because it leads to physical illnesses and other problems, sinning against one's own body. He closed this section by reminding believers that we are indwelt by the Holy Spirit and thus are not our own—"You were bought at a price. Therefore honor God with your body" (1 Cor 6:20).

- In chapter 7, Paul answered questions about marriage. First, he addressed the importance of faithfulness in marriage (1 Cor 7:1–7). Second, he spoke to those who were married to unsaved spouses.

Probably, some who were already married had later became Christians, and they were wondering what they should do.

- Paul stated that if the unbeliever chose to remain, they should stay together (1 Cor 7:12-14). However, if the unbeliever left, the believer should let him or her go (1 Cor 7:15).

- To those who had never been married, Paul advised singleness (spoken as a true-blue bachelor!). Another reason for his suggestion was the present distress against Christians (1 Cor 7:26). You may recall the Lord told Jeremiah not to marry because of the impending persecution of the exile (Jer 16:1-4).

- In conclusion, Paul told his audience that the unmarried or widowed were free to marry as long as it was "in the Lord" (1 Cor 7:39-40.

- In chapter 8 and again in chapter 10, Paul spoke to the issue of eating meat offered to idols, which had created significant confusion and debate in the first-century church. The issue boiled down to one's conscience. If one's conscience permitted the eating of this meat, fine. But if it violated one's conscience, one should not partake

- Furthermore, Paul instructed them not to abuse their personal liberty by flaunting the consumption of this food in front of one who was offended by it. So, just as in Romans, Paul prescribed limiting one's personal freedoms when it would harm another person (1 Cor 8:10-13, 10:23-33).

- Next Paul defended his apostolic authority and explained why he worked while preaching and establishing churches. First, he made it clear that full-time ministers should be remunerated for their work (1 Cor 9:12-13). Second, the reason Paul accepted no payment for preaching the gospel was because he had no choice but to preach it. The sacrifice he gave to God was to preach the gospel free of charge (1 Cor 9:16-18).

- In chapter 11, Paul discussed the importance of a proper attitude about Communion. The Corinthians showed little or no respect at all, even becoming drunk at the Lord's Table (1 Cor 11:21-22). Participating in Communion with a lack of respect led to judgment (1 Cor 11:27-30). For this reason many in the church were sick, and some had even died.

- Paul quoted Jesus, making it clear that the Communion service is a memorial event conducted "in remembrance of me" (1 Cor 11:24-25).

The Pauline Literature (Romans through Philemon)

- The question of spiritual gifts arose in chapters 12 through 14, particularly as it related to the use of tongues in the church. Apparently a number of people were disrupting the church services and creating confusion. Paul wanted this practice to stop.
- A number of important observations emerge: (1) all believers have at least one spiritual gift (1 Cor 12:7); (2) the gifts are sovereignly given by the Holy Spirit to profit or edify the church (1 Cor 12:11); (3) even in the first-century church, not everyone had the gift of tongues (1 Cor 12:20); and (4) spiritual gifts are of true value only when exercised in love (1 Cor 13).
- Some argue that "tongues" was actually an angelic language rather than a known foreign language based upon 1 Corinthians 13:1–3. However, the structure of the passage does not sustain this assertion. It is clearly hyperbole. The first element represented the genuine and the next the exaggerated. Paul spoke in the tongues of men—in other words, foreign languages.
- In chapter 14, Paul outlined a number of important principles. First, the primary purpose of a worship service is to edify or build up believers (1 Cor 14:12). Unintelligible speech, being incomprehensible, does not build up the church (1 Cor 14:9–11). (Note: in chapter 14, the word "prophesying" is basically equivalent to teaching the word of God.) Teaching does build up believers (1 Cor 14:19). Thus, Paul greatly limited the use of tongues in the church (keep in mind that this was the genuine gift of tongues he limited).
- Paul said that two or at the most three could speak in tongues, and their speech needed an interpreter (1 Cor 14:27–28). He suggested that this gift was controllable (1 Cor 14:32). He prohibited women from speaking in tongues in the church (1 Cor 14:34), and he urged orderliness rather than chaos in the church, for God is not the author of confusion (1 Cor 14:33).
- In chapter 15, Paul offered a doctrinal corrective to serious misunderstandings about the resurrection. Apparently some at Corinth taught that there was no resurrection of the body; Paul viewed this as heresy.
- He began by reminding his audience that Jesus Christ rose bodily from the dead, as was witnessed by the apostles and over five hundred others, including Paul himself (1 Cor 15:1–8). He further contended that if Christ was not raised, our faith is vain and we are yet

in our sins (1 Cor 15:12–19). But Paul asserted in the strongest of terms that Christ was raised (1 Cor 15:20, 23–27).

- This was followed by a discussion of the nature of the resurrection body in verses 35 through 50. Paul formed his argument both from terrestrial and celestial examples. The glory of the heavenly bodies differs and so too the glory of the resurrection (this may provide a clue to the kind of rewards we will receive at the Bema Seat Judgment).

- While sown in weakness, the resurrection body will be raised in glory and power.

- One of the most wonderful descriptions of the afterlife appears in 15:51–57. Here death, sin, and judgment are finally conquered and this mortal shall put on immortality (15:53). The rapture of the Church is taught in 1 Cor 15:51–52, which clearly states that some will never taste death but will be transformed instantaneously into the glorified status. I hope to go in this way—how about you?

- The resurrection was intended to serve as a powerful motivator for continuing faithfulness on the part of believers. Paul concluded, "Therefore, my dear brothers, stand firm. Let nothing move you. Always give yourselves fully to the work of the Lord, because you know that your labor in the Lord is not in vain" (1 Cor 15:58).

- Paul concluded the letter by reminding the Corinthians of the importance of the collection to be taken for the poor church at Jerusalem. He hoped to come through Corinth shortly, perhaps with Timothy. He then offered final exhortations and greetings before closing.

Key verses: "Love is patient, love is kind. It does not envy, it does not boast, it is not proud. It is not rude, it is not self-seeking, it is not easily angered, it keeps no record of wrongs. Love does not delight in evil but rejoices with the truth. It always protects, always trusts, always hopes, always perseveres. Love never fails" (1 Cor 13: 4–8a).

2 CORINTHIANS

Paul wrote his second letter to the church at Corinth within one year of writing his first letter. Apparently, the Corinthian church had been infiltrated by false teachers, pseudo apostles who promoted a mixture of legalism with grace. They most likely taught that Jesus was the Messiah but that in order to be saved, one must believe in Christ *and* keep the Mosaic Law and be circumcised. We find the same sort of jousting at the Jerusalem Council recorded in Acts 15. Moreover, these false apostles denigrated Paul to the Corinthians, saying that he was insincere and unreliable. Thus we find Paul frequently defending his apostolic calling and authority throughout the book, making it autobiographical and personal in tone.

- Paul began by reminding the saints at Corinth of God's comforting care for his children in the midst of various distresses. God not only consoles sufferers, but he also equips them through suffering to be comforters of others. Indeed, the care of God is often extended through the care of God's children (2 Cor 1:4).
- Paul reminded the church that as an apostle, he had suffered greatly for Christ (2 Cor 1:8–10), addressing his own hardships more frequently in this book than in any other letter, most particularly to prove his sincerity.
- In 1:12 through 2:2, Paul sought to clear up a misunderstanding. He had told them that he planned to come for a visit in 1 Corinthians 16:5–8. However, he never arrived. His opponents pointed to this as fickleness on Paul's part—that he could not be trusted.
- But Paul explained the reason for his delay; he did not wish to come to Corinth in heaviness of heart due to their misbehavior, nor did he want to administer discipline (2 Cor 2:1–2). He hoped they would receive his counsel and obey so that he could come to them in rejoicing and praise (2 Cor 2:3).
- And indeed, they had obeyed Paul's exhortation to excommunicate the man living in immorality (1 Cor 5). Following their exercise of discipline, the man repented and desired to return to the fellowship. However, they would not let him back. Paul urged them to forgive the offender and reinstate him into the church (2 Cor 2:7–10).

- Forgiveness was important, Paul asserted, not only for the sake of the fallen brother but also to avoid Satan's trap of division and backbiting in the church (2 Cor 2:11).
- Paul concluded the chapter with an affirmation that he, unlike the false apostles, did not corrupt the word of God. We are responsible to evaluate the teaching we receive to determine if it is in accord with Scripture or not.
- In chapter 3, Paul contrasted the New Testament (the gospel message) with that of the Old Testament (the Law system) in some highly instructive ways: (1) The old system kills but the new one gives life (2 Cor 3:6); (2) the old is external but the new is internal (2 Cor 3:3, 7); (3) the old had fading glory and is done away with while the new has eternal glory that increases (2 Cor 3:11–13, 18); and (4) the old condemned but the new gives righteousness (2 Cor 3:9).
- Religion can only control or conform; it cannot transform. Transformation is possible only through the work of the Holy Spirit and the word of God in the heart of a believer (2 Cor 3:17–18).
- Because Paul understood this and had received mercy himself through the gospel, he refused to faint in the work God had entrusted to him (2 Cor 4:1). Chapter 4 deals with the spiritual battle in which Christians are engaged, most especially those who seek to witness for Christ. Satan blinds the minds of those who reject the gospel, lest they should believe and be saved (2 Cor 4:3–4).
- Paul briefly outlined the particular struggles associated with his ministry (2 Cor 4:7–12). Even so, Paul remained resolved to the work, experiencing inner strength and renewal day by day (2 Cor 4:16).
- Paul knew that the affliction of the moment was not worthy to be compared to the glory which would be revealed in the end (2 Cor 4:17–18). Believers must stay focused on the eternal rewards awaiting us if we are to remain steadfast. Paul was not suggesting that the struggles of life were insignificant, rather that the glory was far greater. That is not greed; it is faith.
- He continued this theme into chapter five, speaking especially about the immortal body that believers are anticipating (or should be!). One day, Paul asserted, believers will receive a special body (tabernacle) made by God in which we will live eternally and powerfully (2 Cor 5:4–5).

- For Christians, to be absent from the body is to be present with the Lord (2 Cor 5:6–8). Paul reminded believers that we must all stand before the Judgment Seat of Christ to be assessed for the quality of our service (2 Cor 5:10).

- This thought led Paul to consider his own service and witness, wanting to be approved by Christ. Knowing that Christ will judge the world motivated Paul to persuade people to receive Christ and be saved (2 Cor 5:11). The great sacrifice of Christ compelled Paul to offer his life to the Lord in service (2 Cor 5:14–15).

- Five times in the last four verses of the chapter Paul spoke of the great reconciliation made by God through Jesus Christ. The only way to be reconciled to God is to receive the gift of God—his Son. The innocent Lamb of God took our sins upon himself at the cross and was punished in our place for them. When we receive Jesus, all our sins are immediately transferred to the cross, where God already judged them in the person of his Son. Thus we receive immediate forgiveness and righteousness. Amazing!

- In chapter 6:1–10, Paul once more briefly outlined some of the struggles associated with the apostolic ministry. He concluded this chapter urging the Corinthians to set themselves apart to God and refuse to be unequally yoked with unbelievers. This principle seems to apply to any close union.

- Chapter 7 serves as a bit of a summary: Paul once again asked for their respect based on the hardships and suffering he had experienced for the gospel and reminded them that his first letter was intended for their good.

- The collection for the poor saints at Jerusalem and principles of giving more broadly occupied Paul in chapters 8 and 9.

- He challenged the Church at Corinth by the sacrificial example of the churches of Macedonia (northern Greece, including the Church at Philippi).

- They gave such a generous offering because they first gave themselves to the Lord (2 Cor 8:5). This is a great principle for giving—a devoted heart produces a sanctified budget! A generous gift would prove the sincerity of their love for the brethren, Paul contended (2 Cor 8:8).

- Paul assured them that the offering would be cared for with integrity managed by Titus and other brothers (2 Cor 8:16–22). Paul also gave

Titus a strong character reference. Fiscal responsibility is vital for Christians and congregations.

- Paul also reminded them about key principles for taking their offering.
- First, he shared the principle of sowing and reaping, writing, "Remember this: whoever sows sparingly will also reap sparingly, and whoever sows generously will also reap generously" (2 Cor 9:6). Second, we should plan our giving in accordance with our resources (2 Cor 8:12; 9:7a). Third, we should give cheerfully, recognizing that God loves a cheerful giver (but he also accepts from a grouch!). Fourth, our donations should be offered against the backdrop of God's "indescribable gift" (2 Cor 9:15).
- Once again Paul defended himself in chapter 10 against the accusations and slanders of the wolves. They said that Paul talked tough but that his physical appearance was weak (2 Cor 10:10). But Paul warned unless a repentant spirit prevailed, he would show himself powerful upon arrival (2 Cor 10:11).
- Comparing oneself with others is an age-old practice in which the Corinthians participated. The apostle asserted that this was unwise (2 Cor 10:12). He knew very well that it was not the person who commended themselves who received approval but the one whom the Lord commended (2 Cor 10:18).
- In chapter 11, the confrontation between Paul and the other teachers reached an apex. He told the Corinthians that he was jealous over them with a godly jealousy. He feared that the enemy might beguile them through the same kind of subtlety that he employed against Eve (2 Cor 11:3). The infiltrators were, Paul argued, messengers of another Jesus, false apostles, tools of Satan (2 Cor 11:4, 13–15).
- This chapter contains the most specific and detailed account of the sufferings of Paul for the sake of the gospel found anywhere in the New Testament. The reason for his specificity was to prove his fidelity to the mission of Christ, thus hopefully turning the Corinthians away from doctrinal error.
- How had Paul suffered: (1) he had been whipped five times by the Jews (forty stripes save one)—that's about 195 lashes!; (2) he was beaten three times with sticks; (3) he was stoned with stones on one occasion (at Lystra, according to Acts 14:19); (4) three times he was shipwrecked at sea; (5) often in danger of various kinds and in wea-

riness and watching and in hunger and thirst and in cold and nakedness; (6) furthermore, he carried the responsibility of the churches upon his shoulders daily. Being a servant of Christ surely does not exempt one from hardship and difficulties.

- It seems that those who suffer greatly are comforted greatly too. This was true of Paul, as he recounted a special trip God gave him into Paradise (2 Cor 12:1-6). Paul wasn't even sure if he actually went there in his body or if he had an out-of-the-body experience (2 Cor 12:3). Either way, it was glorious. God has a way of compensating us for our sacrifices.

- A thorn in the flesh was given to Paul to keep him from pride in light of these amazing revelations (2 Cor 12:7). Even though Paul prayed that God would remove this thorn, it remained. The Lord told him, "My grace is sufficient for you" (2 Cor 12:9).

- Affliction is sometimes God's way of keeping us in balance—dependent upon him. Paul gloried in his weakness, realizing that "... when I am weak, then I am strong" (2 Cor 12:10), because the power is of Christ.

- Paul made an important statement about signs and wonders in 1 Corinthians 12:12 saying, "The things that mark an apostle—signs, wonders and miracles—were done among you with great perseverance." This is in harmony with statements found throughout the book of Acts asserting that miracles were principally the domain of the apostles.

- This statement is in the context of a warning that extends from 12:11 to 13:10. Paul wanted to come to them with encouragement, not with discipline. The decision regarding the manner of his arrival was in their hands, based upon their attitude and actions.

- The book concludes with a warm farewell. Paul offered an early Trinitarian formula at the very end writing, "May the grace of the Lord Jesus Christ, and the love of God, and the fellowship of the Holy Spirit be with you all" (2 Cor 13:14).

Key verses: "For our light and momentary troubles are achieving for us an eternal glory that far outweighs them all. So we fix our eyes not on what is seen, but on what is unseen. For what is seen is temporary, but what is unseen is eternal" (2 Cor 4:17-18).

GALATIANS

The book of Galatians was written to a cluster of churches in the region of Galatia, including those at Derbe, Lystra, and Iconium. Paul visited this area on both his first and third missionary journeys, as discussed in the book of Acts (Acts 13:51—14:23; 18:23). At the time of Paul's writing, these churches faced a dual threat: (1) legalism negating the doctrine of grace; and (2) impure conduct infiltrating the church community. Thus Paul wrote a letter of correction and warning to these groups, urgently reminding them of his message of salvation by grace through faith in Christ alone. The deviation in Galatia was so severe that Paul failed to commend them for anything in the opening of the letter—the only such letter from Paul.

- Paul identified himself and his readers, offering a brief doxology of the greatness of the plan of God to redeem us through Christ (Gal 1:4–5). This served as a fitting reminder to this wavering community.

- He launched quickly into the purpose of his writing: "I am astonished that you are so quickly deserting the one who called you by the grace of Christ and are turning to a different gospel" (Gal 1:6).

- However, this other gospel was not a real gospel (it was not good news) but a forgery and heresy. So distorted was this blend of legalism with grace that Paul pronounced judgment upon all those who proliferated this message—whether a man or an angel. Any who preached any other gospel than that which Paul preached, he urged, should be eternally condemned (Gal 1:9).

- In 1:10–24 Paul reminded the Galatians of his conversion and calling as an apostle of Christ. One of his main points in this section was to confirm that Jesus Christ directly delivered the gospel message Paul now preached. Thus Paul announced the unblemished and pure message of the true good news from God (1:10–12).

- Religion appeals to the pride of mankind, but the gospel is an offense. Paul spent his preconversion life enmeshed in Judaism, and indeed, he had profited from his zeal (Gal 1:14). However, he rejected that life in favor of the gospel of grace in which righteousness was offered as a gift, not a reward. He stressed throughout this section that he was discipled by the Lord himself, but that he also had important apostolic contacts, most notably with Peter and James (Gal 1:18–19).

- Chapter 2:1–10 seems to be a glimpse behind the events at the Jerusalem Council (Acts 15), wherein the early church fought off Judaizing legalists. Paul had received the call to preach to the Gentiles just as Peter had received a commission to preach to the Jews. Because of the controversy over grace and works, Titus, a Greek, refused to be circumcised.

- Events often dictate appropriate action. Another associate of Paul, Timothy, was circumcised because of the Jews, according to Acts 16:3. Why this apparent discrepancy?

- In the case of Titus, some false teachers were arguing for the need to be circumcised in order to be saved. Thus Paul and Titus opposed this idea, refusing to appear to accommodate this message. However, in Acts there was no such debate. Not wanting to put up any unnecessary obstacles to their witness, Timothy was circumcised. Titus and Timothy did precisely opposite things—but they were both exactly the right thing to do under the circumstances.

- Peer pressure is not just for teenagers, as we discover in 2:11–14. Here Paul revealed a moment of weakness experienced by both Peter and Barnabas regarding the Gentiles.

- Before certain religious Jews arrived in Antioch, Peter and Barnabas, as well as others, ate with the Gentiles. However, after these elite came to Antioch, Peter and Barnabas separated themselves from the Gentile believers. Paul rebuked them for their hypocrisy (Gal 2:14).

- He probably raised this issue for a couple of reasons: (1) to illustrate the sinister and pervasive nature of wrong thinking and (2) to demonstrate his apostolic authority in confronting one of the chief apostles, Peter.

- In the closing section of chapter 2, Paul clearly articulated the path to true righteousness, stating, "A man is not justified by observing the law, but by faith in Jesus Christ. So we, too, have put our faith in Christ Jesus that we may be justified by faith in Christ and not by observing the law, because by observing the law no one will be justified" (Gal 2:16).

- Paul argued that if we could be justified by any law, there was no reason for Christ to be crucified, noting, "I do not set aside the grace of God, for if righteousness could be gained through the law, Christ died for nothing" (Gal 2:21).

- As chapter 3 opened, Paul addressed the Galatians as those under a spell—as bewitched by the false teachers. They began their new life in Christ by the Spirit; did they expect to now be made complete through the law? That made no sense, Paul reasoned. Furthermore, Abraham was justified by God 430 years before the law was delivered to Moses.

- Just as he did in Romans 4:3, Paul quoted Genesis 15:6 "Consider Abraham: 'He believed God, and it was credited to him as righteousness'" (Gal 3:6). Indeed, the Abrahamic covenant foreshadowed the gospel stating, ". . . All nations will be blessed through you" (Gal 3:8).

- Paul went on to argue that those who sought to be justified by the law lived under the curse of the law, being incapable of obeying it. If someone hoped to be made just by law keeping, he or she had to obey all of it, all of the time, and not just the pieces that appealed to him or her, Paul explained (Gal 3:10).

- Thankfully, Paul noted, "Christ redeemed us from the curse of the law by becoming a curse for us . . ." (Gal 3:13).

- God made the promise to bless the whole world through Abraham but had Christ in mind, according to Galatians 3:16.

- If the law is unable to produce righteousness, then what was its purpose? Paul anticipated and answered this logical question, saying, "So the law was put in charge to lead us to Christ that we might be justified by faith" (Gal 3:24).

- Now there is nothing wrong with the law. Indeed, it is a partial expression of the character of God. Furthermore, it certainly helped maintain order in the theocracy under which Israel lived.

- The problem is with human beings; we are sinners incapable of observing the law perfectly. Once we sin, the law can no longer help us—it can only condemn us. It is in this way that the law leads one to Christ. It makes our guilt unmistakably clear, revealing our need of a Savior.

- In order to emphasize the availability of the gospel to all, Paul stated that in Christ there is neither Jew or Gentile, there is neither bond or free, there is neither male or female; for ye are all one in Christ. Obviously, Paul did not intend to dissolve all social relationships. His point was simply that everyone is on equal footing regarding salvation.

- We are no longer under tutors, Paul asserted in 4:1–3, because we have received the adoption of sons (Gal 4:4–5).

- Since they now know God and are known by God, Paul puzzled over their readiness to go back under the yoke of bondage to various rules and rituals (Gal 4:8–11).

- The law brings bondage, and Paul concluded chapter 4 illustrating this principle from the example of Isaac (the son of promise) and Ishmael (the bondwoman's son). These two systems are incompatible; they cannot be blended together. If one follows a works system, one loses grace.

- This led Paul to exhort his friends to stand firm in their liberty in Christ and refuse the yoke of slavery (Gal 5:1).

- Reasoning with them about their potential error, Paul stated one had to fulfill the whole law if one hoped to be justified by works—and in the process had fallen from grace (Gal 5:3–4). This was merely hypothetical, since no one can observe it all.

- Employing a play on words about circumcision, Paul wished that those troubling the Galatians would themselves be cut off. Such was the disdain with which the apostle viewed these false teachers.

- From 5:14 to 6:10, the apostle stressed the importance of the Spirit-led life for Christians and churches. Love fulfills the law, Paul argued, regarding our relationship one to another. Legalistic churches tend to "... bite and devour one another ..." (Gal 5:15). If driven by the flesh, lambs can indeed turn carnivorous and tear into others in the body of Christ.

- A litany of the works of the flesh is offered in verses 17 through 21. This implies that believers are capable of committing any of these sins if we quench and grieve the Spirit and follow the promptings of the old nature—a somber warning.

- Instead, God wants the Spirit to produce fruit in the lives of Christians, "But the fruit of the Spirit is love, joy, peace, patience, kindness, goodness, faithfulness, gentleness, and self-control ..." (Gal 5:22–23).

- Love leads to patience with others rather than criticism and judgment (one of the Spirit's fruits is longsuffering or patience with people). Thus Paul turned to the issue of fallen comrades in the faith. If someone stumbles into sin and it becomes known to the church, those who are spiritual are exhorted to restore such a one in a spirit of meekness (Gal 6:1). Of course, this prescription implies a repentant attitude on the part of the fallen person.

- No one is exempt from temptation or impervious to spiritual danger. Indeed, even in restoring a fallen brother the perils of pride are present. We are called to prove or test our own works and rejoice in them rather than in the failure of another (Gal 6:4).
- The principle of sowing and reaping is set forth in verses 7 through 9. It is certain that the farmer reaps what he sows—if he plants corn, he assuredly won't reap beans. The same is true in our lives; we are to sow to the spirit. Because of the certainty of this principle, Paul stated "Let us not become weary in doing good, for at the proper time we will reap a harvest if we do not give up" (Gal 6:9).
- He then wished peace and mercy upon all those who trust in Christ alone for salvation as he concluded.

Key verse: "May I never boast except in the cross of our Lord Jesus Christ, through which the world has been crucified to me, and I to the world" (Gal 6:14).

The Pauline Literature (Romans through Philemon)

EPHESIANS

The books of Ephesians, Philippians, Colossians, and Philemon are called the Prison Epistles because Paul wrote them while detained under house arrest at Rome (Acts 28:16–31). Ephesians offers a grand exposition of Christian truth, teaching the exalted position of the believer by the grace of God and the duties that accompany such a position. Chapters 1 through 3 deal principally with doctrinal matters, and chapters 4 through 6 focus on the walk and warfare of the believer. Paul clearly understood the inextricable connection between believing, behaving, and becoming.

- Chapter 1:1–14 deals with our exalted position "in Christ" in the heavenlies because of the grace of God. Following a brief and friendly greeting by Paul, the apostle reminded Christians of the great inheritance awaiting us in heaven, speaking as though we had already taken possession of it—and indeed, in God's sight we have—"Praise be to the God and Father of our Lord Jesus Christ, who has blessed us in the heavenly realms with every spiritual blessing in Christ" (Eph 1:3).

- Regarding the doctrine of election, verse 4 could be taken in one of two ways: (1) that each individual believer has been chosen before the foundation of the world to be holy and blameless before God in love, or (2) that God has chosen the mechanism of salvation to be his Son from before the foundation of the world, and that all who believe in him will be holy and without blame before him in love. Either way, the marvelous grace of God is necessary to redeem sinners.

- The prepositional phrase "in Him" or "in Christ" or "in the beloved" or "in whom" appears at least nine times in these opening verses, making it clear that only through our union with Christ are we redeemed and made right with God—"In him we have redemption through his blood, the forgiveness of sins ..." (Eph 1:7).

- Verse 13 offers us a chronology of the actual events accompanying salvation, stating that first we must hear the gospel, then we must believe on Christ, immediately after which we are sealed by the Holy Spirit of promise.

- The imagery of the seal is used twice by Paul in this letter, signifying both security and authenticity. It is used again in 4:30 when Paul says believers are sealed unto the day of redemption. This imagery and that statement strongly support the idea of the eternal security of the believer.

- Paul offered a prayer on behalf of his friends recorded in verses 15 through 23. Prominent themes of this prayer included a request for wisdom and knowledge about God, hope regarding the glorious inheritance awaiting us, and an understanding of the great power working for us and in us and through us—the same power that raised Christ from the dead. The prayer ends with a doxology praising Jesus Christ, the head of the Church (Eph 1:21–23).

- Chapter 2 begins by contrasting our unsaved and saved conditions, asserting that by nature we were all the children of wrath (Eph 2:3). But God intervened on our behalf because of his mercy and his love and rescued us even when we were dead in our trespasses and sins.

- A classic statement on salvation appears in Ephesians 2:8–9, which reads, "For it is by grace you have been saved, through faith—and this is not from yourselves, it is the gift of God—not by works, so that no one can boast."

- The rest of chapter 2 deals with the new unity among the Jews and the Gentiles found in Christ. Both are rescued in the same manner—through the great sacrifice of Christ for sins. At one time the Gentiles were aliens and strangers, having no hope and without God in the world (Eph 2:12). But by faith in Christ, they were brought near to God and have become fellow heirs with all the saints, being made members of the household of God.

- Paul asserted that the gifts of apostle and prophet were temporary, being foundational in nature. Continuing the imagery of building a house, Paul stated that Jesus Christ was the chief cornerstone. Just as Jesus finished his work, so the apostles and prophets have accomplished their work (Eph 2:20).

- In chapter 3:1–12, Paul defended his mission to the Gentiles, saying that in this new dispensation (which at one time was a mystery) God was bringing in the Gentiles by the gospel (Eph 3:2–6). Paul was given a special mission by God to go to the Gentiles and preach Christ.

- Life is ironic isn't it? Here we see a former zealous Pharisee, saved by the grace of God, sent to the very people he once loathed but now loved! The gospel changes things.

- Chapter 3 concludes with the apostle once again offering a prayer on behalf of his friends. The essence of his prayer was: (1) that they might be strengthened with might by his Spirit on the inner person; (2) that Christ might dwell comfortably in their hearts; (3) that their foundation would be love; (4) that they might know the immensity of the love of Christ, and (5) that they might be filled with the fullness of God (Eph 3:16–19). I find it interesting that Paul wanted them to know what he was praying for them.

- Some of the duties and responsibilities of believers, who enjoy the great privileges just announced, are set forth in the remainder of the book. Doctrine directs practice. Paul alluded to his captivity again in 4:1 (see 3:1), stating that he realized he was actually the prisoner of the Lord.
- A call to humility, patience, and unity appears first in verses 2 through 7. We have unity in the Spirit, and Paul called us to keep it in the bonds of peace.
- The resurrected Christ has bestowed gifts to his church, and they are to be used to strengthen it and build it up. In this case, Paul spoke of gifted people: apostles, prophets, evangelists, and pastor/teachers.
- The purpose of the pastor/teacher is to "prepare" the saints. This word means to equip them; it was used of mending nets in the gospels and of setting a broken bone in other literature. It carries the sense of making something strong and useful—being mature and fully functional.
- How is this accomplished? Col 1:28 tells us that it is through faithfully preaching the word of God to those with receptive hearts and ears.
- This is the main work of a pastor/teacher.
- As the saints mature under the hearing of the word of God, they become increasingly ready for various aspects of the work of the ministry. Thus pastor and people are all to be engaged in the work, all using our gifts for service, heading toward the same goal, becoming increasingly like Christ (Eph 4:13).
- As all the members of the body serve the body, it is built up and strengthened in love (Eph 4:16).
- He exhorted the Gentile believers against falling back into their former lifestyles (Eph 4:17–21). Instead, they were to "put off" the old self and "put on" the new one.

- This indicates the need for conscious action and decision on our part. The new life is neither automatic nor easy, but it is possible to live it as we choose to submit to the new nature.
- Paul concluded this chapter by urging Christians not to grieve the Holy Spirit (Eph 4:30–32).
- Chapter 5 continued his discussion of this new life. He urged them to "Be imitators of God, therefore, as dearly loved children" (Eph 5:1). We are to love as Christ loved us, having offered himself as a sacrifice for us. Immoral living is to be avoided, knowing that such actions produce the wrath of God upon the children of disobedience (Eph 5:6).
- We are called to walk as children of the light, reproving the works of darkness. We can only do this as we are controlled by the Spirit of God (Eph 5:18). The mandate to be filled by the Spirit is a call to relinquish control of our own lives to God and allow him to lead and use us.
- Once saved, we have the Holy Spirit. Filling pertains to control, not volume. We are not ordered to get more of the Spirit but to allow the Spirit to get more of us.
- We can interrupt God's work in our lives by quenching and grieving the Holy Spirit—in other words, saying no to his promptings.
- The imagery of wine is appropriate and instructive. Just as wine controls a drunkard, making him act differently, so we are to allow the Spirit to control and change us. This is a moment-by-moment decision of our will.
- A section on right relationships follows from 5:21 to 6: 9. We should all humbly defer to one another in appropriate settings (Eph 5:21).
- He then turned to wives, exhorting them to respect and honor their husbands, submitting to their authority. Husbands, in turn, should love their wives even as Christ loved the church and gave himself for it, sacrificing for the welfare of the wife.
- It is right for children to obey their parents in the Lord. Parents are the first authority children encounter; it is important they learn to respectfully submit to and obey parents. Yet, parents must be careful not to provoke their children with unreasonable demands and expectations.
- Slavery was a part of the ancient world and so Paul spoke to slaves and masters, not endorsing the institution but revealing that the Christian faith can be lived out in any social setting.

- Servants should honor their masters and serve them faithfully, knowing that the Lord will reward them. Masters should treat their slaves with respect and dignity, knowing that they too have a master in heaven. These are good principles to take into the workplace.
- The spiritual warfare of the believer is set forth in 6:10–18. Paul made it clear that we are currently engaged in an unseen but very real conflict with Satan and his army.
- Our fight is against spiritual wickedness in high places (Eph 6:12). And our enemies want nothing less than our destruction. Since they cannot sever us from the love of God in Jesus Christ, they seek to neutralize us, destroying our witness and ruining our lives. The devouring enemy wants to swallow us up in one of a hundred different ways. The devil has a strategy, and we need one too.
- We need to stand fast against our opponents, using the weaponry assigned by God. Paul exhorted us to be strong in the Lord and in the power of his might. The apostle used the actual armor of his Roman guard as an analogy to the Christian's system of defense. Putting on the armor of God allows us to stand fast against the attacks of our enemy, honoring Jesus Christ and accomplishing his work. But it is not automatic; we must take action.
- Paul spoke of the belt of truth, the breastplate of righteousness, the boots of the gospel, the shield of faith, the helmet of salvation, and the sword of the Spirit, which is the word of God. Interestingly, our weaponry begins and ends with Scripture.
- These provisions must be put on daily if we are to enjoy spiritual success. We don't win every battle, but we really can experience consistent victory as we war in God's strength. Thankfully, the ultimate victory is already won by the great work of Christ at the cross on our behalf!
- The book concludes with Paul requesting prayer of the saints that he might preach the gospel boldly as he ought to, alluding again to his bonds (Eph 6:18–21). Tychicus, a faithful friend, apparently delivered this letter to those in Asia (Eph 6:21–22).

Key verses: "For it is by grace you have been saved, through faith—and this not from yourselves, it is the gift of God—not by works, so that no one can boast. For we are God's workmanship, created in Christ Jesus to do good works, which God prepared in advance for us to do" (Eph 2:8–10).

PHILIPPIANS

Written under house arrest, Philippians is also one of the prison epistles produced by Paul from a Roman jail cell. It is a letter directed toward a group of believers with whom Paul felt great kinship and friendship. Paul established the church at Philippi during his second missionary journey (Acts 16:2). It was home to Lydia, with whom the missionaries stayed while there, as well as the Philippian jailer who was converted along with his household under Paul's ministry. You may recall that Paul and Silas were prisoners at that time as well, being rescued by an earthquake. It would seem jail time and the gospel sort of went together—like cheese and crackers!

- Paul was thankful for these dear saints, and his appreciation came through during his greeting. Unlike his letters to the Romans, Corinthians, Galatians, and Ephesians, Paul failed to appeal to his apostolic authority in the opening; there was no need to defend himself to these friends. Instead. he addressed himself as a servant of Jesus Christ.

- The church had developed nicely since Paul's initial trip, as evidenced by his recognition of both elders and deacons in the assembly (Phil 1:1). The saints are all those who have received Jesus Christ as their sin-bearing Savior, trusting in the risen Christ for forgiveness and salvation. This is why Paul addressed the entire church as the "saints."

- He expressed gratitude for their fellowship and confidence in their continuing faithfulness to Christ. In 1:8–11, he articulated his hopes regarding their spiritual growth: (1) that their love might abound with discretion and judgment; (2) that they might approve excellent things; (3) and that they might be filled up with the fruits of righteousness by Jesus Christ unto the glory of God.

- The apostle next alluded to his status as a prisoner, wanting his friends to realize that though things looked bad, they were really good! Paul's prison term had provided him with many opportunities to share the gospel with people he never would have met except for his confinement. He stated, "Now I want you to know, brothers, that what has happened to me has really served to advance the gospel" (Phil 1:12).

- Imprisoned in the capital, Paul was guarded by an elite group of Roman soldiers known as the Praetorian Guard. These crack troops protected the city and its officials from rogues and marauders and stood ready to battle any challengers, keeping order with a firm hand. These men guarded Paul—and listened to him as he shared the gospel with them. Clearly, some believed, and they in turn took the message further into the palace, penetrating even into the household of Caesar himself (Phil 4:22).

- Paul had a great attitude, seeing the good even in personally difficult and frustrating circumstances. Perhaps this was because his focus was so squarely upon Christ. The name Jesus, or Jesus Christ, or Lord appears some fifty times in this brief epistle of 104 verses.

- He realized that his confinement had other consequences, too. Some of the brethren gained confidence from Paul's willingness to suffer for the cause, speaking the word of God boldly. Unfortunately, others wanted to depress Paul and preached out of envy and jealousy. Even so, Paul rejoiced that the gospel was proclaimed, regardless of the motive behind the proclamation.

- Though imprisoned, the terms joy and rejoice are constantly employed by Paul, appearing frequently in the book.

- Paul explained that to be absent from the body was to be present with the Lord—and frankly, Paul was ready to go. However, he calculated that he would remain alive for a season in order to help build up God's people (Phil 1:21-24).

- The chapter concludes with an exhortation to conduct oneself in a manner worthy of the gospel of Christ—even in suffering.

- Chapter two opens with an appeal to live humbly with one another and to defer to each other rather than demanding one's rights. The motivation to do so was the example of Jesus Christ.

- In chapter 2:5-11, Paul reminded his readers of the gentle and humble countenance of the Savior of the world. This is the "Kenosis" passage in which we learn of Christ's great sacrifice: temporarily setting aside his glory to become a human being.

- Jesus not only became a man, but also a servant and a sacrifice for sin. He died the most reprehensible of all deaths for us, the death of the cross. He did not cling to his rightful position but instead willingly relinquished it for our sake.

- The mind of Christ is to be the believer's new model—a mind that sees others, serves others, and sacrifices for others. Indeed, the humble mind is the pathway to greatness in God's economy—"Therefore God exalted him to the highest place and gave him the name that is above every name, that at the name of Jesus every knee should bow, in heaven and on earth and under the earth, and every tongue confess that Jesus Christ is Lord, to the glory of God the Father" (Phil 2:9–11).

- Not wanting God's plans to be frustrated, he encouraged his friends to "work out" their salvation in fear and trembling, realizing that it was God at work in and through them.

- Christians are to shine as lights, offering a beacon of hope to the lost.

- Paul explained the plight of Epaphroditus in 2:25–30. The church at Philippi had apparently sent him to Paul to encourage the apostle, but he became sick and returned to Philippi.

- Paul wanted the people to know that he had been a great comfort and commended him to his home church with the highest of recommendations, "because he almost died for the work of Christ, risking his life to make up for the help you could not give me" (Phil 2:30). Paul also hoped to send Timothy to them.

- Chapter 3 opens with a warning to his friends to beware of the Jewish legalists who sought to confuse them about the gospel (Phil 3:2).

- They trusted in the physical mark of circumcision to make them right with God and demanded adherence to the Law of Moses. Paul countered their distorted teaching, asserting that we place no confidence in the flesh. Though if anyone could be justified by the flesh, Paul argued that he could.

- He then offered a litany of items true of himself and in which the Jews trusted: circumcised the eighth day, of the tribe of Benjamin, a full-blooded Hebrew, a Pharisee, a zealous persecutor of the church, and externally blameless. That list would impress any legalist.

- However, he went on to say that compared to the righteousness found in Christ, all those other things were nothing but rubbish—incapable of granting any real righteousness with God.

- Paul knew that one could not win Christ while trusting in works. No matter how sterling the pedigree, nothing but Christ could make one right with God. Paul wanted to be "... found in him, not having a righteousness of my own that comes from the law, but that which is through faith in Christ—the righteousness that comes from God and is by faith" (Phil 3:9).

- The apostle also realized that true transformation occurred as a result of personal communion with the risen Christ. Paul knew that he had not fully arrived spiritually, but he was pursuing this with great vigor (Phil 3:13b–14).
- He called the mature to pursue the very same goal. There are always obstacles to such pursuits, and Paul warned the Philippians against false teachers.
- The section concluded with a reminder of the return of Christ and the glory of the coming resurrection of the body (Phil 3:20–21).
- Two women in the church, Euodia and Syntyche, apparently had a feud, and Paul exhorted them to put their differences aside for their own sakes and for the sake of the church.
- One of the truly great counseling passages occurs in 4:6–7. If worry is one of your problems, memorizing this passage may prove helpful.
- Paul offered a great remedy to worry—prayer. This doesn't condone irresponsible behavior, but once we have done what we can do—and the issue (whatever it is) is beyond our control—we are called to pray rather than fret.
- Paul directed us toward wholesome thinking in verse 8 and offered a great teaching thought in verse 9, writing, "Whatever you have learned or received or heard from me, or seen in me—put it into practice . . ." Teachers not only dispense information but also serve as models for their students.
- Paul thanked the Philippians for their generous donation. Though Paul had learned to live with contentment in any situation, he was very happy to receive their assistance, not only because it helped him, but also because he knew his friends would receive a reward (Phil 4:17).
- In light of their generous gift, he reminded them that God would supply all their needs. God honors those who honor him and his work. The letter concluded with a warm farewell, in which Paul made it clear that his witness had borne fruit—all the way to Caesar's household (Phil 4:22).

Key verse: "For to me, to live is Christ and to die is gain" (Phil 1:21).

COLOSSIANS/PHILEMON

The book of Colossians was written by Paul to a group of believers he had never personally met (Col 1:7; 2:1). The church may have been founded by Epaphras, who is mentioned a number of times in this letter as a faithful servant (Col 1:7; 4:12, 13). This person was probably led to Christ by Paul during his stay at Ephesus. It is wonderful to see one's spiritual children leading others to Christ!

- Paul wrote this book to combat an insidious heresy that had invaded the Church at Colosse and which later developed into Gnosticism (from the Greek word "gnosis," meaning "knowledge").
- Early Gnostics believed that a chain of spiritual beings existed between God and earth and that Jesus was one of these lesser beings. They devalued his atoning work, arguing that a worship of angels and personal asceticism was necessary to acquire God's approbation.
- In rebuttal, Colossians exalts the person of Christ as thoroughly as any New Testament letter, claiming for him, in contrast to the heretics, all preeminence.
- Paul extended a warm greeting to the saints at Colosse, of whose faith he had heard through Epaphras. Once informed about their faith, Paul prayed regularly for them.
- As in Ephesians, Paul informed them of the content of his prayer: that they might have knowledge and wisdom, that they would walk worthy, that they would be fruitful, that they would be strong in the Lord, that they would be thankful, and that they would embrace their freedom from the power of darkness to live for God.
- Much of Colossians sounds quite similar to Ephesians. For instance, in 1:14, Paul wrote of Christ, "In whom we have redemption, the forgiveness of sins." This sounds a lot like Ephesians 1:7.
- In 1:15–23, Paul set forth the preeminent glory of Jesus Christ in contrast to the false teaching of the heretics. Paul stated that all things were created by him and for him and that he is above all things (Col 1:16–17). Some have wrongly imagined that Christ was also a created being based upon Paul's use of the term "firstborn" in verse 15.
- The term "prototokos" may refer to priority of position rather than origin, meaning he is the greatest of all. This interpretation is in complete accord with the context, which goes on to assert that Jesus

created all things, is before all things, holds all things together, and is the head of the church. The emphasis throughout is on his exalted position.

- Through the "blood of his cross," he has reconciled all believers, making peace with those who were at one time alienated and enemies of God. Through his sacrificial death we have become "holy and unblameable and unreproveable in his sight!"

- Paul expressed his love and concern for Gentile believers and explained his work in the ministry, "We proclaim him, admonishing and teaching everyone with all wisdom, so that we may present everyone perfect in Christ" (Col 1:28). The word "perfect" does not mean sinless, but rather mature. This was the apostle's great labor and God's great commission to him (Col 1:29).

- While the Gnostics claimed to possess secret knowledge, Paul contended that all the treasures of wisdom and knowledge are in Christ (Col 2:3).

- We are offered insight into the kind of false philosophy infiltrating Colosse in chapter 2. It involved following dietary restrictions and keeping special days (Col 2:16), worshipping angelic beings (Col 2:18), and other ascetic practices (touch not, taste not, handle not—2:21). These kinds of practices look spiritual, but they do not make one right with God—instead, they only satisfy the flesh (Col 2:23).

- Religious rituals of whatever kind appeal to the pride of the human heart.

- In stark contrast to such ideas, Paul reminded his friends that they are complete in Christ (Col 2:9–10).

- Faith in the crucified and risen Christ alone makes a sinner right with God—nothing else (Col 2:14). As a matter of fact, in his great cross work, Christ completely overwhelmed spiritual forces of darkness, making a public spectacle out of them after the resurrection (Col 2:15).

- Colossians 3 begins with an exhortation to think about eternal things. In light of our glorious future, let us live like citizens of heaven while on earth, Paul urged.

- The rest of Colossians 3 sounds strikingly like Ephesians chapter 5, aligning with it in almost every important way.

- First, Paul exhorted his readers to reject worldliness, asserting that for these things the wrath of God is revealed against the children of disobedience (Col 3:5–6).
- Next, Paul encouraged believers to put off the old man and put on the new man (Col 3:8–15).
- A section outlining relationships appears next in which Paul offered the same commands as in Ephesians to husbands, wives, children, servants, and masters, though with some minor differences (Col 3:18—4:1).
- Paul requested the prayers of his friends, that many opportunities to witness might present themselves to him and that he might speak the gospel clearly and boldly.
- In the same manner, Paul exhorted his friends to be ready to speak for God when the door opened. Make sure your speech is seasoned with salt, he told them, and be wise, redeeming the time.
- In 4:7–18, Paul mentioned a number of friends and associates in the work of the gospel, most particularly Tychicus and Onesimus, who probably delivered the epistle for Paul. Of course, Onesimus was the runaway slave who Paul led to Christ and sent back to his master, Philemon.
- He also named Epaphras, who was a great prayer warrior on behalf of the Colossians (Col 4:12–13). Prayer is a wonderful and necessary ministry.
- Luke and Demas also sent their greetings to those in Colosse. Sadly, we read about the defection of Demas in 2 Timothy 4:10. Paul had apparently already forgiven Mark for his premature departure on the first missionary journey, commending him to the Colossian believers (Col 4:10).
- Paul wanted his letter to the Colossians to be read at the church in Laodicea and the Laodicean letter to be read at Colosse. It seems likely that the Laodicean epistle to which Paul alluded is the letter to the Ephesians, since Ephesus was in the general vicinity of Laodicea.
- Lastly, Paul encouraged Archippus to take heed to the ministry he received from the Lord, that he would fulfill it (Col 4:17). He then closed the letter, asking for prayer for his time in prison.

Key verse: "For by him all things were created: things in heaven and on earth, visible and invisible, whether thrones or powers or rulers or authorities; all things were created by him and for him" (Col 1:16).

The Pauline Literature (Romans through Philemon)

PHILEMON

The Letter to Philemon was also written by Paul during his Roman imprisonment. The occasion for writing was to advocate on behalf of Onesimus, a runaway slave, with his former master. Onesimus, an escaped slave, met Paul in Rome, and the apostle led him to Christ (v. 10). He then encouraged Onesimus to return to Philemon, a wealthy citizen of Colosse. In order to smooth the return, Paul wrote the letter to Philemon, a masterful little piece of diplomacy in which Paul asked Philemon to lovingly receive the escaped slave, who was now a brother in the Lord.

- After assuring Philemon of his prayers, Paul expressed the purpose of his letter—to ask a favor. He asked Philemon to deal gently with the returning slave (v. 10).
- Paul said that he would have kept Onesimus with him to help in his imprisonment, but that he did not want to infringe on the rights of Philemon. Therefore, Paul sent him back, hoping that he would be received with kindness. Perhaps his escape was providential, Paul suggested, "Perhaps the reason he was separated from you for a little while was that you might have him back for good—no longer as a slave, but better than a slave, as a dear brother. He is very dear to me but even dearer to you, both as a man and as a brother in the Lord." (v. 15-16).
- Paul urged Philemon to put any wrong incurred in this escape on his account and he would repay it, though he was quick to remind Philemon that he owed Paul his very life (v. 17-19).
- Paul closed by saying that he soon hoped to come and stay with his old friend following his confinement—implying that he hoped all would be peaceful and happy when he arrived. He then closed his appeal, including greetings from a number of fellow workers in the gospel.

1 AND 2 THESSALONIANS

Both 1 and 2 Thessalonians were written by Paul very early in his ministry, being among the first of his inspired writings. He penned 1 Thessalonians shortly after he founded the Church at Thessalonica, as recorded in Acts 17:1–10. Incredibly, Paul ministered in Thessalonica for less than one month. He preached in the synagogue there on three consecutive Sabbaths, but because of persecution, he was forced to leave. In this abbreviated time span, Paul not only led this fledgling group to Christ, but he also taught them many important doctrines, most particularly about the second advent of Christ and the rapture of the Church. Indeed, the return of Christ and the rapture are both prominent themes in these letters, such that every chapter in both 1 and 2 Thessalonians contains a reference to the return of the Lord.

1 THESSALONIANS

- Upon hearing of their steadfast faith and continuing questions from Timothy (1 Thess 3:1–3), Paul wrote them this letter, in which he sought to encourage, comfort, and instruct them more fully—especially about things to come.

- Paul offered thanks for them as he opened, citing three reasons for his appreciation: (1) their work of faith; (2) their labor of love; and (3) their patience of hope (1 Thess 1:3). These phrases might be translated as: their work, which was the product of faith; their love, which labored; and their endurance, produced by hope. These qualities are vital for all believers to possess, and Paul was surely happy that such qualities were apparent at Thessalonica.

- The gospel erupted powerfully in Thessalonica as the Spirit of God moved among these early converts (1 Thess 1:5). The result was that these new believers became followers of Paul and his missionary team, becoming examples of the faith to others in the region (1 Thess 1:8).

- Their transformation resulted in their turning to God from idols to serve the true God and "to wait for his Son from heaven, whom he raised from the dead—Jesus, who rescues us from the coming wrath" (1 Thess 1:10).

- Chapter 2:1–12 is a general call to walk worthy of the new calling. Paul used himself and the other members of his team as examples worthy of emulation by the Thessalonians (2:1–11).

- Paul next contrasted the openness of the Thessalonians with the stubbornness of his own countrymen, the Jews. The Thessalonians had received their words as the very words of God—which indeed they were (1 Thess 2:13), while the Jews had repeatedly resisted God's messengers, the prophets, killing and persecuting them (1 Thess 2:14–15). Indeed, these same people were prohibiting Paul from speaking forth the gospel to the Gentiles, provoking the wrath of God (1 Thess 2:16).

- The enemy had hindered Paul in his quest to return and visit his friends, but he continued to rejoice in them (1 Thess 2:19–20).

- Paul addressed one of the key questions the Thessalonians had asked his young associate, Timothy. They wondered if they were currently in the tribulation period of which Paul spoke, since they were experiencing various trials, most especially a rash of deaths among the believers.

- Paul did not answer their inquiry fully until chapters 4 and 5, but the rest of chapter 3 is filled with thankful sentiments toward his friends, including a reminder that Paul and his company were praying earnestly for their faith (1 Thess 3:9–13).

- The first part of chapter 4 contains several exhortations to right living, including a call to abstain from fornication (1 Thess 4:3–7). Perhaps some reasoned that immorality was of little importance since the body was of secondary concern to God. Paul urged that this was incorrect (1 Thess 4:8).

- He also mandated hard work and industry among the people of God, in which they responsibly cared for their own concerns without meddling in the affairs of others (1 Thess 4:9–12).

- First Thess 4:13–18 offers what is surely one of the most comforting of all passages regarding believers and death, offering us a glimpse of the coming rapture of the Church.

- A number of saints had recently passed away at Thessalonica, causing both grief and concern among the assembly. Were the survivors in the Tribulation? Paul offered a touching and incisive response to their angst, comforting his friends with the truth of end-time doctrine.

- Paul offered them three comforting words: a comforting word of rest, a comforting word of resurrection, and a comforting word of reunion.
- First, Paul addressed those who had died in Christ as those who had fallen asleep (1 Thess 4:13–15). By this he did not intend to say that the dead in Christ were experiencing some sort of soul sleep. Sleep is a euphemism for death, indicating a peaceful existence free from all pain or distress.
- At the moment of death, the soul of the believer enters into the presence of the Lord (see also Phil 1:23; 2 Cor 5:1, 8). At the rapture of the church, soul and body are reunited together and glorified.
- The bodies of the dead in Christ will be raised first, and then those who are still living on earth will be translated (in a moment—in the twinkling of an eye) and glorified as they rise to meet the Lord in the air (1 Thess 4:16–17).
- Last, Paul spoke of a grand reunion between those who had passed on and those yet living—the likes of which this world has never witnessed. Glorified and reunited, the Bride of Christ, his Church, will finally receive her rewards and dwell eternally in the presence of her King!
- No wonder Paul wrote, "Therefore, encourage each other with these words" (1 Thess 4:18).
- Paul continued to assure them in chapter 5 that they were not experiencing the Great Tribulation.
- The Day of the Lord, which will come unexpectedly, had not yet arrived.
- You may remember the term "the Day of the Lord" or "that day" from the prophets. It will be a day of great vengeance and judgment, as the wrath of God will be poured out upon all mankind.
- However, God has not appointed believers to go through this period of wrath. Instead, we will be spared from it, according to 1 Thessalonians 5:9.
- Final exhortations follow from 5:12–22. First, he urged the brethren to honor those in spiritual authority over them (1 Thess 5:13).
- Next, among other things, Paul encouraged them to rejoice, remain prayerful, and be thankful in everything (1 Thess 5:16–18). Notice

that Paul said be thankful "in," not "for" everything. (Little prepositions make a big difference in meaning.)

- After requesting prayer himself, Paul charged that this letter be read to all the holy brethren.

Key verse: "For the Lord himself will come down from heaven, with a loud command, with the voice of the archangel and with the trumpet call of God, and the dead in Christ will rise first" (1 Thess 4:16).

2 THESSALONIANS

- In many respects, 2 Thessalonians is a continuation of the first letter, written shortly after it. The Thessalonian believers were still confused about the Day of the Lord, wondering if it was upon them. This was particularly unsettling to them, since they had been taught to expect deliverance from it.

- The key issue emerges in chapter 2 where Paul wrote, "Concerning the coming of our Lord Jesus Christ and our being gathered to him, we ask you, brothers, not to become easily unsettled or alarmed by some prophecy, report or letter supposed to have come from us [apparently a forged letter had also served to upset them], saying that the day of the Lord has already come" (2 Thess 2:1–2).

- Paul clarified what must occur before the Day of the Lord arrived: (1) there would be a great falling away or apostasy; (2) the man of sin must be revealed (the antichrist); (3) this person will establish himself as God and defame the temple with his presence, claiming deity; and (4) that which restrains the power of evil must removed. Many believe that this refers to the indwelling Holy Spirit in the Church, meaning that the people who comprise the Church will be removed via the rapture.

- The Lord will destroy this deceiver with the splendor of his coming (2 Thess 2:8). But antichrist will deceive much of the world with lying wonders and signs and miracles. Remember that miracles are not the exclusive domain of God. The enemy deceptively uses them also. The test of truth is not miracles but the word of God.

- God will send a strong delusion upon those who refuse the truth, that they might believe a lie. These will receive damnation and judgment along with the antichrist (2 Thess 2:11–12).

- In stark contrast, believers will stand safely with the Lord when he returns (2 Thess 1:8–10).

- Deliverance from jeopardy and judgment are prominent themes in the Thessalonian letters. Those who know Christ are safe.

- Paul asked for prayer that the word of God might be effective and that he and his friends might be kept safe from enemies and opponents.

- Twice as he concluded his letter, he exhorted his friends to withdraw from disorderly brethren (2 Thess 3:9, 14), however, he said they should not treat them as enemies but admonish them as brothers.

What constituted "disorderly conduct"? In this case, it included refusing to work, freeloading off of other people, and intruding into concerns that did not really concern them (2 Thess 3:6–11).

- Scripture consistently endorses a strong work ethic and sternly rebukes laziness: "For even when we were with you, we gave you this rule: 'If a man will not work, he shall not eat'" (2 Thess 3:10).
- Paul concluded his letter wishing peace from the Lord Jesus Christ to be with his friends (2 Thess 3:16).

Key verse: "May our Lord Jesus Christ himself and God our Father, who loved us and by his grace gave us eternal encouragement and good hope, encourage your hearts and strengthen you in every good deed and word" (2 Thess 2:16–17).

1 TIMOTHY

The pastoral letters are 1 and 2 Timothy and Titus. They were penned by Paul near the end of his life and were written to two young pastors, explaining matters related to church order, polity, and doctrine. As more churches were established, more and more questions arose about how things should function in the assembly. These are the only epistles that concentrate on the specifics of these issues and thus represent an important source of inspired information on church life. Many things we might expect to be included are omitted, such as style of music and order of service—whew! Such things Paul considered rather peripheral. However, other issues, like the importance of teaching the word of God and establishing appropriate church leadership, are discussed at some length.

- Unlike most of his letters, Paul wrote not to a church or a group of churches but to a particular person, "To Timothy my true son in the faith . . ." (1 Tim 1:2). Does this indicate that Paul led Timothy to Christ? Probably not, since according to Acts 16:1–3, Timothy was already active in the church and received a strong letter of reference from its leaders. More probably it means that Paul had a close friendship with this younger man and thought of him as a father thinks of his son. Since Paul was a bachelor, he had no children of his own.

- Paul urged Timothy to assess teachers and make certain that they taught sound doctrine. Some, the apostle feared, wanted the position of teacher without possessing the qualifications to fulfill this vital calling (1 Tim 1:7)

- Paul reminded Timothy of his own personal testimony and of some of the challenges still facing the apostle. Christ himself had placed Paul into the ministry entrusting the gospel to his care. Paul marveled over this, since by his own admission he was a terrible blasphemer and persecutor of the church.

- Indeed, this confession indicates Paul's firm belief in the deity of Christ, for surely as a dedicated Pharisee, Paul never blasphemed God the Father. He can only be referring to his words and actions against Jesus.

- Paul was the recipient of great mercy, a truth of which he was very much aware, "Here is a trustworthy saying that deserves full acceptance: Christ Jesus came into the world to save sinners—of whom I am the worst" (1 Tim 1:15).

- This led him to compose a brief doxology to the glory of God, after which he turned to a mandate to Timothy—that his young protégé might war a good warfare and hold fast to the faith.
- Some, Paul noted, had capitulated. He then mentioned two such people who were no doubt familiar to Timothy, Hymenaeus and Alexander. These two Paul delivered unto Satan that they might learn not to blaspheme (1 Tim 1:20).
- Wrong doctrine is like a disease that destroys and spreads (2 Tim 2:16–18).
- Paul exhorted Timothy to keep praying for the souls of men, most particularly those in authority. Pray also that believers might be able to lead a quiet, peaceable, and godly life, Paul wrote (1 Tim 2:2).
- Paul clearly indicated that God wants all men to be saved. Jesus is the mediator between God and human beings, Paul stated. His ransom paid the sin debt entirely and is the only means whereby we are forgiven and made right with God. Of this glorious message, Paul was ordained a preacher, an apostle, and a teacher of the Gentiles (1 Tim 2:7).
- From verses 9 to 15, Paul spoke to the role of women generally and particularly to their demeanor in the church. Modesty is an abiding principle for godly women (1 Tim 2:9). One can be stylish and modest.
- Good works of various kinds should also be evident among believing women. Paul did not want women to teach men or to usurp male authority in the church. His rationale is a bit difficult to follow, but it goes like this: Adam was formed first and then Eve, and Adam was not deceived in the transgression, but Eve was deceived. Is Paul claiming some form of innate difference between male and female? It appears so.
- A rather ambiguous passage appears at the conclusion of the chapter in which Paul states that "women shall be saved through childbearing . . . ." Obviously this does not mean that women receive spiritual salvation by having children. So what does it mean?
- Well, some commentators believe that it means women find their greatest fulfillment in the home and raising a family rather than having positions of authority in the church. Others think it means

that women are sanctified by childbearing and its subsequent responsibilities.

- In chapter 3, Paul turned from the role of the woman to the role of qualified men to lead the church. In 3:1–10 (as well as in Titus 1:5–9) qualifications for elders are set forth (the terms bishop and elder are used of the same office).

- The character of life is emphasized above particular gifts or skills. However, clearly some elders were called to teach while others served as administrative overseers (1 Tim 5:17). In general, elders must be faithful men with good judgment, temperate, having their household under good control, and mature in the faith.

- Qualifications for the office of a deacon appear next, with an emphasis once more upon character and faithfulness—dependability and level headedness.

- The wives of both elders and deacons must be women of good character as well, not gossips or slanderers (1 Tim 3:11).

- The key verse of the book is 1 Timothy 3:15, which reads, "… You will know how people ought to conduct themselves in God's household, which is the church of the living God, the pillar and foundation of the truth."

- Chapter 4 opens with a warning that in the end times a general falling away in the church will occur, as people give heed to seducing spirits and doctrines of devils (1 Tim 4:1). Some of their false teaching will include forbidding people to marry and placing undue emphasis on dietary restrictions; we have encountered such problems before. Paul's prescription to such misguided doctrine was to "refuse it" (1 Tim 4:7).

- Limited atonement doctrine seems refuted by what Paul says next, "… We have put our hope in the living God, who is the Savior of all men, and especially of those who believe" (1 Tim 4:10). Paul's statement suggests that God will save anyone and does in fact save all those who believe the gospel.

- Once again Timothy was commanded to teach faithfully (1 Tim 4:11).

- Though young, Paul cautioned Timothy not to let his youth prevent him from fulfilling his calling. Rather, Paul urged him to be an example of the believer to others and give himself fully to his ordination calling (1 Tim 4:12–16). The verbs in this section are forceful: neglect not, be diligent, watch, and persevere.

- In chapter 5, Paul explained that we are to treat the older men as fathers, the older women as mothers, and the younger women as sisters. He also offered a lengthy discussion on widows in 5:4–16.
- Undoubtedly, the church had acquired a reputation of being a compassionate community. Some likely tried to take advantage of that concern.
- Thus Paul spoke directly to it. First, Paul noted that if the widow had family members nearby, they should care for her (1 Tim 5:4). Paul had strong words for family members who abnegated such responsibility, saying, "If anyone does not provide for his relatives, and especially for his immediate family, he has denied the faith and is worse than an unbeliever" (1 Tim 5:8).
- A widow who the church was to assist had to be in genuine need, a faithful member of the church, one who had served the church, was at least sixty years old, a faithful woman, and of good report (1 Tim 5:5–10).
- Paul advised younger widows to remarry, have children if possible, take good care of their home and family, and refrain from using their free time to meddle in the affairs of other people (1 Tim 5:11-15).
- Paul iterated the need for family members to take responsibility in caring for their aged parents or relatives (1 Tim 5:16).
- The church does not have unlimited resources, and Paul wanted them to be used wisely, not frivolously.
- Paul turned again to some matters pertaining to elders in 5:17–22. Elders who fulfilled their responsibilities well were to receive a double honor, especially, Paul noted, those who labored in the word and doctrine (1 Tim 5:17). This probably referred to some form of remuneration (1 Tim 5:18).
- Accusations against an elder were to be binding only if substantiated by two or three witnesses. Positions of authority sometimes produce animosity and slanderous comments.
- If an elder has done something wrong, the others should rebuke him (1 Tim 5:20).
- This should be done fairly and without personal preferences clouding the issue (1 Tim 5:21).

- It is important to get to know people well before entrusting them to positions of authority (1 Tim 5:22).
- Paul then encouraged Timothy to use wine for medicinal purposes because of his weak stomach (1 Tim 5:23).
- Chapter 6 contains instructions regarding servants and masters and about money and material wealth.
- The unbridled pursuit of wealth is not the path to lasting happiness—quite the contrary, Paul stated. If God blesses us economically, let us be thankful and use it productively (1 Tim 6:17–18).
- Paul's charge is probing: "But godliness with contentment is great gain, for we brought nothing into the world, and we can take nothing out of it. But if we have food and clothing, we will be content with that" (1 Tim 6:6–8). I have never seen a U-Haul following a hearse!
- Instead of pursuing wealth greedily, Paul pointed Timothy in a different direction "But you, man of God, flee from all this, and pursue righteousness, godliness, faith, love, endurance and gentleness" (1 Tim 6:11).
- Paul concluded by charging Timothy before Jesus Christ that he would keep the commandment and be a faithful minister of that which had been entrusted to his care (1 Tim 6:13–21).

Key verses: "Don't let anyone look down on you because you are young, but set an example for the believers in speech, in life, in love, in faith, and in purity. Until I come, devote yourself to the public reading of Scripture, to preaching and to teaching" (1 Tim 4:12–13).

2 TIMOTHY/TITUS

Perhaps the most personal of all Paul's letters, 2 Timothy was likely the apostle's final epistle. Whereas in 1 Timothy Paul expressed hope of seeing his son in the faith shortly, in 2 Timothy he appears to be awaiting execution at the hands of Nero as "the time has come for my departure" (2 Tim 4:6). Still, Paul hoped to catch a glimpse of his dear friend before he went to heaven, hoping that Timothy would arrive before winter and visit him (2 Tim 4:9). Titus is much like 1 Timothy in tone and content, emphasizing as it does church polity and the role of women in the assembly.

- Paul opened with a warm greeting, addressing Timothy as his dear son (2 Tim 1:2).
- Paul greatly missed his young associate and yearned to visit with him once again. He also expressed thanks for Timothy's strong Christian upbringing at the hands of his grandmother Lois and his mother Eunice (2 Tim 1:5). Apparently, Timothy's father was an unbelieving Greek (Acts 16:1).
- Immediately following these endearing opening remarks, Paul offered an exhortation to his friend: "For this reason I remind you to fan into flame the gift of God, which is in you through the laying on of my hands" (2 Tim 1:6). This does not mean Paul magically bestowed a gift on Timothy. It likely refers to Timothy's ordination service in which the apostle had laid hands on him, identifying with his ministry and confirming his approval of Timothy's work of teaching, preaching, and leading the church.
- Timothy was not a natural born leader, as made plain by some of his character qualities: emotional (2 Tim 1:4), timid (2 Tim 1:7), sickly (1 Tim. 5:23), youthful (1 Tim.4:12—a problem that time eventually solves), and easily discouraged (2 Tim 1:8).
- However, he did have some great qualities, namely, a godly heritage, a gift from God, and a helpful mentor.
- Paul urged Timothy to be unashamed of Christ, offering his own testimony as encouragement to Timothy. Paul clearly differentiated between the gift of apostle, preaching, and teaching, stating that he had all three gifts (2 Tim 1:11).
- Paul was neither ashamed nor discouraged, though he had been deserted by a large number of believers in Asia. This occurred, no

doubt, at the envious promptings of Phygellus and Hermogenes, who Paul mentioned by name in 1:15.

- However, Onesiphorus sought Paul out at Rome and offered him refreshment—probably physical, emotional, and spiritual in nature. He was not ashamed of Paul's imprisonment. Paul prayed that his household might receive mercy from the Lord.

- As Paul had instructed Timothy in the things of the Lord, now Timothy had to continue teaching others. The faith is always just one generation from extinction. God's plan is that faithful men might transmit to other faithful men and so on. This probably referred to cultivating pastoral leadership in the church—developing pastors/teachers to lead other congregations in sound doctrine and living.

- This sort of faithful work requires endurance, Paul explained. He offered three metaphors that underscore qualities necessary for successful pastoral ministry: the soldier, the athlete, and the farmer (2 Tim 2:3–7).

- The soldier metaphor emphasizes courage and loyalty; the athletic metaphor stresses strength and integrity; and the farming metaphor expresses the need for endurance/patience. As Paul stated, pastors need to "endure hardship" for the cause of the work.

- Indeed, Paul recognized that trouble often accompanied the bold declaration of the gospel, but he was determined to endure (2 Tim 2:9).

- Right teaching is absolutely essential and the main pastoral work to be done. False doctrine is like a disease that spreads, confuses, and destroys. Thus Paul urged his friend, "Do your best to present yourself to God as one approved, a workman who does not need to be ashamed and who correctly handles the word of truth" (2 Tim 2:15).

- In contrast, the false teachers led people astray (2 Tim 2:16–18). Timothy was to oppose them and their wrong doctrine, though he needed to do so with a proper attitude (2 Tim 2:25–26), hoping to win them over to the truth.

- One of the best ways to deal with temptation is to flee from it (and don't leave a forwarding address!). While running from temptation, one should pursue other things like righteousness, faith, love, and peace (2 Tim 2:22).

The Pauline Literature (Romans through Philemon)

- Chapter 3:1–9 contains some of the most specific teaching about the character of the end times. As Paul noted, it will be most terrible indeed. People will be self-absorbed. Paul offered some twenty unflattering descriptions of the end time populace, most particularly that they will hate those that do good and that they will love pleasure more than God.

- It's not that they will be irreligious. No, they will have a form of religion—but they will deny the power of it. Thus they will have rituals but no gospel. Paul urged Timothy to turn away from these sorts of people.

- These are they who creep about from house to house and lead people into error and confusion (2 Tim 3:6). Peddling themselves as experts, they fail to ever really comprehend the truth. They are like Jannes and Jambres, who withstood Moses at some point. In the end, their folly shall be clear to all.

- Paul used himself as an illustration in contrast to such self-serving teachers, exhorting Timothy to use him as an example.

- The apostle refuted prosperity doctrine ideology, knowing very well that sometimes faithful believers will suffer, noting, "In fact, everyone who wants to live a godly life in Christ Jesus will be persecuted" (2 Tim 3:12).

- Even so, Paul encouraged Timothy to press forward and be faithful and obedient to his calling.

- One of the great texts on the divine authorship of Scripture appears next "All Scripture is God-breathed [the literal rendering] and is useful for teaching, rebuking, correcting and training in righteousness, so that the man of God may be thoroughly equipped for every good work" (2 Tim 3:16–17).

- Maturity is produced through the word of God.

- So concerned was Paul about the faithful preaching of the word of God that he formally charged Timothy before Christ that he would, "Preach the word; be prepared in season and out of season; correct, rebuke and encourage—with great patience and careful instruction" (2 Tim 4:2).

- Timothy was to do this even though some people would refuse to listen (2 Tim 4:3). The time will come, Paul warned, when people would not tolerate sound doctrine but after their own lusts will find teachers who will tell them what they want to hear.

- Realizing that his time on earth was short, Paul employed military and athletic imagery once more, announcing, "I have fought the good fight, I have finished the race, I have kept the faith" (2 Tim 4:7). Paul finished well; may that be true of all of us.
- The apostle was excited about his future reward for faithful service, thinking no doubt of the Judgment Seat of Christ to which he had often referred (2 Tim 4:8).
- Our hope of a future reward should motivate us to faithfulness in the present.
- Paul hoped Timothy would visit him soon.
- Indeed, Demas, a former ally, had defected.
- Only Luke was with Paul at this time. Paul asked Timothy to bring Mark when he came. God had not given up on Mark, and Paul now recognized the error of his original verdict, judging the young man too harshly.
- As winter was settling in, Paul requested a cloak, some books, and especially the parchments—perhaps some inspired writings (2 Tim 4:13, 21). The coppersmith, Alexander, had been a fierce opponent of Paul and the gospel. Paul warned Timothy about him.
- Paul testified of the Lord's faithfulness to him through everything, strengthening him to preach the gospel fully to the Gentiles. He dedicated his life into the strong and loving hands of the Lord, knowing that Christ would preserve him all the way to his heavenly kingdom (2 Tim 4:18). He offered final greetings to some of his friends, once again urging Timothy to "Do your best to get here before winter..." (2 Tim 4:21).
- We do not know if they ever had that final reunion on earth, because Paul was executed shortly after writing this letter; he was beheaded by Nero for his faith, refusing all opportunities to recant, trusting the Lord to preserve him unto his heavenly kingdom. Thankfully, these two surely had a warm reunion in heaven.
- **Titus:** The reason Titus remained on the isle of Crete was to appoint church leaders—elders. The terms elder and bishop are nearly synonymous, with the former referring to the person and the latter to their work of overseeing. Paul wanted Titus to appoint elders in the churches on the island of Crete.

- We discover that it is through preaching that God planned to make manifest his word (Titus 1:3), suggesting that one of the key roles of the elders was preaching.

- The qualifications for elders appear again in Titus 1:6–10, sounding very much like those offered in 1 Tim 3:1–7. The book of Titus stresses the teaching ministry of elders more than 1 Timothy, probably because Crete was known to have many false teachers and deceivers against whom the leaders would undoubtedly contend (Titus 1:10–16).

- One does not envy Titus in his assignment when we hear Paul describe the Cretians "Even one of their own prophets has said, 'Cretans are always liars, evil brutes, lazy gluttons'" (Titus 1:12). Paul agreed, saying, "This testimony is true. Therefore, rebuke them sharply, so that they will be sound in the faith" (Titus 1:13).

- In chapter 2, Paul outlined the proper work of older men, older women, younger men and women, and servants. Paul urged the elder women to teach the younger women to love their husbands and children, to take good care of their homes, and to honor their husbands' authority—challenging modern counsel.

- Paul wanted all God's children to keep anticipating the glorious return of our Savior Jesus Christ—the blessed hope. The gospel not only saves us from sin, but it should incite a zeal for good works as well (Titus 2:14b). Paul stressed the importance of maintaining good works—not to get saved or even to stay saved but because we are saved (see especially 3:1, 8, 14).

- Paul was not confused about the mechanism of salvation stating, "He saved us, not because of righteous things we had done, but because of his mercy. He saved us through the washing of rebirth and renewal by the Holy Spirit, whom he poured out on us generously through Jesus Christ our Savior" (Titus 3:5–6).

Key verses: "While we wait for the blessed hope—the glorious appearing of our great God and Savior, Jesus Christ, who gave himself for us to redeem us from all wickedness and to purify for himself a people that are his very own, eager to do what is good" (Titus 2:13–14).

7

Hebrews through Revelation

HEBREWS

The writer of the book of Hebrews is anonymous. This fact caused some in the early Church to question its inspired status. Genuine books of disputed canonicity are called the "antilegomena" books. Sometimes counterfeit books were circulated by deceptive writers hoping to advance their personal agenda, claming inspired authority. Church leaders correctly dismissed many such works as spurious. These books are called the "pseudepigrapha," or false books. Other times the internal nature of a book produced a certain amount of suspicion, leading some to question even truly inspired literature. Can you imagine any other New Testament books that might have been questioned for one reason or another?

The short list includes Hebrews, James, and Revelation. However, these books were all ultimately and rightly admitted into the New Testament canon.

- Speculation abounds regarding the author of Hebrews. Some suggest that the apostle Paul wrote it, and others argue for Apollos. Some contend that it was Barnabas, and still others suggest Pricilla. The fact is we do not know who it was.
- I think Apollos is a pretty good guess, since this book contains some of the most eloquent (and difficult) Greek in the New Testament and makes elaborate use of the Old Testament in its argument, and we know that Apollos was an eloquent man and mighty in the Old Testament Scriptures.
- The book was written to a community comprised of mostly Jewish Christians, some of whom appear to be vacillating in their faith and

considering defection back to Judaism. The writer feared that still others in the assembly had never actually received Christ by faith, and he urged them not to turn away.

- Whoever wrote this book possessed a masterful knowledge of the Old Testament and used that knowledge to seek to convince his audience of the superiority of Jesus Christ and the Church.

- Indeed, one of the important key words in the book of Hebrews is the word "superior." The writer employed comparison/contrast constantly to demonstrate that the good things of Judaism pale in comparison to the superior things of Christ and the New Covenant message. Keeping this in mind can help the interpreter follow the argument of the book of Hebrews.

- From the instant the book opens, the author established the pre-eminence of Jesus Christ: he is the creator of all things, the express image of God, and the redeemer who purged our sins, and he has taken his seat at the right hand of God the Father. (The right hand makes reference to the position of power and authority).

- Furthermore, the Son is far superior to the angels, who are his obedient servants. Hebrews 1:8 is one of the great claims to the deity of Christ in which God the Father calls the Son God.

- It's comforting to know that one of the major aspects of the angelic mission is to serve those who shall be heirs of salvation (Heb 1:14)!

- Because Jesus is so superior to the angles, we should pay close attention to his message of salvation. If we fail to listen, there will be no escape (Heb 2:1–4). For if the word of an angel was reliable, how much more so is the word of the Lord?

- Furthermore, God confirmed the apostolic message, using signs and wonders and various miracles, affirming the way of salvation (Heb 2:1–4).

- Jesus became a man for the mission of redemption (Heb 2:9). Human beings, imprisoned by the fear of death, are delivered by Jesus Christ (Heb 2:14b–15).

- Having lived as a man, Jesus is a merciful and faithful High Priest for his people, understanding all our struggles. He graciously offers help for those who are tempted (Heb 2:17–18).

- Jesus is superior to Moses; that is the main argument of chapters 3 and 4. Moses was a faithful servant, but Jesus is the ruling Son.

- The writer then picked up on the wandering experience under Moses to implore his readers not to harden their hearts against the message of God. The wandering generation failed to enter the rest of the promised land. Our writer urged his readers not to make a similar mistake (Heb 4:10).

- Those who failed to enter in under Moses did so because of unbelief (Heb 4:6). Do not harden your own hearts against the better rest offered by Jesus, the author argued.

- The word of God is powerful indeed, the writer asserted, sharper than any double-edged sword. Thus let us respond in faith to the gospel. Wonderfully, our high priest is sympathetic to our weaknesses and calls us to come before his throne to find mercy and grace in time of need (Heb 4:15–16).

- One does not apply to be the high priest—one must be chosen. God chose Christ to serve in this exalted capacity. One of the major functions of the high priest was to offer sacrifices for himself and the people. However, in the case of Christ, he was the sacrifice—the perfect sacrifice. This point will be greatly stressed later.

- Those to whom the author wrote had been treading water. They should have been teachers but instead were still in need of basic instruction. It was time to move on to maturity, according to the writer. This thought led to chapter 6.

- Some of the most difficult verses in the New Testament are found in 6:4–6. On the basis of these statements, some have concluded that salvation is contingent and can be lost.

- However, I do not think that is the best rendering of this text. Of course, when confronting puzzling passages, we must bring our general knowledge of Scripture into the equation. There are many passages that seem to teach that once an individual is truly saved, he or she is a child of God forever (Eph 4:30; Rom 8:1; 1 John 5:13; John 10:27–29, etc.).

- I suspect this passage was addressed to those who had been in the church for some time but had as yet failed to accept Christ. They were teetering on the brink, and the writer was seeking to instill something of the sense of urgency surrounding their delay.

- It is critical to note the following: (1) the main assertion is "it is impossible . . . to be brought back to repentance," and (2) the writer makes a distinction between the people of whom he spoke in verses 4 through 6 and genuinely saved people.

- As to number one above—the people of whom he spoke do not get saved multiple times. They turn away and don't come back. Their heart is gradually hardened over time against the gospel, and finally they reject it completely and walk away.

- The text says it is impossible for the people under consideration to repent—it does not say it is impossible for them to be saved. Indeed, all those who humbly turn to Christ for forgiveness are saved, but these people do not turn to him—they harden their hearts against him.

- As to number two above—after making these somewhat mystifying statements, the writer declared "Even though we speak like this, dear friends, we are confident of *better things* in your case—*things that accompany salvation*" (Heb 6:9; emphasis added). This implies that the writer made a clear distinction between those who were saved (of whom he thought better) and those of whom he spoke in verses 4 through 6—the not quite saved!

- It seems likely that he was speaking of those who attended the church but were not yet "in Christ." His hope was to warn them against delay.

- In chapters 7 through 10, Jesus was contrasted with Aaron and the Levitical priesthood. Jesus is far better. The writer first articulates the flaws inherent in the Levitical system: the priests could perfect nothing (Heb 7:11); they died (Heb 7:23); their system has been replaced (Heb 8:7–13); the rituals and furnishings of the Old Covenant were mere types of the true (Heb 9:1–10); their sacrifices could not remove sins (Heb 10:2–4); and their work was never finished (Heb 10:11).

- The work of Christ is far superior, he contends: Christ offered his own blood for our cleansing, not the blood of animals (Heb 9:12–14); His sacrifice perfects forever them who are sanctified by it (Heb 10:14); and Christ offered himself once and forever—no more sacrifice is ever needed (Heb 9:28; 10:12).

- In short, the writer argued that the work of Christ is perfect, finished, and powerfully efficacious to cleanse us from every sin forever (Heb 10:12, 14).

- Because of the absolute, total, and perfect cleansing we receive in Christ, we have direct access to the Father (Heb 10:19–22). We have the amazing privilege of entering into the holy of holies—the very presence of God—because of Christ!

- It is surely worth noting that under the Old Covenant, only the high priest had such a privilege and then only one day in the year. But believers can meet before their heavenly Father at any moment of any day because of the finished work of Christ on our behalf.
- Hebrews 10:26 has been a scary verse for many, demanding, so some assert, sinless perfection after salvation. Thankfully, that's not what it means. In context it means something like, if one willfully rejects the perfect sacrifice of Christ, choosing instead to return to Judaism, no sacrifice in that system is able to remove sins. Thus, there is nothing but a fearful looking toward judgment.
- The hall of fame of faith appears in Hebrews 11. The section begins with a brief definition of faith (11:1) and then establishes the superiority of faith over ritual and works. In context, the chapter is even more forceful, since it is the writer's attempt to convince his readers to either "hold fast" or "take hold" of faith in Jesus Christ.
- Verse 6 is the key verse, which reads, "And without faith it is impossible to please God, because anyone who comes to him must believe that he exists and that he rewards those who earnestly seek him."
- Genuine faith influences our actions—a concept much in harmony with what James asserted. The actions do not save us, but they reveal our faith in God and his word. For instance, by faith Noah *built* the ark, by faith Moses *forsook* the land of Egypt, etc.
- Chapter 12:1–3 is perhaps the best-known section in the book of Hebrews. These Bible heroes testify to us of the superiority of the life of faith. Thus the writer exhorted us to run our race with endurance, looking unto Jesus, the object of our faith.
- Considering Christ's endurance at the cross can help us endure too. He then urged his readers to accept the chastening of God, knowing that such discipline proves God's fatherly concern.
- Chapter 13 contains a number of final brief exhortations, such as the importance of marriage and the need to submit to legitimate spiritual authority (Heb 13:7, 17).
- We are called to offer the spiritual sacrifices of praise and thanksgiving to God. These offerings please God.

- The book concludes with a final wish for the readers' spiritual growth and maturity.

Key verse: "And without faith it is impossible to please God, because anyone who comes to him must believe that he exists and that he rewards those who earnestly seek him" (Heb 11:6).

THE GENERAL EPISTLES

The seven letters of James, 1 and 2 Peter, 1, 2, and 3 John, and Jude are often referred to as the General Epistles or sometimes the Catholic Epistles (not as in the denomination but in the sense of "Universal"). Unlike the Pauline literature, which was directed to particular churches or individuals, the General Letters were addressed to clusters or groups of people.

JAMES

- The book of James was one of the antilegomena books whose status was questioned by some in the early Church. The main reason for this concern was directed at the alleged contradiction of James with Paul's great message of salvation by grace through faith. Martin Luther supposedly considered James a "strawy epistle"—in other words, fit to be burned. However, the differences between Paul and James have been overrated.

- It is a matter of perspective between the writers. Paul emphasized the actual mechanism of salvation while James focused on the proofs attending genuine faith. Indeed, as we saw in Hebrews 11, true faith influences our actions. The actions do not save us. but they are evidences of saving faith. As James says so aptly, ". . . Faith by itself, if it is not accompanied by action, is dead" (Jas 2:17, 20, 26)—in other words, it is not real faith.

- James was the half brother of Jesus our Lord and thus viewed as the natural leader of the first-century church (as seen in the book of Acts and the activity at the Jerusalem Council). Apparently, James became a believer following the resurrection of Christ, who appeared to his brother in glory (1 Cor. 15:7). Wow—what a mind-blowing experience that must have been!

- James addressed his letter to the twelve tribes scattered abroad—so to Hebrew Christians in dispersion. Jewish converts to Christianity often experienced persecution for their defection, being ostracized from the community and generally viewed as traitors. This same theme is prominent especially in 1 Peter. Thus James began his letter, putting trials and suffering into their proper perspective for these displaced sojourners.

- In what is a grand paradox, James wrote, "Consider it pure joy, my brothers, whenever you face trials of many kinds" (Jas 1:2). We tend to be joyful when everything runs smoothly, with no complications. Why should we be joyful in trials? Because, James asserted, it is through trials that we develop perseverance or endurance (Jas 1:4).
- James urged believers to ask God for wisdom. Happily, God helps us when we turn to him in faith.
- A warning to the rich was offered in 1:9-11. Since wealth and life itself are fleeting, it is important to place one's faith in God, who is eternal, James exhorted.
- God will give a special crown to those who endure the trials and temptations of life (Jas 1:12). The hope of future rewards should influence present activity; that is not greed—it is faith.
- Neither should anyone blame God for temptations, since God is not tempted with evil and never tempts anyone to sin. However, God does test our faith—not to seduce us to fail but to approve our loyalty and faith. Many such examples of this are found in the Bible, such as Abraham (and the offering up of Isaac) and the calamity of Job.
- The real problem of sin emerges from our own lustful predisposition (Jas 1:14-15).
- His mandate, "Do not merely listen to the word, and so deceive yourselves. Do what it says" (Jas 1:22) is the theme of the book. Over and over James stressed the importance of actions commensurate with our profession.
- This led him to discuss true religion, which for James consisted of controlling our speech, visiting the destitute, and remaining unpolluted by the world (Jas 1:26-27).
- Showing partiality for selfish motives received a stern rebuke by James in 2:1-9. Instead, we should love our neighbor, rich or poor, as ourselves.
- One of the very important statements about the futility of law keeping is offered in 2:10, where James stated, "For whoever keeps the whole law and yet stumbles at just one point is guilty of breaking it all." Statements like this clearly indicate that James was not advocating salvation by works in his letter.
- He urged the need for an active faith—a faith that works because it is genuine. This was his point in 2:14-26. The repeated "a man may

say" (2:14, 15, 18) is a key to the kind of faith he derided—it is only skin deep, lacking real substance.

- Another clue to his complaint is in 2:19, in which he condemned mere intellectual assent, writing, "You believe that there is one God. Good! Even the demons believe that—and shudder." Intellectual assent is not saving faith.

- For James faith was more than head knowledge—some form of catechism—and it was more than something talked about; it influenced life. Faith that does not produce some change is dead, according to James.

- It is here that James turned the Abraham story on its head, asserting that Abraham was justified by works in offering up Isaac. The Isaac event occurred in Genesis 22.

- However, Genesis clearly states that Abraham was justified well before this. Genesis 15:6 says, "Abram believed the LORD, and he credited it to him as righteousness." Thus Abraham was justified long before he obediently offered Isaac.

- James was essentially saying that God rightly justified Abraham (Gen 15:6) because his faith was real, as evidenced by his obedience in the critical test of offering up Isaac. Abraham really trusted God, and his subsequent actions proved it. That is what James was emphasizing.

- Chapter 3 sets forth one of the most extensive discussions on the importance of controlling our speech anywhere in Scripture. Indeed, a little bit controls a horse and a little rudder steers a ship, and a little member, the tongue, is mighty indeed. It has the capacity to destroy and bless.

- Speech driven by envy and strife breeds destruction and confusion. Instead, let us use our words to build one another up and be at peace among ourselves, James urged.

- Evil speaking is an evidence of evil desires, according to James's continued discussion in chapter 4. Wars and fighting are unfortunately common among God's people. This saddened James. He attributed their cause mostly to selfish lusts that wage war in our members (Jas 4:2). He sternly rebuked his audience for self-absorbed praying (Jas 4:3).

- We do not know precisely what concerned James except it appears clear that an increase in worldliness was creeping in among the Hebrew believers.

- He reminded them that the Spirit in us wants to control us—but we must let Him.
- James counseled, "Submit yourselves, then, to God. Resist the devil, and he will flee from you. Come near to God and he will come near to you." (Jas 4:7–8a).
- If we humble ourselves before the Lord, he will lift us up. Part of humility is realizing our dependence on God. Therefore, we should not presume upon the future but commit our plans to God, trusting him to help us (Jas 4:13–17).
- Those who trusted exclusively in riches received a forceful rebuke from James in 5:1–6. "Your gold and silver are corroded. Their corrosion will testify against you and eat your flesh like fire ..." (Jas 5:3).
- Now there is nothing wrong with wealth honestly and industriously acquired so long as it is maintained with thanksgiving and used, at least partially, for the work of God.
- Wealthy people should not look down upon those less fortunate, and in fact, should have a generous and giving spirit, realizing that their wealth is a blessing and a trust from God.
- As the book concludes, James offers a charge to persevere in the faith. "As you know, we consider blessed those who have persevered. You have heard of Job's perseverance and have seen what the Lord finally brought about. The Lord is full of compassion and mercy" (Jas 5:11). Indeed, the need for a persevering faith is a recurrent theme throughout Hebrews and James and other General Epistles.
- The final few verses endorse the power of prayer and the need to pray for one another in terms of spiritual growth and physical wellness. If someone is sick, he may call upon the elders of the church to come and anoint him with oil, laying hands upon him and praying. The emphasis is upon the prayer of faith (Jas 4:15).
- James clearly believed that prayer changes things. Has it changed anything for you?
- He encouraged believers to seek to reclaim the wayward if possible; sadly, it is not always possible. However, if one does, one has covered a multitude of sins. The question revolves around whose sins—the backslidden or the counselor? Good question—perhaps both. James then abruptly closed his letter.

Key verse: "Do not merely listen to the word, and so deceive yourselves. Do what it says" (Jas 1:22).

1 AND 2 PETER

Peter wrote his first epistle to believers undergoing persecution and suffering and sought to encourage them to stand fast and take hope in the glorious future awaiting them. Indeed, God permits trials to come our way, but he wants to approve our faith through them and reward us for our endurance. As James wrote to the scattered twelve tribes, Peter addressed his message to the scattered strangers in Pontus, Galatia, Cappadocia, Asia, and Bithynia—large regions to the north and northwest of Jerusalem.

- Peter wrote his message from Babylon, according to 5:13, but some believe this is a term for Rome, emphasizing its decadence.

- From the outset of the book Peter sought to comfort and encourage these sojourners regarding their election of God and forgiveness of sins (1 Pet 1:2). He drew their minds to the mercy they had received, the resurrection of Jesus Christ from the dead, and their inheritance awaiting them on the other side (1 Pet 1:3–4).

- This inheritance is undefiled and incorruptible, reserved in heaven for them. Moreover, they were kept secure by the power of God through faith. This glimpse of the future was intended to bring the recipients hope.

- However, Peter also realized that their current condition was one of hardship and trial. Even here, he sought to give his friends an eternal perspective on these issues, writing, "These have come so that your faith—of greater worth than gold, which perishes even though refined by fire—may be proved genuine and may result in praise, glory, and honor when Jesus Christ is revealed" (1 Pet 1:7).

- This is a key verse explaining why God permits his people to suffer. He wants to reward us for our loyalty and faith. Only under adverse conditions can these qualities be fully examined and rewarded.

- Neither the prophets of old nor the angels understood the gospel—the sufferings of Christ for the forgiveness of sins, Peter asserted (1 Pet 1:10–12). But we do understand it and rejoice at the love and mercy of God for our salvation.

- We know the mechanism of redemption. "For you know that it was not with perishable things such as silver or gold that you were redeemed . . . but with the precious blood of Christ, a lamb without blemish or defect" (1 Pet 1:18–19).

- Since we do understand the great sacrifice of Christ for us, let us live as obedient children, striving after holiness. This was considered especially important in light of the brevity of life (1 Pet 1:24–25a).

- Peter used the imagery of the temple to argue that we are living stones in the spiritual house God is now constructing. Not only are we the stones, but we are the priesthood serving in the temple as well (1 Pet 2:5). Jesus Christ is the cornerstone (1 Pet 2:6–7).

- Those who believe are "a chosen people, a royal priesthood, a holy nation, a people belonging to God, that you may declare the praises of him who called you out of darkness into his wonderful light" (1 Pet 2:9).

- Peter concluded chapter 2 with a plea to live honorably among the Gentiles, submit to proper authority, and with a special appeal to servants to be obedient to their masters (1 Pet 2:11–19).

- In 2:21–25 Peter set forth Jesus as the great example of honorable suffering: he endured it patiently, and he was innocent of all charges.

- Let us then follow his example and rest in his care as the "… Shepherd and Overseer of your souls" (1 Pet 2:25).

- Peter exhorted wives to submit themselves unto their own husbands—even unreasonable ones. He argued that through a submissive and gentle attitude some husbands at least would be won over to the faith by the modest and loyal demeanor of their wives. Apparently nagging doesn't work very well! Husbands should respect and honor their wives as well (1 Pet 3:1–7).

- A series of other exhortations follow, most especially to do good and to be ready to suffer for the faith if need be (1 Pet 3:16–17).

- One of the most difficult sections of the New Testament appears in 3:18–21. Some argue that this section endorses baptismal salvation. It doesn't.

- Remember that Peter was offering comfort to Christians suffering for their obedience to God. Peter used the Noah illustration to confirm God's faithful deliverance from such antagonists.

- Just as the flood rescued Noah and his family from the hostile environment in which they lived, so too baptism rescues people from their former manner of life, serving as a point in time (at least humanly speaking) in which they choose to enter the church.

- The key parallel is between the flood and baptism, and the agreement is found in the establishment of a pristine new environment in which to live for and serve God.

- Since Christ suffered in the flesh, should we be surprised if we must do so, Peter asked. Besides, suffering has a cathartic character, he argued. "... He who has suffered in his body is done with sin" (1 Pet 4:1). This does not mean that sufferers are sinlessly perfect, but it does suggest that if we suffer for our faith, our conviction and commitment grows.

- Our unsaved friends will likely be surprised by our changed life in Christ and may well express their shock in derogatory comments (1 Pet 4:4).

- Don't give in to them, Peter urged, for they will give an account to the judge of the living and the dead.

- In light of the future judgment, remain steadfast in the faith, Peter continued. Be sober, prayerful, and fervent in love, for love covers a multitude of sins.

- Be hospitable and use your gifts to minister to one another, he told them. And don't "be surprised at the painful trial you are suffering, as though something strange were happening to you. But rejoice that you participate in the sufferings of Christ, so that you may be overjoyed when his glory is revealed. If you are insulted because of the name of Christ, you are blessed" (4:12–14a).

- If we experience suffering for our faith, we should commit the keeping of our souls to our faithful creator (1 Pet 4:16, 19).

- Peter offered an encouraging word to elders in 5:1–4. One might suspect that these leaders bore some of the brunt of the persecution. Peter exhorted them to keep feeding the flock (continue to meet and teach them the word of God), not for personal gain or as lords over it, but as examples. The chief Shepherd, Peter told them, will be sure to reward such loyalty (1 Pet 5:4).

- Deference to one another and a spirit of humility are also endorsed (1 Pet 5:5–6).

- The enemy would use hardship to discourage and defeat us. We must not let that happen, the apostle noted. "Be self-controlled and alert. Your enemy the devil prowls around like a roaring lion looking for someone to devour. Resist him, standing firm in the faith" (1 Pet 5:8–9a).

- Peter concluded his first letter with a wish that God would perfect, establish, strengthen, and settle them in the midst of their suffering. He then offered final greetings and closed his epistle.

Key verse: "These [trials] have come so that your faith—of greater worth than gold, which perishes even though refined by fire—may be proved genuine and may result in praise, glory and honor when Jesus Christ is revealed" (1 Pet 1:7).

2 PETER

The second letter of Peter has some similarities with 2 Timothy in that both writers appear to have been awaiting martyrdom (2 Pet 1:14). This book exalts the Holy Scriptures and offers a stern warning against false teaching.

- Peter informs us that we possess all we need for life and godliness through the Scripture (2 Pet 1:3).
- He also reveals that our faith in Christ is but the beginning of the Christian life, imploring us to add a number of important virtues to our faith (2 Pet 1:5–7).
- If we exhibit such qualities, we assure ourselves of having eternal life (2 Pet 1:11).
- Peter did not apologize for reminding his hearers of previously taught truths, noting the importance of repetition as an effective teaching device (2 Pet 1:12–13).
- Peter's message was no fable but was an accurate reporting of an eyewitness account. He referred to the Mount of Transfiguration, asserting that God himself offered clear testimony to Jesus as his Son. Though he heard a voice from heaven, Peter asserted that we have an even more sure word of prophecy in the Scripture.
- Thus Peter clearly equated the Scripture with God's word and endorsed its complete reliability, writing, "For prophecy never had its origin in the will of man, but men spoke from God as they were carried along by the Holy Spirit" (2 Pet 1:21).
- Chapter 2 is a warning against false teachers in which Peter used a variety of powerful images and Old Testament allusions to make his point. First, they deny the Lord who offered himself for them, so their heresy is works oriented. Many will believe their false teachings, appealing as they do to human pride. However, they will eventually receive judgment.
- Neither did God spare the wicked world in Noah's day. Sodom and Gomorrah testify further to the eventual judgment of those who treat God's Son and salvation lightly. These teachers are like Balaam, a typical prophet for hire who would say whatever brought him the highest price.

- They were wells without water, promising refreshment but delivering emptiness. They promised liberty but were themselves the servants of corruption. Indeed, they knew the gospel but had turned from it (perhaps akin to the situation about which the writer of Hebrews warned his hearers), becoming more inveterate in their sinful ways and awaiting greater judgment because of the light they had received but rejected.
- Peter likened them to pigs and dogs, which were considered among the lowest of all animals among the Jews (2 Pet 2:22).
- Chapter 3 is a reminder to his friends of the coming scoffers who walk after their own lusts. They taunt believers who hope in the Lord by saying: "Where is Christ? Why has he not returned?"
- Peter reminded his audience that time is inconsequential to the Lord. He will return at the right time. The scoffers said much the same to Noah before the flood devoured them. The day of the Lord will come as a thief in the night. The heavens will pass away with a great noise, and the elements will melt with fervent heat.
- Keep looking for the New Heavens and New Earth in which righteousness will dwell, Peter exhorted. Since all these things are temporal, be diligent to be found in him and unspotted.
- Peter elevated Pauline literature to the status of inspired writ in 3:15–16. Keep growing in the knowledge of our Lord and Savior Jesus Christ, Peter urged and then closed his letter.

Key verse: "For prophecy never had its origin in the will of man, but men spoke from God as they were carried along by the Holy Spirit" (2 Pet 1:21).

1, 2, AND 3 JOHN/JUDE

These four short epistles are devoted largely to combating heresy and doctrinal deviation of various forms. First John is the most comprehensive, but all the letters indicate the great concern uniformly expressed by church leaders against false teaching infiltrating the assemblies.

- First John begins in a way quite similar to the gospel of John. One is not surprised, since the three epistles of John were composed by the gospel historian. Jesus Christ, the Word of Life, was from the beginning. This eternal God is the very one who visited earth as a man. This fact was stoutly defended by John, asserting as he does that he heard, saw, looked upon, and touched this real person.

- The heresy against which John wrote was a pre-Gnostic kind of teaching that denied Jesus was the unique Savior of the world, contending that he was a lesser kind of deity.

- They also contended that the body was evil and thus deity could not really have become a man. Instead, he only appeared to be human; actually, he was a phantom of some kind. Thus they denigrated the life and especially the sacrificial death of Jesus. This doctrine is known as Docetism, which became an important tenet in later more advanced Gnosticism.

- Key passages in 1 and 2 John in which this concern appears include the following: 1 John 2:18-19; 2:22; 4:1-3; and 2 John 1:7.

- In light of the false doctrine confronting him, John set forth a number of important theological themes he wanted to emphasize: the very real problem of sin, the remedy for the problem in Christ, the need for separation from worldliness, the importance of looking for the return of Christ, the quest for brotherly love, and the comfort of knowing we have eternal life.

- Some pre-Gnostics argued that sin was itself a phantom, endorsing immorality and arguing that only the spirit mattered to God. However, John stated, "If we claim to be without sin, we deceive ourselves and the truth is not in us" (1 John 1:8).

- Instead of living in self-deception, John urged believers to maintain a close relationship with the Father via regular confession of our sins. "If we confess our sins, he is faithful and just and will forgive us our sins and purify us from all unrighteousness" (1 John 1:9). This is a wonderful verse to memorize.

- As the Judge, God is fully satisfied with the atonement of Christ for every sin. Believers are cleansed from all sin at the moment of faith in Christ and will never be charged with any of them before God as Judge (Rom 8:1). But as our Father, God is aware of our actions, and fellowship is broken when we sin. Thus the charge to confess is in order to remain "in the light" or in close fellowship with our Father.

- The theme of Christ's advocacy for sin continues into chapter 2, "We have one who speaks to the Father in our defense—Jesus Christ, the Righteous One. He is the atoning sacrifice for our sins and not only for ours but also for the sins of the whole world" (1 John 2:1b–2).

- The word propitiation is used twice in 1 John. It means to satisfy or appease someone, in this case God. The sacrifice of Christ has completely satisfied the righteous anger of God against sin toward all those who have received the Son.

- We know that we know God when we abide by his word (2:3–14). John especially stressed the need to love our brothers in this section. He then warned against loving the world. The lust of the flesh, the lust of the eyes, and the pride of life are not of the father but of the world—and the world is passing away (1 John 2:15–17).

- John then offered a warning against following the teachings of the apostate false teachers who apparently left the church to form their own assembly.

- From 2:28 to 3:3, John exhorted believers to keep looking for the return of Christ, asserting that when we see him we shall be like him and that this hope purifies all those who keep it. Of course, living in light of meeting the Lord does indeed keep us walking carefully and wisely.

- In John 3:4–24 John argued that those who know God should live righteously and love their brethren. Those who practice sin show themselves to be false. Instead, we should give heed to the commands of God, chief of which is offered in 3:23: "And this is his command: to believe in the name of his Son, Jesus Christ, and to love one another as he commanded us." This sounds nearly identical to John 6:29, 40 and 13:34.

- Chapter 4 warns against the heretics and exhorts believers to love once again. The motive behind our love should be God's great love for us. "This is love: not that we loved God, but that he loved us and sent his Son as an atoning sacrifice for our sins." (1 John 4:10).

Indeed, since God loved us in this way, we are challenged to show love to God and others.

- It is wonderful to know that God is not angry with us anymore because of Christ. And it is humbling to know that the reason he is not is because his precious, innocent Son willingly offered himself as our substitute and endured the Father's judgment for us at the cross.
- "Everyone who believes that Jesus is the Christ is born of God" (1 John 5:1).
- Chapter 5 begins with yet another exhortation to love God and the people of God. This passage also contains a great assurance section, indicating that we can rest in our salvation right now if we have truly received Christ as our Savior.
- John wrote, "And this is the testimony: God has given us eternal life, and this life is in his Son. He who has the Son has life; he who does not have the Son of God does not have life. I write these things to you who believe in the name of the Son of God so that you may know that you have eternal life" (1 John 5:11–13).
- Second John was addressed to the "elect lady"; this was either a well-known female Christian or most probably a way of addressing a church congregation. This seems particularly the case in light of the concluding remarks in the final verse "The children of your chosen sister send their greetings" (2 John 1:13). This likely referred to the members of a sister church.
- We are not surprised that the apostle of love also included a brief exhortation to follow the command we have had from the beginning "that we love one another" (2 John 1:5). He was delighted to hear that those to whom he wrote were living rightly (2 John 1:4). John hoped to either see this person or visit this congregation shortly and speak more with them at that time.
- Third John contains sparse information about three people: Gaius, Diotrephes, and Demetrius. Gaius was a good friend of the apostle, one to whom John offered warm greetings at the outset. Again John rejoiced to hear that many walked in the right path (3 John 1:4).
- A man in the church named Diotrephes rejected John's authority, loving the preeminence of leadership. Apparently, Diotrephes spoke maliciously against John and would not receive him or other Christian brothers. John warned Gaius against his evil actions and words.

- In contrast to Diotrephes was a man named Demetrius who was well reported of by all. John likewise commended him as a godly man. We can only speculate on what is going on here. Perhaps these men were both vying for leadership in this unnamed assembly and John commended the one above the other. In any event, John stated that he hoped to see his friends in the near future.
- Jude was another half brother of Jesus. His letter is a rather scathing missive directed at false teachers seeking to lead people astray. It was addressed to those sanctified by God and preserved by Jesus Christ.
- Jude challenged his audience to "contend for the faith that was once for all entrusted to the saints" (Jude 1:3). This was needed because of the intrusion of various heretical teachers. Their error seemed to be an endorsement of immorality due to the transient nature of the body and the eternal value of the soul. They were changing "the grace of our God into a license for immorality" (Jude 1:4). Sounds something like the problem in Romans 6 in which people abused the grace of God to continue sinful lifestyles.
- He used many illustrations and metaphors to condemn them.
- They not only "defiled the flesh," but they also spoke evil of authority (Jude 1:8). This is a serious sin. Jude used Michael the archangel as his illustration of respect. As he debated with Satan over the body of Moses, he said, "The Lord rebuke you!" (Jude 1:9). We are not given any further information about this mysterious confrontation.
- These heretics, however, were bold in their denigration of authority and spoke against things they did not understand. They pursued the way of Cain and ran greedily after the error of Balaam and Korah. These were wells without water, fruit trees without fruit, plucked up by the roots, raging waves of the sea, wandering stars reserved for the blackness of darkness forever, etc. Jude denounced these false teachers in many strong terms.
- But the lord will come to execute judgment against the ungodly, Jude assured his readers. He concluded by exhorting his friends to stay strong in the Lord and keep sharing the faith, even pulling some out of the fire.
- In a moving doxology, Jude commended them to the safekeeping of the only wise God our Savior and ascribed to God "glory, majesty, power and authority, through Jesus Christ our Lord, before all ages, now and forevermore! Amen." (Jude 1;25).

Key verse: "And this is the testimony: God has given us eternal life, and this life is in his Son. He who has the Son has life; he who does not have the Son of God does not have life. I write these things to you who believe in the name of the Son of God so that you may know that you have eternal life" (1 John 5:11–13).

REVELATION

The book of Revelation is the inspired account of the consummation of history in which the rebellious world is judged and Jesus Christ returns visibly and bodily in glory in order to establish his Millennial Kingdom on earth. The book closes with the creation of the New Heavens and New Earth following the Millennial reign. This represents the eternal state of glory. As the Lion of Judah, Christ conquers all his enemies, including Satan and his followers, casting them into the Lake of Fire. In Revelation, unlike in the gospel accounts, Jesus is seen reigning and glorified—powerful and majestic, receiving the glory, honor, and praise due to his holy name. Revelation teaches us that Jesus wins and all those with him share in his glorious victory.

- The book of Revelation was written by the apostle John. He received his message while an exile on the island of Patmos, a desolate and rocky piece of land upon which John wandered, eking out a meager existence (Rev 1:9). It was here that Jesus Christ appeared to John and told him, "Write, therefore, what you have seen, what is now and what will take place later" (Rev 1:19). A special blessing is offered to those who read and keep the sayings of this book (Rev 1:3).

- Revelation is addressed to the seven churches that were in Asia from Jesus Christ (Rev 1:5). John declared that when Jesus does return to earth, "... Every eye will see him, even those who pierced him; and all the peoples of the earth will mourn because of him ..." (Rev 1:7).

- The book makes great use of symbols and prophecies, making it difficult to understand in every detail. However, much can be discerned even from its often enigmatic passages.

- As John was in the Spirit on the Lord's Day, he heard a great trumpet blast and the Lord Jesus appeared to him in magnificent splendor. He stood in the midst of seven golden candlesticks (later identified as the seven churches [Rev 1:20]).

- He was glorified—hair like wool, white as snow, eyes like fire, and feet like finely burnished bronze. He wore a garment down to his feet and a golden breastplate. His voice was rich and resonant, like the sound of many waters. In his right hand he held seven stars (later identified as the angels of the seven churches [Rev 1:20]). Out of his mouth went a sharp, two-edged sword, and his overall countenance was as the sun shining in all its brilliance!

- We are hardly surprised to hear that when John saw him, he fell down as dead. Jesus placed his right hand on John and said, "... Do not be afraid. I am the First and the Last. I am the Living One; I was dead, and behold I am alive for ever and ever! And I hold the keys of death and Hades" (Rev 1:17–18).
- Chapter 2:1 to 3:22 records the Lord's messages to the seven churches in Asia: Ephesus, Smyrna, Pergamos, Thyatira, Sardis, Philadelphia, and Laodicea.
- It appears that these were actual churches in existence at the time of John's writing, though the lessons gleaned are applicable to all churches throughout the Church Age.
- To each is offered a commendation, except to the church at Laodicea, which was a tepid congregation (Rev 3:15–16). Jesus wished they were either hot or cold. To each is also offered a warning, except to the church at Philadelphia, which received only praise for their faithfulness to the word of God and Christ (Rev 3:8).
- Interestingly, Laodicea was rich by the world's standards but not in Christ's eyes, and Philadelphia was poor humanly speaking but was wealthy in Christ's sight.
- Ephesus was urged to return to their first love; Smyrna was encouraged to endure times of suffering; Pergamos was exhorted to deal with the false doctrine of the Nicolaitans; Thyatira was to confront Jezebel, a false prophetess who seduced some to commit fornication; Sardis received a mandate to "... Strengthen what remains and is about to die ..." (Rev 3:2). Only a few in Sardis had remained faithful. And the Laodiceans were commanded to become zealous again for God.
- We learn that Jesus is very much aware of what takes place in his church in whatever locale. He stands in and among the churches, assessing them and encouraging them to be faithful and zealous. The angels of the churches may be actual angels or the leaders of the churches. They are held in his strong right hand.
- The church is not mentioned in the section of Revelation in which the Tribulation is unveiled from 4:1 through 19:21. One would think that during such world-wide cataclysmic events, the church would be mentioned if it was present. The silence is deafening, suggesting that the church will be raptured prior to the Tribulation.

- The remainder of the book may be briefly outlined in the following manner: The Tribulation Period (Rev 4:1—19:21); the Millennial Reign and the Great White Throne Judgment (Rev 20:1—15); and the New Heaven and New Earth and the eternal state (Rev 21:1-22:21).
- The Tribulation Period is discussed from Revelation 4:1 to 19:21. It is important to keep in mind that the events from 4:1 and following are all future. A series of sevens characterizes this major division: seven seals (Rev 4:1—8:1), seven trumpets (Rev 8:2—11:19), and seven bowls (Rev 15:1-16:27). In between these sections appear various parenthetic scenes related to the Great Tribulation.
- Chapters 4 and 5 offer us a glimpse into heaven itself, immediately focusing upon God the Father as one seated upon a great throne. John's description is one of brilliance and incomparable glory. As he tried in human language to capture and explain the incredible glory before him, he appealed to precious gems.
- The one on the throne was like a jasper and sardius stone surrounded by an emerald rainbow. Twenty four seats surrounded the throne, upon which the elders sat worshipping God. They were wearing white garments and golden crowns.
- Before the throne was a sea of glass like crystal and four living beasts that announced, "... Holy, holy, holy is the Lord God Almighty, who was, and is, and is to come" (Rev 4:8). The elders too fell down to worship him upon the throne (Rev 4:11).
- God the Father held in his right hand a book sealed with seven seals that no one could open (Rev 5:1-4). John was very upset that none could open or read the book. However, one of the elders told him to stop crying, for "... the Lion of the tribe of Judah, the Root of David, has triumphed. He is able to open the scroll..." (Rev 5:5).
- Next John saw in the midst of the throne and the beasts and the elders a Lamb as if it had been slain. He came and took the book from the right hand of him that sat upon the throne. (Here we see the Father and the Son together in heaven.)
- All those in heaven, angels and saints, offered praise to the Lamb for his sacrificial death and great redemptive work throughout the world, making the redeemed kings and priests to God (Rev 5:9).
- In chapter 6, the first six seals are opened, creating war, worldwide famine, destruction of 25 percent of the world's population, martyrdom of many of the saints on earth, and natural disasters like

earthquakes and astronomical upheavals, such as falling stars. All this generates intense fear among the inhabitants of the earth.

- Chapter 7 is something of a parenthesis in which we have the sealing of the one hundred forty-four thousand Jewish witnesses (Rev 7:4). Indeed, this is Israel being grafted back in, just as Romans 11 described.
- Next is a scene in heaven of all the saints martyred during the Tribulation Period finding comfort and rest in heaven (Rev 7:9–17). Clearly, many people will be redeemed during the Tribulation Period, but many of them will die for their faith.
- The seventh seal was opened in 8:1, leading to silence in heaven for about a half an hour.
- From 8:2 to 9:21 the first six trumpets are sounded, bringing various judgments against the world. The trumpets were sounded by angels.
- The first trumpet produced fire and hail mingled with blood, destroying a third part of grass and trees. The second hurled a great mountain-like object burning with fire into the sea, causing a third part of aquatic life to die. The third trumpet sent a great burning star splintering into many pieces to fall into other water areas, turning the water bitter. The fourth trumpet created celestial signs, blotting out a third of the stars and a third part of the moon (8:7–13).
- The fifth trumpet unleashed hordes of stinging locusts upon the earth that had the power to torment men for five months. Those sealed by God were not hurt by these creatures. In these days, men would long to die but would not be able to die (Rev 9:1–12).
- The sixth trumpet unleashed four angels bound at the Euphrates River who were specially prepared for this exact year, month, day, and hour (Rev 9:15). They led an army of two hundred million strong (Rev 9:16). By these a third of the remaining inhabitants on earth were killed. Amazingly, the people of the world did not repent of their wickedness even in light of all these judgments (Rev 9:20–21). The human heart is very hard.
- Chapter 10 is another brief parenthesis in which we see that John was not permitted to reveal all that he saw. Here he was expressly prohibited from writing some of the Revelation he witnessed (Rev 10:4). He was told to eat the little book, which tasted sweet in his

- mouth but turned sour. The angel then told him to prepare to write again.
- The precise length of time in which the Gentiles would trample down the temple area was forty-two months—or three and a half years. This is the second half of the Great Tribulation Period.
- In this period of time, two powerful witnesses arose, testifying for Christ to the world. Their witness lasted for 1,260 days—or forty-two months (of thirty days each)—or three and one half years. The exact time period is stated repeatedly—it is forty-two months as stated in Revelation 11:2 and 13:5, and 1,260 days in Revelation 11:3 and 12:6. The Tribulation lasts for seven years (the one week of Daniel 9:27). It is further divided into two equal periods of three and a half years each.
- The witnesses were slain after their ministry was completed, and all the people of the earth rejoiced over their demise. They were so happy that they did not bury them but celebrated over their dead bodies. However, after three and a half days, the witnesses rose up, causing no small commotion on earth. They then ascended into heaven (Rev 11:11-12). At the same time a great earthquake hit, killing many.
- The seventh trumpet was sounded in 11:15, signaling the coming reign and conquest of Christ. Joy in heaven is starkly contrasted with the anger of the nations on earth at this event, for their judgment is at hand.
- From chapters 12 to 14, various important people or groups are identified. Chapter 12 introduces Israel as the woman who delivered the child (the Messiah) and is pursued by the devil, the great dragon. Satan will torment Israel for 1,260 days during the last half of the Tribulation (Rev 12:6).
- A war in heaven between Michael and his angelic army and Satan and his army is detailed in 12:7-12. The great dragon was cast down and earth bound, leading to his great wrath (Rev 12:12). So the dragon pursued the woman (Israel) and her remnant.
- The rise of the two evil beasts is recorded in chapter 13. The first beast, empowered by Satan, rises to power.
- He received an apparently fatal head wound but miraculously recovered. People will literally worship this beast as deity. All who are not written in the Lamb's book of life worship the beast.

- A second beast arises, working miraculous wonders. "And he performed great and miraculous signs, even causing fire to come down from heaven to earth in full view of men. Because of the signs he was given power to do on behalf of the first beast, he deceived the inhabitants of the earth . . ." (Rev 13:13–14).

- He also caused everyone to place a mark of allegiance on their right hand or their forehead so that no one could buy or sell unless they had the mark of the beast. The mark is six hundred threescore and six (Rev 13:18). It will require wisdom to understand the number of the beast.

- In contrast to these evil people, chapter 14 records the happiness and fellowship of the one hundred forty-four thousand witnesses in the presence of the Lord. They too have a mark, being sealed by the Father. They enjoy wonderful fellowship with God.

- Three angels are heard from. The first announced the everlasting gospel to those on earth, the second announced the fall of Babylon, and the third declared judgment upon those who worship the beast or his image or who take his mark. This judgment will be eternal and terrible. Chapter 14 concludes with a glimpse of Armageddon (more fully described in chapter 19).

- Chapters 15 and 16 discuss the seven bowl judgments of God upon the earth. These last plagues pour further judgment on the lost. "I saw in heaven another great and marvelous sign: seven angels with the seven last plagues—last, because with them God's wrath is completed" (Rev 15:1).

- John was offered a look into heaven just prior to the judgments of the seven bowls. The martyred Tribulation saints were singing praise to God, and one of the four elders delivered seven golden vials to the seven angels from the temple in heaven in which was stored the wrath of God.

- Poured out, the first bowl produced painful sores upon the people of the earth who had the mark of the beast and worshipped the image of the beast (Rev 16:1–2). The second vial poured out caused the sea to become as blood, creating widespread death and destruction. Likewise, the third bowl caused further destruction of various water tributaries, turning them to blood also. The fourth angel poured his bowl upon the sun, generating intense heat that scorched the people of the earth.

- In all this, the earth's inhabitants refused to repent, instead blaspheming God (Rev 19:9). The fifth vial seems to be directed at the beast and his ruling cabinet, producing painful sores upon them. After the sixth angel poured out his vial, the Euphrates River dried up.
- Once again Armageddon is foreshadowed as three spirits like frogs emerging from the mouth of the dragon, the beast, and the false prophet, luring the kings of the earth toward Armageddon (Rev 16:13–16).
- Then the seventh vial was poured out, producing great hail stones weighing about sixty pounds each. Their destructive force pounded the mountains flat and literally destroyed islands (Rev 16:20–21).
- Chapters 17 and 18 outline the destruction of Mystery Babylon. It is a difficult section to interpret. However, in chapter 17 the religion of Babylon is destroyed by the false beast, and in chapter 18 the city itself is decimated. On both counts, the question concerns the identity of the city.
- It is likely either Rome or actually Babylon. In chapter 17 we find that this Babylon has created a widely accepted religion—perhaps Catholicism, though that is disputed.
- Some of its descriptions suggest such an interpretation. "The woman was dressed in purple and scarlet, and was glittering with gold, precious stones and pearls. She held a golden cup in her hand, filled with abominable things and the filth of her adulteries" (Rev 17:4). This woman was drunk with the blood of the saints and martyrs of Christ. It had influenced the whole earth and is called the great harlot.
- However, in the middle of the Tribulation Period, the beast will destroy this other counterfeit system, demanding that the entire world worship him (Rev 17:14–18).
- In chapter 18, the actual city is destroyed, causing all the merchants of the earth to wail because business is lost.
- In chapter 17, the religious system emanating from the city is overthrown by the beast, and in chapter 18, the social and economic aspects of this city are ruined.
- Unlike the people of the earth, the citizens of heaven are found rejoicing over its demise (Rev 18:20—19:6).

- The rest of chapter 19 deals with the Battle of Armageddon. Here we find Jesus leading the armies of heaven to do combat with the beast and his armies. It is not a close battle—not one casualty is recorded on the Lord's side. In stark contrast, all his enemies are utterly destroyed. The conquering Christ is seen riding a white horse. From his mouth proceeds a sharp sword and with it he smites the nations and rules them with a rod of iron. And on his thigh a name is written "KING OF KINGS AND LORD OF LORDS" (Rev 19:16).

- An angel invited all the fowls of the air to come and dine upon the flesh of the vanquished. The beast and the false prophet were taken and cast alive into the lake of fire and brimstone. The rest of the armies are cut down by Jesus and his sharp sword (Rev 19:21). Indeed, the Lord of armies is the greatest of all warriors.

- Next, Satan is bound and cast into a bottomless pit for a thousand years, after which time he will be loosed for a short season (Rev 20:1–3).

- The saints will live and reign with Christ for a thousand years (Rev 20:4, 5, 6).

- After the millennial reign, Satan is once again loosed for a season and goes forth to deceive the nations. How is this possible? Who is he deceiving? It appears that those believers who manage to live through the Tribulation Period enter the millennium as human beings.

- These people will have families, bearing children. And those children will marry and produce more children. Over the course of a thousand years, a fairly substantial human population will emerge. When Satan is set free, he will go forth to deceive some of these people. Even in a perfect environment, one in which Christ is present; people will still rebel against the Lord. This surely demonstrates the hardness of the human heart.

- These rebels will follow Satan against the holy city but will be devoured with fire from God out of heaven. Thus human and satanic rebellion against God will finally cease. This event leads to the Great White Throne Judgment as recorded in 20:11–15.

- The devil that deceived the human rebels will be cast into the lake of fire where the beast and false prophet are and will be tormented day and night forever and ever (Rev 20:10). After this all the lost dead are assembled for their final judgment before the Great White Throne.

All of the lost are then judged according to their works and cast into the lake of fire.

- Chapter 21 records the creation of the New Heavens and the New Earth. Wonderfully, God will create a new paradise in which we will live with him forever and ever. The New Jerusalem comes down from heaven to earth—an incredible city that serves as the center of the new creation. Indeed, it is a city the like of which we have never seen nor imagined.

- It was a huge square—surrounded by a massive wall with twelve gates. An angel was stationed at each gate, and each gate had the name of one of the tribes of Israel upon it. This immense wall of the city also had twelve foundations, and upon each foundation was the name of one of the apostles. Thus a distinction between Israel and the Church is maintained, but this city seems to be home for both.

- An angel measured the city with a golden rod. It is truly full of unspeakable glory. As mentioned, it is a perfect square, measuring about 12,000 stadia (or furlongs) square (Rev 21:16). In other words the city was fourteen hundred miles on each side. Incredible! But what is even more incredible is that the city is fourteen hundred miles high too! One might reasonably infer from such dimensions that the saints will possess the capacity to fly. Can you imagine taking the stairs!

- Precious gems were the only earthly things to which John could appeal in describing the walls of the city and the city itself—pure gold as clear as glass, the gates as pearls, the streets of the city as pure gold like crystal (Rev 21:18, 21), etc.

- There was no temple in this glorious city because in it the Lord God Almighty and the Lamb dwelt. There was no darkness there at all—it was always light and always safe and always bustling with all kinds of activity. The kings of the earth will bring their glory and honor into the city, as will the nations (Rev 21:24–26). John offers a picture of social life filled with excitement and activity.

- Nothing that defiles or works abomination or makes a lie shall ever enter the New Jerusalem—only they written in the Lamb's book of life (Rev 21:27).

- Furthermore, a river as clear as crystal proceeds from the throne of God and the Lamb. On either side of the river stands the tree of life that yields twelve different fruits every month. The curse is forever removed, and the servants of God will serve him face to face. And his name shall be in their foreheads forever. God will give the city light.

- The last message of the Bible appears in Revelation 22:6–19. John affirmed that he had seen these things and heard them via angelic pronouncement and said that blessed are all those who keep the prophecies of this book. John fell down at the angel's feet but the messenger told him not to do so but to worship God alone.

- Three times in this closing section Jesus announced, "Behold, I am coming soon" (Rev 22:7, 12, 20). A warning is given against tampering with the message of the book (Rev 22:18–19). From his captivity on Patmos, John yearned for the return of Christ, "Come, Lord Jesus" (Rev 22:20). He then closed his message wishing that "the grace of the Lord Jesus Christ be with God's people. Amen."

Key verse: ". . . You are worthy to take the scroll and to open its seals, because you were slain, and with your blood you have purchased men for God from every tribe and language and people and nation. You have made them to be a kingdom and priests to serve our God, and they will reign on the earth" (Rev 5:9–10).

www.ingramcontent.com/pod-product-compliance
Lightning Source LLC
Chambersburg PA
CBHW062015220426
43662CB00010B/1346